THE COLLECTED WORKS OF VINCENET

Recent Researches in the Music of the Middle Ages and Early Renaissance is one of four quarterly series (Middle Ages and Early Renaissance; Renaissance; Baroque Era; Classical Era) which make public the early music that is being brought to light in the course of current musicological research.

Each volume is devoted to works by a single composer or in a single genre of composition, chosen because of their potential interest to scholars and performers, and prepared for publication according to the standards that govern the making of all reliable historical editions.

Subscribers to this series, as well as patrons of subscribing institutions, are invited to apply for information about the "Copyright-Sharing Policy" of A-R Editions, Inc., under which the contents of this volume may be reproduced free of charge for performance use.

Correspondence should be addressed:

A-R Editions, Inc.
315 West Gorham Street
Madison, Wisconsin 53703

RECENT RESEARCHES IN THE MUSIC OF THE MIDDLE AGES AND
EARLY RENAISSANCE • VOLUMES IX and X

THE COLLECTED WORKS OF VINCENET

Edited by Bertran E. Davis

A-R EDITIONS, INC. • MADISON

For Betty Hunt

Copyright © 1978, A-R Editions, Inc.

ISSN 0362-3572

ISBN 0-89579-110-2

Library of Congress Cataloging in Publication Data:

Vincenet, Johannes, d. 1479?
   The collected works of Vincenet.

  (Recent researches in the music of the Middle Ages and early Renaissance ; v. 9-10 ISSN 0362-3572)
    CONTENTS: Mass, Sine nomine.—Mass, Eterne Rex Altissime.—Mass, Entrepris suis par grant lyesse.—Mass, O gloriosa Regina mundi. [etc.]
    1. Masses—Vocal scores. 2. Part-songs, Secular. 3. Motets. I. Davis, Bertran E. II. Bruolo, Bartolomeo, fl. 1400-1440. Entrepris suis par grant lyesse. 1978. III. Touront, Johannes. O gloriosa Regina mundi. 1978. IV. Series.
M2.R2383 vol. 9-10 [M2011] [M1579] [(M2092.3)]
  ISBN 0-89579-110-2 780'.902s [784]   78-21899

Contents

Preface   vii

THE COLLECTED WORKS OF VINCENET

[1] Mass: [sine nomine]   1

[2] Mass: Eterne rex altissime   28

[3] Mass: Entrepris suis par grant lyesse   75

[4] Mass: O gloriosa regina mundi   114

[5] Villancico: La pena sin ser sabida   159

[6] Rondeau: Triste qui spero morendo   162

[7] Rondeau: Ou doy je secours querir   165

[8] Rondeau: Fortune, par ta cruaulté   167

SONG MODEL SOURCES

Rondeau: Entrepris suis par grant lyesse   173
    Bartholomeus Bruolo

Song-motet: O gloriosa regina mundi   176
    [Jo. Touront]

Preface

The Composer

The passing of almost 500 years has left varying amounts of evidence related to music and musicians of the Quattrocento. In the case of Vincenet, an important collection of music has survived, but a comparable fund of biographic data is lacking. Aside from the ascriptions in the manuscript sources of the music, only a few references to the composer are known to exist in documents dating from the fifteenth century. Indeed, these references are so few and so widely separated in time and place of origin that any proposal linking the "early" and "late" documentary records must be considered tentative. The "late" evidence, which includes the chief manuscript sources of the music (all copied ca. 1480) and documentary references whose dates range from 1466 to 1479, may or may not be related to "early" data found in Papal records dating from 1424 to 1429. A biographic statement based on such fragmented evidence must be provisional. On the other hand, the deficiencies of the biography should not obscure the importance of the musical works as a new and rich treasure of early Renaissance polyphony.

The following discussion incorporates recently published data not included in this editor's article on Vincenet in *MGG* and represents a revision of the biographic portion of that article.[1] No attempt is made to standardize the different spellings of the composer's name as they occur in particular documents, and such variant spellings appear in italics. When a generalization is necessary, the form "Vincenet" is given using Roman type.

The earliest documentary evidence concerning the composer occurs in records (dating from April, 1424, through May, 1429) related to the Papal Choir which refer to the singer and priest *Johannes Vincinetti*; these records are the only sources where the Christian name Johannes occurs. The uncertainty surrounding attempts to establish conclusive relationships between the early and late data is largely due to the absence of a Christian name in all except the Roman records. Only the surname Vincenet (or variant spellings) is used in the late records, including the ascriptions found in the manuscripts containing the music.

The late evidence consists mainly of facts related to the musical style and to the copying (around 1480) of the chief manuscript sources of the music; there are also a few brief references made in documents written after the middle of the century. When considered in relation to dates given for the copying of the chief music collections, the most important of the late references is an entry dated 1479 in a register from the Spanish Court at Naples which refers to *Vincinet's* wife, to his position as cantor for the Spanish King, and to his recent death. The close relationship of the dates cited and the fact that the manuscripts and documents mentioned above are for the most part of central or northern Italian origin make it reasonable to assume that the *Vincenet* named in the music manuscripts is identical with the *Vincinet* whose death is referred to in the Naples entry.

Although a Christian name is lacking in the ascriptions in the music manuscripts, there is no reason to doubt that all the compositions attributed to Vincenet are the work of one composer. In light of fifteenth-century spelling practices, the differences in orthography found in the ascriptions (*Vincenet, Vincinet, Vincinecta,* and *Vincineta*) are minimal, and the progressive changes in musical style which can be observed in comparing the different works are of the type one would expect to find in examining the music of a composer active around 1450 and in the decades immediately following. Further, the chief manuscript sources for Vincenet's music are anthologies whose contents are widely accepted as having been written during the third quarter of the century.

The question of whether the *Vincinet* at Naples can be identified with the Papal singer *Vincinetti* (a conclusion that requires the composer to be a contemporary of Dufay) or whether he is more exactly a member of the later Ockeghem generation cannot be resolved conclusively at the present time. Modern opinions differ sharply in their interpretations of the biographical data. Gustave Reese[2] and, more recently, Manfred Schuler[3] have objected to the idea of relating the Papal singer to the *Vincinet* at Naples—Reese bases his opinion on the musical style in the *rondeau Ou doy je secours querir* ([7] in this edition), and Schuler says that it would scarcely be possible to identify the priest with the *Vincinet* at Naples since the latter had a wife. On the other hand, Manfred F. Bukofzer identifies the two as one person without reservation.[4] Most modern scholars simply list the musical works of the composer as they appear in particular manuscripts without reference to biographic considerations. Examples of this type of citation occur in the widely known publications of Ambros, Eitner, Riemann, Peter Wagner, and Johannes Wolf. The usefulness of the chronological assessments relating to fifteenth- and sixteenth-century composers made by Giuseppe Baini in his early monograph on Palestrina are often limited, but it is interesting to note that Baini assigns *Vincenet* to the Ockeghem period.[5]

As far as we know, Vincenet is not mentioned by theorists of the late fifteenth or early sixteenth centuries. Tinctoris, who surely would have known *Vincinet* at Naples[6] and who was himself active there at the time of *Vincinet's* death, does not mention the composer in the numerous citations of musicians made in his theoretical works.

For completeness, mention must be made of the *Vincenet* whose name is listed with others (who may or may not be musicians) in a series of enigmatic puns in the sixth stanza of the poem *Lettres missives de Verjus* by the Burgundian poet Jean Molinet.[7] According to H. Colin Slim, the poem could have been written as early as 1475.[8] If the Vincenet cited in the poem is in fact the composer, this use of his name may indicate that he was widely known in the period; however, nothing else which would add to the biographic data may be drawn from the reference.

The fund of information about the Papal singer *Vincinetti* has been enlarged recently through publication of new data by the German Historical Institute in Rome[9] and through publication by Manfred Schuler of a related article on the choir of Pope Martin V.[10] The newly published data refer to documents which prove that *Vincinetti* was a priest when he came to Rome. An entry taken from a volume now entitled *Liber Officialium 1417—1430* in the State Archives of Rome shows that the singer *Johannes Vincinetti* was a presbyter from the diocese of Toul who was received into the Papal Choir on December 24, 1425:

> In the year of the Lord 1425, the third year of the [cycle of] indiction, of the pontificate of our most holy Father in Christ and our Lord, Lord Martin, by divine providence Pope V, in the ninth year of his [pontificate], the honorable man Johannes Vincinetti, a priest from Toul, was received in the cantor's chapel of our Lord the Pope on the twenty-fourth day of the month of December. He swore in the hands of Lord Benedict, the deputy chamberlain of the pontifical office, of the Reverend in Christ our Father Lord Anthony, Bishop of Sencii, and of Lord John Aezel, cleric of the apostolic chamber. Witness L. Robring.[11]

The *Liber Officialium* contains records of oath-taking ceremonies which occurred during the pontificate of Martin V (November 11, 1417—February 20, 1431), and the editor assumes that the authentic form of the surname is given in this important collection. Documents at the Vatican indicate that provision was made for canonicates and prebends for the singer *Vincinetti* at the cathedrals of Metz and Toul as early as April 25, 1424, and that he continued to receive the income from these benefices and others *(in absentia)* until at least January 23, 1429.[12]

In his monograph on Dufay, F. X. Haberl indicates that the singer's name first appears in the pay records of the Papal Choir (with the abbreviated spelling *Johanni Vicenot*) in January, 1426.[13] This would be the month following the singer's reception into the Choir in December, 1425. In addition, the present editor's research shows that the name is listed in the pay records on a regular monthly basis (as *Vicenot* or *Vincenot*) from January 7, 1426, through May 11, 1429.[14] Vincenet would therefore have known Dufay since the latter's name first appears in the pay records of the Choir on December 20, 1428.[15] Vincenet was probably in the Papal Choir until June, 1429, since the singers were paid a month in advance as shown in the following extract from the above-mentioned pay record for May 11, 1429:

> Disbursements of the month of May, 1429, Rome
> For the singers of our Lord the Pope.
> Showed [exhibited for inspection], Johannes de Reate.
>
> The eleventh day of the said month, the above-mentioned Lord Oddo [de Vacis], treasurer, made payment to the under-mentioned singers of our Lord the Pope for their salary to the month of June next, namely: Egidio L'infant, Johanni Delesme, Toussano de Ruella, Philippo Foliot, Johanni Vincenot, five [florins each]; Johanni Dupassage, six [florins]; Bartholomeo Poignare, Guillelmo Dufay, Galtero Liberti, four [florins each]; and Jacobo Robaille, two gold florins of the chamber. In all, forty-five florins of the same kind. F[lorins] 45.[16]

Variants in the spelling of the name *Vincinetti* in the Vatican documents include the forms *Vinceneti*, *Vincenot*, *Vincenoti*, *Vincennoti*, *Vincencii*, *Vicenont*, and *Vicenot*. The variant used most often in the account books and registers cited as *Registra Lateranensia* and *Supplicationum* (in footnote 12) is the form *Vinceneti*. This preferred usage shows how the spelling *Vincinetti* is transformed even in the early documents into a form almost identical with that seen most often in the late records. The spellings *Vincenot* and *Vicenot* (with the "ot" rather than the "et" suffix) are used exclusively in the pay records found in the *In-*

troitus et Exitus volumes (cited in footnote 14). The "ot" ending was a commonly used variant of the "et" suffix in the Burgundian dialect of the period. The singer's Christian name is used in all Vatican records cited and this (with other facts repeated in the documents) makes it clear that the different entries refer to the same person. The variations shown in the spellings *Vincinecta* and *Vincineta* (both occur in variant copies of the *rondeau Fortune, par ta crualté* [8]) may be viewed simply as diminutives or possibly as reappearances and variations of the name *Vincinetti*. The spelling *Vincenet* is used exclusively in the chief manuscript sources of the music.

Before publication of the new data by the German Historical Institute, one could assume that the *Vincenot* in the Papal Choir was not a priest (since the only known documentary references to him were those cited without clerical rank in the pay records found in the *Introitus et Exitus* volumes of the Papal Court), and that his status was similar to that of Dufay who, on the basis of a fifteenth-century Papal bull published by Haberl in 1885, seems not to have been a priest as late as 1431.[17] In Haberl's opinion, the positions and titles of members of the Roman Curia were customarily made clear in documents of the type cited above. While it seems clear that Dufay was not a priest in 1431, we now know that he is referred to as *diaconus* at Cambrai in 1427.[18]

The date of *Vincinet's* death is known to us through an entry seen by Edmond van der Straeten in a register of the *Cedole della Regia Tesoreria Aragonese* formerly in the *Archivio di Stato di Napoli*.[19] Van der Straeten's transcript shows that *Vincinet* had a wife at the time of his death, that he was lately deceased in 1479, and that he was a cantor for the Spanish King (Ferrante—Ferdinand I, King of Naples from 1458 to 1494): "1479, Vannella, moglia del qº [quondam] Vincinet, Cantor fo del S. R. [Signore Re]."[20] The title "cantor" had more than one meaning in the period. We know, for example, that Dufay is referred to in the archives of the Court of Savoy (in 1450) as a cantor of the Duke of Burgundy [Philip the Good].[21] The term cantor could refer either to a polyphonist or to one more concerned with administrative duties than with music making.[22] If the *Vincinet* at Naples were identified with the Papal singer, the latter definition of cantor would agree well with the age he would have attained by 1479.

The idea that *Vincinetti* would doubtless have been more than seventy years of age by the year 1479 does not in itself exclude the possibility of identifying him with the cantor at Naples. Dufay, for example, would have been near or past the age of seventy when he died in 1474, and several other singers who were active in the Papal Choir early in the century lived into the 1470s.[23]

A discussion of whether the priest *Vincinetti* could or could not have had a wife raises questions which cannot be clearly answered when considered in relation to the realities of clerical life during the pre-Reformation years of the fifteenth century. Most historians familiar with the period describe clerical marriage as a common practice.[24] In the opinion of this editor, it is the absence of data from the middle of the century rather than the fact that the *Vincinet* at Naples had a wife which prevents defining a clear relationship between the priest *Vincinetti* and the cantor *Vincinet*.[25]

The data having the closest chronological relationship to the chief manuscript sources of the music include the Naples entry cited above and material drawn from two letters written after the middle of the century by Jachetto di Marvilla to the youthful Lorenzo de' Medici. Both letters, quoted in full by Bianca Becherini, are important to an assessment of the Naples entry.[26] In the earlier letter, dated September 15, 1566, at Bologna (emended by Becherini to read 1466), Jachetto writes hoping to secure employment and to take part in the re-establishment of the singer's chapel at the church of San Giovanni in Florence.[27] In stating his qualifications, he says that he has been in the chapel of King Alfonso (*el Magnanimo*) and afterward in that of Ferrante (the bastard son of Alfonso) who succeeded his father as King of Naples in 1458.[28] Ferrante was the sovereign served by the cantor *Vincinet* at the time of his death. Jachetto states also that he has been in the chapel of the Pope.

In his second letter to Lorenzo, dated March 22, [1469], at Rome (year supplied by Becherini in view of a reference, in the letter, to Lorenzo's forthcoming marriage),[29] Jachetto outlines a plan to re-establish the choir at San Giovanni, and in the discussion introduces the name *Vincenet* in the following deferential manner: "Then, since I had advised *Vincenet* before he came to Florence that he ought to consider the commission I had from your generous father and from Golino Martelli—that is, to find some fellows for your chapel—I was patient about my place as I had it promised me by your father."[30] Although why or when *Vincenet* came to Florence is not known, his apparent lack of interest in fulfilling the commission was clearly reassuring to Jachetto in the latter's bid for employment with the Medici family. We can assume from the tone of the reference that Lorenzo was familiar with the accomplishments of the Naples cantor. *Vincenet* was undoubtedly known as a composer and, depending on interpretation of the term cantor, possibly also as an administrator in the chapel of King Ferrante. Jachetto's allusion seems to imply that *Vincenet's* recommendation of singers would have been seriously considered by the Medici. These ideas support the conception of *Vincenet* as a venerable servant of the church and one possibly identical with the priest *Johannes Vincinetti* who served Martin V at Rome earlier in the century.

One additional possibility emerges from a review of the data cited in the letters. Since we know from his second letter that Jachetto knew *Vincenet* well enough to discuss personal correspondence with him (perhaps the two first became acquainted during Jachetto's earliest years of service at Naples), and since Jachetto's first letter clearly states that he served Alfonso as well as Ferrante, Jachetto's service at Naples could have begun no later than 1458, the year of Alfonso's death. If Jachetto knew Vincenet at Naples as early as 1458, it is possible that Vincenet entered the chapel of the Spanish King as much as twenty years before the year in which his death is recorded there. This would help to explain Vincenet's activities after his name disappears from the pay records of the Papal Choir and before the approximate date of his death is recorded at Naples.

The Music

The four polyphonic settings of the Ordinary of the Mass and four secular part-songs attributed to Vincenet are included in the present edition, as well as two polyphonic works attributed respectively to Bartholomeus Bruolo and Johannes Touront. The latter two works, the *rondeau Entrepris suis* (Bruolo) and the song-motet *O gloriosa regina mundi* (Touront), serve as models from which melodic material is drawn in the construction of the Vincenet Masses *Entrepris suis, a 4* and *O gloriosa regina mundi, a 4*.

The changes found in comparing individual features of musical style in the different compositions of Vincenet reflect a continuation of the revolution in style which began around 1430. At the same time, the transition from cantus firmus to parody technique seen in the four settings of the Ordinary shows how the composer, writing during the third quarter of the century, expanded the variation principle present in cantus firmus Masses of the late Dufay period. Changes in Vincenet's musical style are seen on a small scale in the secular part-songs; but most of the experiments with new compositional devices (particularly those related to the development of cyclic thematic unity) are carried out within the large polyphonic sections which make up the Ordinary of the Mass. Vincenet's development of parody techniques during the third quarter of the century must be considered both early and progressive.

General features of Vincenet's compositional technique include the careful treatment of dissonance, the use of textures showing the influence of *fauxbourdon*, development of the contratenor bassus, the introduction of new cadence types, the limited use of canonic treatment, and the notation of flowing ternary rhythms in what has been called *tempus* notation (where the imperfect semibreve is the unit of time). The presence of *prolatio perfecta* in the tenor voice part in particular sections of the Mass *Entrepris suis, a 4*, represents an exceptional use of an older mensural (and rhythmic) practice which gradually falls into disuse during the third quarter of the century. The perfect prolation found in this tenor part, a reflection of that found in the song-model for this Mass (the *rondeau Entrepris suis par grant lyesse, a 3*), is used as the rhythmic basis for several different types of augmentation in the Mass.

The frequent occurrence of parallel imperfect intervals (thirds, sixths, and tenths) between the superius and tenor voice parts and the use of stylized textures based on this parallelism attest to the influence of *fauxbourdon*. Canonic or imitative treatment is still in a formative stage in Vincenet's time. When canonic treatment occurs in his music, its use is usually limited to the superius-tenor voice-pair. The new cadence types (widely used after mid-century) are introduced in most of Vincenet's works in conjunction with a downward extension of range in the contratenor bassus part. Chief among the new cadences is that in which the penultimate 6/3 chord found in the older *fauxbourdon*-like cadence is supplanted by the 5/3 built on the fifth scale degree above the final in the lowest voice (interpretations relating the word "chord" or the use of figures to show chord structure to modern harmonic theory are not necessarily intended).

The Secular Part-Songs

Among the secular part-songs, the two *rondeaux a 3, Ou doy je secours querir* [7] and *Fortune, par ta cruaulté* [8], display the most progressive traits. Both are in the three-voice non-quartal style which became popular after about 1460.[31] The *rondeau Triste qui spero morendo, a 4*, [6] and the *villancico La pena sin ser sabida, a 4*, [5] are examples of the new, four-voice Netherlands chanson with contratenor bassus; although the presence of a *si placet* part (the contratenor altus) in *Triste qui spero* points to the origin of this work as a *rondeau a 3*. *La pena* belongs to the type of *villancico* where the text of the *vuelta* (return) is telescoped into that of the *estribillo* (refrain) as shown in the following plan of the rhyme scheme (with the *estribillo* given in capital letters): AB cc aB.[32] In *La pena*, the two parts of the *copla* (stanza) — the *mudanza* (change) and the following *vuelta* — are separated by a brief musical extension of the *mudanza*. The relationship of the two sections of music in the *villancico* (S and T) to the rhyme scheme cited above is as follows:

```
A B   c   c   a B
S     T   T   S
```

In view of the experiments with thematic relationships carried out in settings of the Ordinary by composers such as Vincenet, Faugues, and Barbingant during the third quarter of the fifteenth century, one might expect to find extensive evidence of similar experiments within the secular songs. However, in Vincenet's secular songs there are only two brief examples of thematic recurrence. The second musical section of the *rondeau Ou doy* closes with a relatively exact restatement in the two uppermost voices of melodic material stated at the beginning of the first section of music (cf. p. 165, mm. 3-11, and p. 166, mm. 45-54), and in the *villancico La pena*, the melody found in the uppermost voice at the end of the *estribillo* appears again in varied form in the course of the extended *mudanza* (cf. p. 160, mm. 17-20, and p. 161, mm. 39-44).

Vincenet's use of Italian, Spanish, and French texts in the secular part-songs attests to the cosmopolitan quality of the Spanish Court at Naples. *Triste qui spero morendo* belongs to the relatively small number of *rondeaux* in the period with Italian texts.

The Masses

The indications of gradual change in musical style seen in comparing Vincenet's secular part-songs are confirmed and broadened in a study of the Masses. A logical development occurs in these larger works illustrating stages in the evolution of the parody Mass. From the point of view of history and chronology, the early emergence of the parody Mass is one of the most significant stylistic developments in Vincenet's music.

The Mass [*sine nomine*], a 3, [1] found in Trent MS 91, is the least sophisticated of the Masses in regard to the cyclic use of thematic material, since the different sections of the work seem to be through-composed and are unified only by the use of motto beginnings. More elaborate thematic relationships exist in the three remaining Masses.

In the Mass *Eterne rex altissime*, a 4, [2] (found in MS Cappella Sistina 14 at the Vatican), the melody of the Gregorian hymn of the same name[33] is divided into four sections for use as a cantus firmus in the tenor voice of the Mass, and ternary and binary versions of the melody are used alternately in the tenor throughout the Mass (cf. tenor voice, pp. 34-7, mm. 21-76, and pp. 38-43, mm. 113-214). In addition, motto beginnings contribute to thematic unity. In the edition, Roman numerals mark the beginning of each section of the hymn tune in the tenor part of this Mass. The type of cantus firmus treatment described above is not unusual in the period, but treatment of the remaining voice parts in the Vincenet Mass goes beyond usual practice in that variations based on the initial polyphonic settings of the different sections of the hymn tune (and variations based on the episodic passages leading to the entrance of these sections) recur throughout the Mass. Although the variation treatment is relatively free, a general correspondence emerges when the superius, tenor, and contratenor bassus voices in the different settings of each section of the hymn tune are compared.

The variation process described above foreshadows full parody treatment in that melodic material drawn from several voices of a pre-existing polyphonic setting (originating in this case within the Mass) is re-employed in successive sections of the Mass. The head-motif technique needs no illustration here, but the following example shows the recurrence and variation of the polyphonic sections mentioned above. A comparison of all voices on p. 29, mm 33-4; p. 57, mm. 30-1; and p. 67, mm. 28-9 illustrates the similarity of the episodic material used in the approach to the entrance of section II of the cantus firmus in the Christe, Sanctus, and Agnus I sections of the Mass. In the last two sections named, the measures following those cited illustrate the re-use and variation of the polyphonic setting of section II of the hymn tune, which appears for the first time on p. 30, beginning in m. 35.

The Mass *Entrepris suis*, a 4, Modena, Biblioteca Estense, MS α. M. 1. 13 ([3] in the present edition), is a mixed work with respect to use of structural techniques. The tenor of the *rondeau Entrepris suis par grant lyesse*, a 3, attributed to Bartholomeus Bruolo in the Bodleian codex Canonici Misc. 213, is used as a cantus firmus in the tenor voice in the Kyrie, Gloria, and Credo, and the superius of the *rondeau* is paraphrased in the superius of the Mass in these same sections. This particular combination of paraphrase- and cantus firmus-treatment in the Mass preserves the two-voice structural frame represented by the superius and tenor in the *rondeau* model. At the same time, the canonic treatment of the superius and tenor voices that takes place in the *rondeau* also occurs, in varying degrees, in the same voices in the Mass. The use in the Mass of two voices from the three-voice polyphonic model represents an intermediate stage in the emerging parody technique. A comparison of the superius and tenor voice parts in the *rondeau* (pp. 173-4, mm. 5-12) with a portion of the Mass where these voices are re-worked (pp. 97-8, mm. 90-7) illustrates the relatively strict adaptation of the superius and the usual strict conformance of the tenor to that of the model. The model is divided into three sections in the compositional process within the Mass, and, in the edition, corresponding Roman numerals identify sections of the model with related sections in the Mass.

In the Sanctus and Agnus I sections of the Mass *Entrepris suis*, only the superius of the *rondeau* model is drawn on, and it is freely paraphrased. An unexpected connection between this Mass and the Mass *O gloriosa regina mundi* [4] arises from the fact that the music of Agnus II is identical in both works except that in the Mass *Entrepris suis*, the music is written a fifth lower. In both Masses, the music of Agnus II occurs as new material unrelated to the pre-existent melodies parodied in the Masses.

Parody treatment is broadened in the Mass *O gloriosa regina mundi, a 4,* [4]. All three voices of the song-motet *O gloriosa regina mundi* (attributed to Jo. Touront in Rome, Biblioteca Casanatense, Codex 2856) are drawn on in the Kyrie, Gloria, and Credo of the Mass, and the model is partially re-worked in the Sanctus and Agnus sections. Cantus firmus treatment in the sense of the unvaried repetition of a melody in the tenor voice is abandoned. Since this work is contained in the early layer of the Vatican codex Cappella Sistina 51, compiled between 1471 and 1484,[34] it is one of the earliest-known parody Masses. The type of variation technique applied to the different voice parts of the model can be seen by comparing the beginning measures of the song-motet (pp. 176-7, mm. 1-32) with the opening section of the Gloria of the Mass (pp. 119-20, mm. 1-17). As in the *rondeau Entrepris suis* and the Mass based on it, canonic entries appear for the most part in the superius and tenor voices of the model, and this arrangement is preserved in the Mass.

The structural techniques used in the Masses *Eterne rex altissime, Entrepris suis,* and *O gloriosa regina mundi* represent different stages in the development of a broadly conceived technique of thematic variation. The idea of the repetition and elaboration of a tonal complex related to a *cantus prius factus*, illustrated by the recurrence of material in the Mass *Eterne rex altissime*, is succeeded by the transference of two voices derived from a polyphonic model in the Mass *Entrepris suis*. This type of incipient parody treatment is superseded by the systematic variation of all voices of the polyphonic model in the Mass *O gloriosa regina mundi*, and cantus firmus treatment is abandoned. Parody treatment is used in all three of the Masses cited above—the difference in each case is one of degree rather than kind.

Sources

With one exception, the settings of the Ordinary of the Mass attributed to Vincenet exist as *unica*. The Mass *O gloriosa regina mundi, a 4,* exists in two manuscript sources: (1) a simplified version in Trent MS 91; and (2) the version chosen as the principal source for this edition, found in the Vatican codex Cappella Sistina 51. The unique settings of the other Vincenet Masses are contained in the Vatican codex Cappella Sistina 14 (the Mass *Eterne rex altissime, a 4*); in MS α. M. 1. 13 (Lat. 456) at the Biblioteca Estense in Modena (the Mass *Entrepris suis par grant lyesse, a 4*); and in the newer layer of Trent, Castello del Buonconsiglio, MS 91 (the Mass [*sine nomine*], *a 3*).

The Mellon Chansonnier is the chief source for the four secular part-songs and the only source which contains copies of all the songs. The *rondeau Triste qui spero morendo, a 4,* and the *villancico La pena sin ser sabida, a 4,* are unique to the Mellon manuscript. The *rondeau Ou doy je secours querir, a 3,* exists in only one source other than the Mellon collection (in the late fifteenth-century Pixérécourt Chansonnier), but the *rondeau Fortune, par ta cruaulté, a 3,* is found in seventeen different sources of the late fifteenth and early sixteenth centuries. Most of the variant copies of *Fortune* are found in chansonniers, but three versions are intabulations (two for lute and one for organ). Two of the seventeen variants occur in prints dating from the early sixteenth century (one in *Odhecaton A*, the other in Francesco Spinacino's *Intabulatura de Lauto, Libro primo*). The retrospective or anthological character of the collections cited as principal sources is widely known: in general, they contain music composed during the third quarter of the fifteenth century. With the exception of the variants found in tablature, all sources related to the present edition are written in white mensural notation.

The Mass Sources

The newer layer of Trent MS 91 contains the Vincenet Mass [*sine nomine*], *a 3*, as well as the variant copy of the Mass *O gloriosa, a 4,* mentioned above. This portion of the Trent manuscript is thought to have been copied between 1460 and 1480.[35]

The Vatican codex Cappella Sistina 14, in which

the Mass *Eterne rex altissime, a 4*, is preserved, is thought to have been copied after 1481.[36] This codex also contains a copy of the Dufay Mass *Ecce ancilla Domini*, a work known to have existed at Cambrai as early as 1463,[37] and a Kyrie, Gloria, and Credo belonging to the Dufay Mass *Se la face ay pale* composed about 1450.[38] Such chronological facts prove that the manuscript books containing the music of Vincenet are anthologies and show that dates which may be given for the composition of individual works are not necessarily closely related to those assigned to the copying of manuscript collections containing the works.

No special study exists of Modena, Biblioteca Estense, MS α. M. 1. 13 (Lat. 456) which contains the Vincenet Mass *Entrepris suis, a 4*.[39] This source is among the earliest of the giant choir books; but except for the general assignment to the last quarter of the fifteenth century, no date has been given for the copying of this carefully written manuscript book.[40] The anthological character of the codex is made clear by the fact that it contains a copy of the Dufay Mass *Ave regina caelorum* composed ca. 1464.[41]

The first 200 leaves of the Vatican codex Cappella Sistina 51, which include the folios containing the Vincenet Mass *O gloriosa regina mundi, a 4*, were probably copied between the years 1471 and 1484.[42] Although a model for this parody Mass has not been previously identified, the tenor of the Kyrie carries the incipit *O gloriosa* which proves to be a reference to the song-motet *O gloriosa regina mundi* appearing in at least eleven sources of the period.

Secular Song Sources

The Mellon Chansonnier is the most important source of Vincenet's secular part-songs. It is one of the few chansonniers to reach us in its original state (i.e., unchanged by later scribes). Bukofzer places the copying of the collection at about 1480 and the composition of its contents between 1450 and 1475, "during the latter part of the Binchois and Dufay period."[43] Music of composers in the Josquin and Obrecht generation does not appear in the Mellon Chansonnier. Unique copies of the *rondeau Triste qui spero morendo, a 4*, and the *villancico La pena sin ser sabida, a 4*, appear in the Mellon manuscript, as well as variants of the *rondeaux Ou doy je secours querir, a 3*, and *Fortune, par ta cruaulte, a 3*.

Manuscript books other than the Mellon containing variant copies of the three-voice *rondeau Fortune, par ta cruaulté* are listed below. Three collections containing *Fortune* which (like the Mellon) are assigned approximate dates of compilation are the *Glogauer Liederbuch* (1477-88), Berlin, Deutsche Staatsbibliothek, MS 40098 (Z. 98);[44] Codex Q 16 (1487), Bologna, Biblioteca Comunale, annessa al Conservatorio di Musica "G. B. Martini";[45] and the *Chansonnier cordiforme* (1470-7) at the Bibliothèque Nationale in Paris.[46] *Fortune* is also preserved in Codex 5-I-43 of the Biblioteca Columbina at Seville,[47] and in the Pixérécourt Chansonnier at the Bibliothèque Nationale, Paris.[48] In addition to containing a variant copy of *Fortune*, the Pixérécourt Chansonnier contains the only known variant of the *rondeau Ou doy je secours querir* other than the one in the Mellon collection. Dragan Plamenac has pointed out the similarity of Codex 5-I-43 and the Pixérécourt Chansonnier to Codex Q 16 (all are late fifteenth-century manuscripts of Italian origin whose repertories are chiefly French).[49] Other collections containing variant copies of *Fortune* and dating from the end of the fifteenth century include Codex 431 of the Biblioteca Comunale at Perugia;[50] MS 596, Busta H H, 2$^{1-4}$ (after 1484) at the Biblioteca Universitaria in Bologna;[51] and Grey MS 3. b. 12 at the South African Library in Cape Town.[52] In the Bologna (Biblioteca Universitaria) variant, the superius of *Fortune* is in mensural notation, and the remaining voices are intabulated for lute. Two turn-of-the-century sources containing *Fortune* are Florence, Biblioteca Nazionale Centrale, Banco Rari 229 (ca. 1500),[53] and *Odhecaton A* (1501).[54] The three-voice *rondeau* is also contained in four early sixteenth-century collections: Verona, Biblioteca Capitolare, Codex DCCLVII;[55] the Vatican chansonnier, Cappella Giulia, Codex XIII, 27;[56] Codex Q 18 at Bologna, Biblioteca Comunale;[57] and in Francesco Spinacino's first book of intabulations for lute (1507).[58] The *Fortune* included in the *Buxheimer Orgelbuch* (1465-75) may be an arrangement of the Vincenet *rondeau* although thematic relationships between the organ version and the numerous variants in chansonniers of the period are far from clear.[59]

Song-model Sources

The earliest sources used in the preparation of the present edition are manuscripts containing variant copies of the *rondeau Entrepris suis par grant lyesse, a 3* (from which material is drawn for use in the Vincenet Mass *Entrepris suis, a 4*). The *rondeau* is attributed to Bartholomeus Bruolo in Oxford, Bodleian Library, MS Canonici Misc. 213. Other datable collections containing copies of the *rondeau Entrepris suis par grant lyesse* are the *Schedelsches Liederbuch*, Munich, Bayerische Staatsbibliothek, MS Cim. 351^a (ca. 1461),[60] and three sources mentioned earlier in relation to the *rondeau Fortune*: they are the *Buxheimer Orgelbuch*; the *Glogauer Liederbuch*; and Codex Q 16 at Bologna. The version from Canonici Misc. 213 (with emendations from the variant copy in Bologna, Biblioteca Comunale, Codex Q 16) is the one transcribed in the edition. Canonici Misc. 213 was probably copied in Milan[61] or Venice[62] about 1465; its contents could have been composed as early as 1440.[63]

O gloriosa regina mundi, the song-motet *a 3* which serves as a model for the Vincenet Mass *O gloriosa, a 4*, appears in five previously mentioned fifteenth-century manuscripts: the Pixérécourt Chansonnier; Trent, MS 91; Bologna, MS Q 16; Perugia, MS 431; and Seville, MS 5-I-43. The version of the song-motet given in the edition is that of the Pixérécourt Chansonnier (with emendations from the variant found in Trent, MS 91). Other manuscripts containing a variant copy of the song-motet are Florence, Biblioteca Riccardiana, MS 2356 (late fifteenth century);[64] Paris, Bibliothèque Nationale, Réserve Vm⁷676 (1502);[65] and the sixteenth-century Verona codex MS DCCLVII (already mentioned in relation to *Fortune*). In addition, Plamenac lists a copy of the song-motet in Prague, Strakov Monastery, Codex D. G. IV. 47.[66]

Editorial Method

Transcription

In order to facilitate reconstruction of the original notation, incipits showing rhythmic values, opening pitches, rests, clefs, mensural signs, signs of proportion, the specific names used for the different voice parts, and the flats used as system tones in each voice in the manuscript source chosen for transcription appear at the beginning of major sections of the music. A single horizontal bracket indicates a ligature in the source, while a broken horizontal bracket indicates blackened notes in the source. In the few places where the transcription may be doubtful due to the condition of the manuscript, vertical brackets enclose the area in question.

The octave transposition used in the notation of the tenor in modern vocal scores (where the part sounds an octave lower than written) is used in the transcription of the tenor in three-voice works and in the transcription of the tenor and the contratenor altus in four-voice compositions. The transcription in this edition of both the tenor and contratenor altus, using the type of tenor clef mentioned above, parallels the notational practice of the manuscripts where identical clefs are customarily used in the notation of these voice parts in compositions *a 4* and where both voices occupy approximately the same pitch range. The altus is closely related to the tenor range in this music, and can be realized by a tenor in performance. Although the placement of the overall pitch range is relatively low in the manuscript notation of the Masses *Eterne rex altissime* and *Entrepris suis*, the *rondeau Triste qui spero morendo*, and the *villancico La pena sin ser sabida*, these as well as all other works in the edition are transcribed at the manuscript pitch levels without the use of transposition.

The rhythmic value of the tone concluding each melody in final cadences is realized in the edition. In a few places, ending values of this type are lengthened editorially with the added values placed within editorial brackets. The half-blackened ligature *sine proprietate et cum perfectione* appearing occasionally in final cadences is realized as a *ligatura binaria* rather than by treating the blackened note as an added voice in the final chord. Editorial fermatas appear throughout the edition in conjunction with ending values and without the use of editorial brackets (the few occurrences of the sign in the manuscripts are recorded in the Critical Notes).

The editor has omitted multiple breve-rests in the tenor and contratenor bassus voice parts at the beginning of major sections in the Mass *Eterne rex altissime*. Since these two voices are the last to enter at the beginning of each major section in the Mass cited (after as many as forty-eight breve-rests), most of the breve-rests are omitted in the transcription at these places. All rests of this type are indicated, as they appear in the source, in the incipits at the beginning of each section of the Mass (see pp. 28, 33, 37, 43, 49, 56, and 66).

The use of accidentals, as illustrated in the manuscripts containing the works of Vincenet, differs in no essential way from that usually found in the period. The flats appearing as system tones in the "signatures" are sometimes used in place of particular accidentals in given voice parts, but in other cases they signal transposition of mode. When a flat is occasionally omitted in a "signature," the necessary alterations are often supplied through the use of accidentals. A precedent is provided in the manuscripts, through the use of accidentals, for the editorial alteration of harmonic intervals of the fifth and octave so that these intervals are always perfect and for avoidance of the melodic use of the tritone or diminished fifth. The manuscripts also contain examples of the alteration of one of the tones of an imperfect harmonic interval (the change from a minor to a major third or sixth) in the approach to a perfect consonance. The sign used for the sharp is seldom found. All accidentals in the manuscripts are transcribed in the staff in the edition; all editorial accidentals appear above the staff without brackets. In the few places where a redundant accidental occurs in the manuscripts, the accidental is deleted in transcription but recorded in the Critical Notes.

When partial signatures are used consistently throughout one section of music in the manuscripts, the flats used as system tones (signatures) in the individual voice parts are retained without change in the edition. However, when the number of flats used as system tones varies from staff to staff in one of the voice parts, the signature for this part is standardized in the edition and the variations are recorded in the Critical Notes.

Rhythmic values notated in *integer valor* in the manuscripts are transcribed using a 2:1 rate of reduction; the modern metric signs 3/2 or 2/2 are used in sections of this type in the edition, and the semibreve (the half-note) should be taken as the unit of time at a tempo of 75 to 85 counts per minute. In sections governed by signs calling for simple diminution, rhythmic values are realized using a 4:1 rate of reduction, and the modern metric signs 3/4 or 2/4 are used; the semibreve (here the quarter-note) should be taken as the unit of time, but at a relatively faster tempo (ca. 100 M.M.). In view of the relationship between the semibreve and the tempos suggested above, the sections transcribed using the 4:1 reduction of rhythmic values should not be thought of as strict realizations of *diminutio dupla* or *tripla*. According to Tinctoris in the *Proportionale musices* (ca. 1475),[67] the *virgula* drawn through the mensural sign for *tempus perfectum* or *imperfectum* could be interpreted in two ways: (1) to indicate an acceleration of tempo approximating the 3:2 relationship of *sesquialtera*;[68] (2) to indicate *diminutio dupla*.[69] The editor uses the 3/4 or 2/4 metric divisions in order to call attention to the speeding up of tempo mentioned by Tinctoris rather than to show a strict realization of *diminutio dupla*. These sections could be performed as strict realizations of *diminutio dupla* or *tripla* by taking the half-note (or dotted half) as the unit of time at the tempo suggested for the semibreve in the 3/2 and 2/2 sections (i.e., *alla breve*); but this is not recommended since such performance would produce tempos too fast for an appropriate rendition of note values as small as the semiminim and *fusa*.

Unusual mensural signs and signs of proportion occur only in the Mass *Entrepris suis* where they indicate *prolatio perfecta* and augmentation. The conventional placement of the dot (or point) within the mensural signs governing *tempus* is largely replaced by the number 3 placed after the signs for perfect or imperfect *tempus*. The number 3 may also occur alone in the course of a voice part indicating the place at which perfect prolation should begin.

The notation of the tenor voice part in the *Et in terra* section of the Mass *Entrepris suis* shows the irregular use of the number 3 as a sign of perfect prolation (see p. 80) in conjunction with the canon *crescit in duplo* (it expands in duple). In this case, realization of the canon requires a twofold augmentation of rhythmic values at the level of the minim (pp. 80-6). After realization of the augmentation (and given the rhythmic values shown in the transcription), three semibreves in the tenor part are equal to two in the voices notated in *integer valor* thus creating an effective *sesquialtera* relationship between the tenor and the remaining voices. Although the regular barring of the entire edition is also used in this *Et in terra* section, the augmentation in the tenor part can easily be seen by visualizing the deletion of every other barline beginning with the first. The rhythmic values used in this tenor part should be thought of as a series of half-note triplets (or collectively in larger values as a series of dotted whole-notes). The quarter-rests (minim-rests) in the transcription of the tenor are editorially divided half-rests (semibreve-rests) necessitated by the regular placement of the barline (see p. 82, mm. 27-8, and 31-2).

The realization of the tenor part in the *Qui sedes* of the Mass *Entrepris suis* (p. 86-90) requires continuation of the augmentation applied to the tenor in the *Et in terra* section of the Mass; however, the notational problem is complicated in the *Qui sedes* by the fact that the canon *crescit in duplo* is not restated in the tenor part. A practical transcription shows that the thirty-six breve-rests at the beginning of the tenor part must be transcribed in *integer valor* to allow the part to enter at the place shown by signs of congruence in the other voice parts, but that the remaining rhythmic values in the tenor must be augmented in order to fit logically with the other voice parts throughout the remainder of the *Qui sedes*. The absence in the manuscript of a canon or a *signum augentiae* in the tenor part, at the point where the note values begin, places one notated semibreve of major prolation (equal to three minims) against two notated semibreves of minor prolation (equal to four minims) in the remaining voice parts. The inequality of the rhythmic relationships described above (all are in fact notated in *integer valor*) is an example of the *error Anglorum* mentioned by Tinctoris in the *Proportionale musices*.[70] In examples of the *error Anglorum*, a correct realization of notated rhythmic values requires augmentation, although a sign or canon calling for augmentation is lacking. The reduction in the overall length of the tenor part occurring in the manuscript because of the lack of a *signum augentiae* is corrected in this transcription by editorial continuation of the canon *crescit in duplo* at the place in the *Qui sedes* where the note values begin. In the manuscript, the relationship of equality between the breve-rests, written in *integer valor* under the sign for *tempus imperfectum cum prolatione perfecta* (at the beginning of the tenor part), and the breve-note values, written under the signs for *diminutio dupla* (in all but the tenor voice), indicates that all voice parts in the *Qui sedes* are notated in *integer valor* and that the signs for *diminutio dupla* signal a tempo change rather than the diminution of rhythmic values. The relationships described above confirm the idea expressed by Tinctoris that the sign for *dupla* where the *virgula* is drawn through the mensural sign for *tempus perfectum* or *imperfectum* can be interpreted as indicating an acceleration of the tempo normal to *integer valor* (an acceleration described by Tinctoris as an excited *sesquialtera*) rather than diminution.

The mensural sign for *tempus perfectum cum prolatione perfecta* found in the Mass *Entrepris suis* in the tenor voice of the *Patrem* (p. 90) functions as a *signum augentiae*. Realization of the tenor part given in the manuscript requires threefold augmentation at the level of the minim.

The brief appearance of an added melody in the contratenor altus part in the Credo of the Mass *Eterne rex altissime* (a curious kind of fifteenth-century *Freistimmigkeit*) represents a phenomenon which is rare but not unique in the period (see p. 44, contratenor altus, mm. 10-11).[71] Although in sources where white notation is used added tones of this type are often blackened, the manuscript containing this example (the Vatican codex Cappella Sistina 14, folio 51, staff 1) has the added voice part in white notation.

An eclectic editorial method (one in which variant sources are used to supply music or text missing in the primary source) is used to establish suitable readings of the music for the two polyphonic Mass models, the *rondeau Entrepris suis par grant lyesse, a 3,* and the song-motet *O gloriosa regina mundi, a 3* (neither of which is attributed to Vincenet). This same method is also used to form a text for the above-mentioned song-motet. In addition, the refrain for the Vincenet *rondeau Fortune, par ta cruaulté* (given without further text in the Mellon Chansonnier) is supplemented with the stanza from the variant in the *Chansonnier cordiforme*. The Critical Notes document details of this editorial procedure. Aside from the exceptions listed above, all transcriptions in the edition reflect the readings of text and music found in the primary manuscript sources.

Texts

The spelling, capitalization, and punctuation of the Mass texts have been modernized according to the conventions found in present-day books of the Roman Church. The secular texts (given below with translations) reflect the practice of the source manuscripts. Manuscript abbreviations in the texts of the secular songs are realized as complete words in the edition, and the use of *u* and *v* and of *i* and *j* has been standardized. Conventional spellings in the manuscript copies of the Masses include the shortening of the diphthong *ae* to *e* (for example: *Eterne, bone, celestis, celi, seculi,* and *terre*) and the use of *c* in place of *t* before *i* followed by a vowel (*gracias, tercias, eciam, poncio, deprecacionem,* and *consubstancialem*). Variants in spelling such as *pilatto, pasus, expecto, mondi, Ihesus, Xpriste,* and *Criste* are found as well as the abbreviations *Ihū Xpē* and *Ihm̃ Xpm̃* used to replace *Jesu Christe* and *Jesum Christum,* respectively.

In the Spanish and Italian texts, the shortening of the diphthong occurs in such words as *ben, tene* (*ie* to *e*) and *more* (*uo* to *o*). Great variety exists in the regional spellings of the secular texts (see, for example, the variant spellings of the incipit *Fortune, par ta cruaulté,* Critical Notes, p. xxv). It is not unusual to find that a text given in one language contains single words from another. The polyglot text of the *rondeau Triste qui spero morendo* illustrates this practice (note the interchangable use of *chi* and *qui*).

Several of the verb forms used in the songs deserve special notice. Examples of unusual verb usage are the substitution of *servuto* for *servito* in line 6 of the *rondeau Triste qui spero morendo,* and the use of the form *spero* in relation to the understood third person subject in line 1 which may reflect a street idiom. The meaning of the verb form *armis* in line 8 of the *rondeau Entrepris suis par grant lyesse* is unclear. The word "embraced" is given as a provisional translation.

The poor correlation of text and music often found in music manuscripts dating from the second half of the fifteenth century is well known. In the source manuscripts for this edition, the division of words into syllables is the exception rather than the rule. As the facsimiles included here show, the manuscript texts are usually written under the voice parts in a prose style with little attention given to the coordination of notes and syllables. However, the difficulties of aligning the text with the music are more apparent than real if we allow for small adjustments of the type that would doubtless have occurred in the period in different performances using the same manuscripts. Minor adjustments are tacitly made in the placement of text in the edition, but all major changes related to the placement of text are recorded in the Critical Notes.

Although theoretical treatises dating from the fifteenth century do not include rules governing text underlay, a few relatively close relationships between text and music can be observed in the manuscripts containing the music. For example, there is often good correspondence between canonic (imitative) entries in the music and the placement of words (and sometimes syllables) of the text. First and final words (or syllables) of text phrases are often placed logically in relation to melodic structure. In working with these manuscripts the coordination of musical rhythm and normal language accents helps to reduce the number of alternatives when there are more tones than syllables. Where there are more syllables than tones, dividing rhythmic values in order to accommodate the text is necessary (all such divisions are recorded in the Critical Notes).

In the few places in the manuscripts where words are divided into syllables, the placement so indicated has been followed in the edition. Of particular interest are the examples in the manuscripts where the alignment of text and tones indicates that the final syllable of a word is enunciated before reaching the final tone in the cadence. Thus, the first of the following realizations would be preferable to the latter:[72]

no-   bis____

rather than

no-   bis

An interesting formulation of this principle appears in the retrospective sixteenth-century treatise *De musica verbali* attributed to Gasparis Stoqueri and recently described by Edward Lowinsky.[73] Another practice described in *De musica verbali* and confirmed by a few examples in the source manuscripts for this edition is the assignment of a final syllable to the first note of a final ligature.[74]

In most of the manuscript sources for both the Masses and the secular songs, a complete text is found only in the uppermost voice. In voices other than the superius, the text is usually fragmentary and sometimes omitted altogether; however, the quantity of text present in a given manuscript should not prohibit editorial addition of text in the lower voice parts. In cases where numerous copies of one work exist, such as the fourteen variant copies (other than tablatures) of the Vincenet *rondeau Fortune, par ta cruaulté*, the quantity of text given varies from a complete text for all voices to a total omission of text. With these conditions in mind, text has been added editorially at selected places in the edition (in both Masses and secular songs) in order to show how text might have occurred in the period, not only in variant manuscript sources, but also extemporaneously in performance. Such editorially added text appears in brackets in the Masses; but the emendations to the secular texts are recorded in the Critical Notes where individual explanations are given for the several types of emendation required in editing these texts. For example, the manuscripts sometimes include supplemental stanzas on folios containing the music transcribed but set apart from the textual underlay (as in the *rondeaux Ou doy* and *Entrepris suis*). In these cases, editorial emendation consists only of alignment of the supplemental text with the music. In another example, the stanza found only in the *Chansonnier cordiforme* is used to supplement the refrain of the *rondeau Fortune* (given without stanza in the Mellon manuscript). Other reasons for emendation of the secular texts include the correction of spelling errors and, in the case of the song-motet *O gloriosa regina mundi*, the completion of a text using an editorial method which draws on variant manuscript sources for words lacking in the source selected for transcription. A complete text is added editorially in the tenor voice part of the *rondeau Ou doy je secours querir* and in the tenor of the song-motet *O gloriosa regina mundi*; the manuscript sources selected for transcription give only the text incipits for these voice parts. Italics are used in the transcriptions of the music to show the exact manuscript placement of fragments of text in the lower voices when such fragments are not completed editorially (see, for example, the italicized text in the tenor and contratenor bassus voice parts in the Gloria and Credo of the Mass *Eterne rex altissime* [2]). In the cases of the voice parts cited above, text is not added editorially because of the decided instrumental character of the melodic lines (shown by the presence of long rhythmic values and, particularly in the contratenor bassus, the frequent and consecutive use of large melodic intervals). In the following presentation of the secular texts, the refrains are given in italics.

Texts and Translations of the
Secular Part Songs:

[5] *Villancico — La pena sin ser sabida, a 4* (Vincenet)
Mellon Chansonnier, fols. 57ᵛ-59 (*olim* pp. 112-15)

1. *La pena sin ser sabida
Es incurable dolor,
Mas quien es de mi servida
Ben sabe que por su amor
Soy triste toda mi vida.*

2. Et finge de non saber
La causa de mi tristura,

3. Por que mas a su plazer
Me pene su fermosura.

4. La gente non intendida
Non sabe mi disfavor,
*Mas quien es de mi servida
Ben sabe que por su amor
Soy triste toda mi vida.*

1. (Pain without being known
   Is an incurable suffering,
   But she who is served by me
   Knows well that because of her love
   I am sad all of my life.
2. (And she pretends not to know
   The cause of my sadness,
3. In order that her beauty, to her pleasure
   [Should] pain me more.
4. (People [who] don't understand
   Don't know of my misfortune,
   But she who is served by me
   Knows well that because of her love
   I am sad all of my life.)

[6] *Rondeau* — *Triste qui spero morendo*, a 4 (Vincenet)
Mellon Chansonnier, fols. 56ᵛ-57 (*olim* pp. 110-11)
Rubric: *Contratenor* [*altus*] *Si placet alius*

1. *Triste qui spero morendo*
   Finire ogni dolore.
   Triste qui jamay non more
   Va de foco in foco ardendo.
2. *Triste qui tene sperança*
   A lo suo tempo servuto.
   Triste chi mai nulla avança
   Sinon pena per aiuto.

1. (Sad is he who hopes, while dying,
   To end every sorrow.
   Sad is he who never dies,
   [Who] goes from blaze to blaze burning.
2. Sad is he who has hope,
   [After] he has served his time.
   Sad is he to whom nothing is left,
   Except pain for help.)

[7] *Rondeau* — *Ou doy je secours querir*, a 3 (Vincenet)
Mellon Chansonnier, fols. 31ᵛ-32 (*olim* pp. 60-1)

1. *Ou doy je secours querir,*
   Sinon par vous requerir,
   Ma seulle damme et maistresse.
2. *Aultrement ne puis lyesse,*
   Ne resconfort acquerir.
3. *San vous je ne puis cherir,*
   Et suy content de mourir,
   En angoisseuse destresse.
4. *Ou doy je secours querir,*
   Sinon par vous requerir,
   Ma seulle damme et maistresse.
5. *Faictes vers moy accourir,*
   Grace pour moy secourir,
   Et moustres vostre noblesse.
6. *Puisque vous estes princesse,*
   Pour faire ung monde fleurir.

7. *Ou doy se secours querir,*
   Sinon par vous requerir,
   Ma seulle damme et maistresse,
8. *Aultrement ne puis lyesse,*
   Ne resconfort acquerir.

1. (Where should I seek help,
   Except by beseeching you,
   My only lady and mistress,
2. Otherwise I can gain neither happiness
   Nor comfort.
3. (Without you I cannot thrive,
   And am content to die,
   In anguished distress.
4. (Where should I seek help,
   Except by beseeching you,
   My only lady and mistress.
5. (Make grace come running to me,
   To aid me,
   And show your nobility,
6. Since you are a princess,
   In such a way as to make a world bloom.
7. (Where should I seek help,
   Except by beseeching you,
   My only lady and mistress,
8. Otherwise I can gain neither happiness
   Nor comfort.)

[8] *Rondeau* — *Fortune, par ta cruaulté*, a 3 (Vincenet)
Refrain (lines 1-5) from Mellon Chansonnier, fols. 23ᵛ-24 (*olim* pp. 44-5); supplemental text from the *Chansonnier cordiforme*, fols. 34ᵛ-36

1. *Fortune, par ta cruaulté,*
   Pour dueil ou pour adversité,
   Ne pour doleur que tu m'avance,
2. *Je ne perdray ma pacience,*
   Et ne penseray lasceté.
3. *Plus tu as contre moy heurté,*
   Moins suis doubteux, plus ay seurté,
   Car j'ay le baston d'esperance.
4. *Fortune, par ta cruaulté,*
   Pour dueil ou pour adversité,
   Ne pour doleur que tu m'avance.
5. *J'ay bien maulgré ta malheuirté,*
   J'ay ris de ta diversité,
   J'ay plaisir de ton actavance,
6. *J'ay fierté contre ta puissance,*
   Car tout me vient de loyaulté.
7. *Fortune, par ta cruaulté,*
   Pour dueil ou pour adversité,
   Ne pour doleur que tu m'avance,
8. *Je ne perdray ma pacience,*
   Et ne penseray lasceté.

xviii

1. (Fortune, by your cruelty,
   Because of anguish or adversity,
   Nor because of pain you impose on me,
2. I shall not lose my patience,
   Nor shall I think evil.
3. (The more you have buffeted me,
   The less I am uncertain, the more sure am I
   For I have the rod of hope.
4. (Fortune, by your cruelty,
   Because of anguish or adversity,
   Nor because of pain you impose on me,
5. (I am well despite your ill will,
   I have laughed at your variety,
   I take pleasure in your actions,
6. I stand proudly against your power
   For all comes to me out of loyalty.
7. (Fortune, by your cruelty,
   Because of anguish or adversity,
   Nor because of pain you impose on me,
8. I shall not lose my patience,
   Nor shall I think evil.)

Rondeau — *Entrepris suis par grant lyesse, a 3* (Bartholomeus Bruolo)
Oxford, Bodleian Library, MS Canonici Misc. 213, fol. 39ᵛ

1. *Entrepris suis par grant lyesse,*
   En regardant sans autre adresse,
   Le dous contiens de son cler vis,
2. *En repensant il m'est avis,*
   Qu'el soit la flour de gentilesse.
3. Tenir l'avoye pour ma maistresse,
   D'ele servir fai je proumesse,
   Puisque mon [coeur], le siens armis.
4. *Entrepris suis par grant lyesse,*
   En regardant sans autre adresse,
   Le dous contiens de son cler vis,
5. He! Dieu d'amours de grant noblesse,
   Qui vrais amans tiens en fermesse,
   Soustiens mon [coeur], ne soit guerpis,
6. De sa doucheur, par ta mercis,
   Car y le maul que tant me blesse.
7. *Entrepris suis par grant lyesse,*
   En regardant sans autre adresse,
   Le dous contiens de son cler vis,
8. *En repensant il m'est avis,*
   Qu'el soit la flour de gentilesse.
1. (*I am seized by great happiness,*
   Upon looking without other address,
   At the sweet expression of her fair face,
2. *In thinking back it is my opinion,*
   That she is the flower of gracefulness.

3. I had to have her for my lady,
   To serve her I pledged,
   Because my heart [embraced] hers.
4. *I am seized by great happiness,*
   Upon looking without other address,
   At the sweet expression of her fair face.
5. Oh! God of great nobility,
   [You] who hold true lovers under your protection,
   Sustain my heart, let it not be abandoned,
6. By her sweetness, by your mercy,
   Because there the pain hurts so much.
7. *I am seized by great happiness,*
   Upon looking without other address,
   At the sweet expression of her fair face,
8. *In thinking back it is my opinion,*
   That she is the flower of gracefulness.)

Song-motet — *O gloriosa regina mundi, a 3* [Jo. Touront]
Paris, Bibliothèque Nationale, fonds français, MS 15123, fols. 3ᵛ-4 (Pixérécourt Chansonnier); for emendations to text see Critical Notes, p. xxvii.

1. *O gloriosa regina mundi,*
   Succurre nobis, pia, ad te clamantibus,
   Quia tu genuisti
   Salvatorem in gentibus.
2. *Ave virgo pulcherrima,*
   In gratiis uberrima,
   Ave virgo regia,
   Salutem protulisti.
1. (O glorious queen of the world,
   Help us, pious one, as we call on you,
   Because you gave birth
   To the Saviour among the nations.
2. (Hail virgin most beautiful,
   Abounding in grace,
   Hail royal virgin,
   You have provided salvation.)

Critical Notes

In the commentary for each composition, the editorial treatment of the source is described first under the heading "Transcription." When applicable, these notes are followed by a concordance of manuscripts and early printed works, by references to modern publications of the music, and by a list of variants. For an explanation of the abbreviations used in the Critical Notes and elsewhere see the following "*Sigla* and List of Manuscripts, Early Prints, and Reference Works."

In the Critical Notes for the secular part-songs,

the different voice parts in each variant copy are listed consecutively in one paragraph with the manuscript *sigla* placed at the beginning of the commentary. In the Critical Notes for the Masses, the same plan is followed except that a separate paragraph is used for each of the five major divisions of the Ordinary. In references to the quantity of text given, a complete text is indicated by the symbol (t), the presence of an incipit, or incipits, by (i), and the omission of text by the symbol (-). In listing variants, the individual entry begins with citation of the measure number. When a second number is given following the measure number, it refers to the note within the measure where the variation begins; and when this number is omitted the comment refers to the entire measure. A given variation may be limited to one change, or it may consist of several consecutive changes beginning at the place first cited (consecutive changes may involve more than one measure, but only the place where the variations begin is cited). When several variations occur in one measure the measure number is not repeated. The abbreviation *lig* used without further qualification refers to the *ligatura binaria* known as the c.o.p. *(cum opposita proprietate)*. For example; "19, 1 sb, 2 lig; 22, 2 lig 3" is to be read "measure 19, semibreve in place of first note, c.o.p. beginning with the second note in the same measure; measure 22, *ligatura ternaria* beginning with the second note in the measure." In addition, "71, 4 dotted sb g' and two sm a' c''" reads "measure 71, a dotted semibreve on g' occurs in place of the fourth note in the measure and is followed by two semiminims on a' and c'', respectively." In counting within the measure cited, tied notes are counted, but rests are not counted. The note values cited are those of the manuscript sources. Pitch is indicated in accordance with the following plan: C - B, c - b, c' (middle c) - b', c'' - b''.

A reference list of the variant copies of the Mass models appears at the end of the commentary; full critical notes are not given for these works since they are not attributed to Vincenet.

Sigla and List of Manuscripts,
Early Prints, and Reference Works

MANUSCRIPTS

BU	Bologna, Biblioteca Universitaria, MS 596, Busta H H, 2[1-4]
BUX	Munich, Bayerische Staatsbibliothek, Cim. 352[b] (Mus. MS 3725) *Buxheimer Orgelbuch*
CAS	Rome, Biblioteca Casanatense, Cod. 2856
CG	Vatican City, Biblioteca Apostolica Vaticana, Cappella Giulia, Cod. XIII, 27
CORD	Paris, Bibliothèque Nationale, Chansonnier de Jean de Montchenu (H. de Rothschild Collection) *Chansonnier cordiforme*
CS 14	Vatican City, Biblioteca Apostolica Vaticana, Cappella Sistina 14
CS 51	Vatican City, Biblioteca Apostolica Vaticana, Cappella Sistina 51
CT Grey	Cape Town, South African Library, Grey MS 3. b. 12
F229	Florence, Biblioteca Nazionale Centrale, Banco Rari 229 (Magliabecchiana XIX, 59)
FP	Florence, Biblioteca Nazionale Centrale, Cod. Panciatichi 27
FR	Florence, Biblioteca Riccardiana, MS 2356
GLO	Berlin, Deutsche Staatsbibliothek, Mus. MS 40098 (Z. 98) *Glogauer Liederbuch*
MEL	New Haven, Conn., Yale University Library, Mellon Chansonnier
MNS	Munich, Bayerische Staatsbibliothek, Cim. 351[a] (Mus. MS 3232) *Schedelsches Liederbuch*
MOD	Modena, Biblioteca Estense, MS α. M. 1. 13 (Lat. 456)
OC	Oxford, Bodleian Library, Canonici Misc. 213
OS	Oxford, Bodleian Library, MS Selden B 26
P676	Paris, Bibliothèque Nationale, Réserve Vm[7] 676
PER	Perugia, Biblioteca Comunale, Cod. 431 (G. 20)
PIX	Paris, Bibliothèque Nationale, fonds français, MS 15123, Pixérécourt Chansonnier.
PRA	Prague, Strakov Monastery, Cod. D. G. IV. 47
Q16	Bologna, Biblioteca Comunale annessa al Conservatorio di Musica "G. B. Martini," Cod. Q 16
Q18	Bologna, Biblioteca Comunale annessa al Conservatorio di Musica "G. B. Martini," Cod. Q 18
SEG	Segovia, Catedral, Codex (without number)

SEV	Sevilla, Biblioteca Colombina, Cod. 5-I-43	*RMI*	*Rivista musicale italiana*
TR 91	Trent, Castello del Buonconsiglio, MS 91	*Sta E*	*Early Bodleian Music, Sacred and Secular Songs.* Edited by Sir John Stainer. 2 vols. London: 1902.
VER	Verona, Biblioteca Capitolare, Cod. DCCLVII	*SzMw*	*Studien zur Musikwissenschaft*
		TVNM	*Tijdschrift der Vereeniging voor Nederlandsche Muziekgeschiedenis*

Early Prints

ODA	*Harmonice musices Odhecaton A.* Venice: O. Petrucci, 1501 [*RISM I*, 1501], and 1504 [*RISM I*, 1504²]
FPn	*Intabulatura de Lauto / Libro primo* (Francesco Spinacino), Venice: O. Petrucci, 1507 [*RISM I*, 1507⁵]

VfMw	*Vierteljahrsschrift für Musikwissenschaft*
York B	*Breviarium ad usum insignis ecclesie Eboracensis.* 2 vols. The Publications of the Surtees Society. Vol. 71 (1880) and Vol. 75 (1883).
ZfMw	*Zeitschrift für Musikwissenschaft*

Reference Works

AfMw	*Archiv für Musikwissenschaft*
AM	*Acta musicologica*
AnM	*Annales musicologiques*
Britt H	*The Hymns of the Breviary and Missal.* Edited by Dom. Matthew Britt, O.S.B. New York: 1948.
Chev U	Chevalier, Ulysse. *Repertorium hymnologicum.* 6 vols. Louvain, Brussels, Paris: 1892-1921.
CMM	*Corpus mensurabilis musicae*
Cous S	Coussemaker, C. E. H. *Scriptorum de musica medii aevi, nova series.*
Dreves A	*Analecta hymnica.* Edited by G. M. Dreves, C. Blume, and H. M. Bannister. Leipzig: 1886-1922.
DTOe	*Denkmäler der Tonkunst in Österreich*
GR	*Graduale sacrosanctae Romanae ecclesiae de tempore et de sanctis.* Rome: 1924.
IMAMI	*Istituzione e Monumenti dell'Arte Musicale Italiana*
JAMS	*Journal of the American Musicological Society*
JMT	*Journal of Music Theory*
Julian D	*A Dictionary of Hymnology.* Edited by John Julian. Second revised edition. New York: 1957.
MD	*Musica disciplina*
MfMg	*Monatshefte für Musikgeschichte*
MGG	*Die Musik in Geschichte und Gegenwart*
MMB	Harrison, Frank, L. *Music in Medieval Britain.* London: 1958.
MQ	*The Musical Quarterly*
RISM I	*Répertoire international des sources musicales.* Vol. 1: *Recueils imprimés des XVIe et XVIIe siècles.* Munich: 1960.

Abbreviations

a 2, a 3, a 4	*a due, a tre, a quattro*
acc	accidental
bl	black or blackened
br	breve
C^1, C^2	C-clef on line 1, line 2, etc.
c.o.p.	*cum opposita proprietate*
CTA	contratenor altus
CTB	contratenor bassus
cum-sine	*cum proprietate et sine perfectione*
ed	editorial or editorially
F^4, F^3	F- clef on line 4, line 3
Fer	fermata
fu	fusa
imp	imperfect or imperfected
Jg	Jahrgang
lg	long
lig	*ligatura binaria (c.o.p.)*
lig 3	*ligatura ternaria*
lig 4	*ligatura quarternaria*
m	minim
Nu	numeral
om	omitted
p.d.	*punctus divisionis*
per	perfect
S	superius
sb	semibreve
s.c.	*signum congruentiae*
sf	semifusa
sig	signature
sine-sine	*sine proprietate et sine perfectione*
sm	semiminim
T	tenor

[1] Mass—[*sine nomine*], a 3

TRANSCRIPTION: *TR 91*, fols. 179-184ᵛ, Vincenet, unicum.

Kyrie— Superius: sharp on d' before m. 22 refers to f' m. 22.

Gloria— Tenor: flat on f' before m. 51 refers to e' m. 52. Contratenor: 29, Nu 3; 52, b-flat on f' space treated as e'-flat; 164-72, b-flat om in sig; 164, 3 b-flat acc.

Credo—Superius: 78, 1 b'-flat acc. Tenor: 71-8, *et propter nostram salutem descendit de caelis* lacking in all voices in MS, added ed; 256-88, b-flat om in sig. Contratenor: 67, 1 b-flat acc; 188, b-flat acc.

Sanctus— Superius: 50, 3 b'-flat acc. Tenor: 107, misplaced sharp on c'-line in MS refers to f' m. 108; 138, flat before f' refers to e' m. 139.

Agnus Dei lacking in MS.

[2] Mass—*Eterne rex altissime*, a 4

TRANSCRIPTION: *CS 14*, fols. 47ᵛ-56, Vincenet, unicum.

Kyrie— Superius: 47, ℂ. Contratenor altus: 32, misplaced *Kyrie* replaced by *Christe* in m. 36; 47, ℂ. Tenor: 47, ℂ. Contratenor bassus: 47, ℂ; 54, b-flat after br A refers to m. 56.

Gloria—Contratenor bassus: 52, b-flat acc after br A refers to per br on b in m. 53.

Credo—Superius: 49, 4 two m on a equal sb in source MS; 60, reads *et propter nos homines salutem* with *nostram* om; 145-51, *cujus regni non erit finis* lacking in all voices, added ed; 190, 2 two m on f' equal sb in source MS; 196-202, *qui locutus est per Prophetas* lacking in all voices, added ed; 230, two sb on f' equal MS br. Contratenor altus: 11 both Fer in MS; 29, 2 two m and one sb on a equal MS imp br; 32, 2 two m equal MS sb; 33, 1 two m equal MS sb; 37, 1 two m equal MS sb; 49, 1 two m equal MS sb; 53, 5 two m equal MS sb; 54, 1 two m equal MS sb; 54, 3 two m and one sb on g equal MS imp br; 55, 1 two m equal MS sb; 59, 1 two sb equal MS br; 68, 2 two sb equal MS br; 76, two m equal MS sb; 132, 2 two sb on b equal MS imp br; 156-226, ed added text ends with the following phrase which is lacking in all voices: *Et unam sanctam . . . in remissionem peccatorum*; 169, two sb equal MS br. Contratenor bassus: 68, 1 Fer used as s.c.

Sanctus—Superius: 46, after 3 b-flat acc given here in MS refers to m. 48, 2.

Agnus Dei—Tenor: 17, br-rest added ed to conform to s.c. in CTA m. 18. Contratenor bassus: 17, br-rest added ed as in T above; 115, after 3 b-flat acc given here in MS refers to m. 120; 122-7, unusual ligature *maxima-longa*; both *modus maximarum* and *modus longarum* are imperfect as shown by the grouping of the rests before m. 80.

The cantus firmus is the hymn *Aeterne Rex altissime* used in the Roman liturgy as a hymn at Matins for Ascension-day and daily until Pentecost; Sarum rite uses this cantus firmus as a hymn at Vespers on the Vigil of the Ascension and daily to Whitsuntide, and also at Matins on Ascension-day and in the Procession for Corpus Christi; occurs also in Ambrosian and Mozarabic use, see: *Britt H*, pp. 146-7; *Chev U*, Vol. 1: 40-1; *Dreves A*, Vol. 27: 96-7, 291; *Julian D*, pp. 26-8; *York B*, Vol. 1, col. 475; two-part setting in *Sta E*, facsimile in vol. 1: xci with transcription in vol. 2: 163 (cf. *MMB*, p. 382).

[3] Mass—*Entrepris suis par grant lyesse*, a 4

TRANSCRIPTION: *MOD*, fols. 55ᵛ-69, Vincenet, unicum.

Kyrie—Superius: 12, Fer; 20, ○3; 25, ○; 38, Nu 3; 45, ○; 48, after 5, Nu 3. Contratenor altus: 20, after 2, ○3. Tenor: 32, 3 Fer. Contratenor bassus: 21, ○3; 38, ○3; 44, ○; 49, ○3.

Gloria—Superius: 79, 2 Fer; 141, redundant syllable -a to show placement of final syllable (first-a in m. 134); 155, Nu 3 after br. Contratenor altus: 31, after 3, Nu 3; 33, after 3, ○; 42, *Deus* used in MS in place of *Fili*; 79, 2 Fer; 166, Nu 3 after br-rest. Tenor: 27-8 and 31-2, quarter-rests are ed divided half-rests; 39, ○ before br; 40, ○3 before first imp br; 44 *Crescit i duplo ut prius*; 78, 2 Fer. Contratenor bassus: 25, after 1, Nu 3; 26, after 2, ○; 31, after 2, Nu 3; 33, after 3, ○; 79, 1 Fer; 115, *Tu*; 118, *solus*; 121, *altissimus*; 155, Nu 3 after br.

Credo—Superius: 1-23, a b-flat in sig; 23 (after 3)-43, b-flat and e'-flat in sig; 44-6, no flats in sig; 46-85, a b-flat in sig; following 85, *Et resurrexit* lacking; 91, 2 two sm equal MS m; 104, ϕ3. Contratenor altus: following 85, *Et resurrexit* lacking. Tenor: following 85, *Et resurrexit* lacking; 111, b-flat in sig om. Contratenor bassus: 83, 1 b-flat acc; following 85, *Et resurrexit* lacking.

Sanctus—Superius: 1-6, a b-flat in sig; 7-38, b-flat and e-flat sig. Contratenor altus: 1-6, a b-flat in sig; 7-38, b-flat and e-flat sig; 62, 5 b-flat acc; 80, Nu 3 after B; 95, ₵ after sb. Tenor: 86, Nu 3 after br; 95, ₵ after br.

Agnus Dei—Superius: 1-7, no flats in sig; 8-30, a b-flat in sig. Contratenor altus: 1-15, a b-flat in sig; 16-30, b-flat and e-flat in sig. Contratenor bassus: 28, after 2, Nu 3.

[4] Mass—*O gloriosa regina mundi*, a 4

TRANSCRIPTION: *CS 51*, fols. 27ᵛ-36, Vincenet.

Kyrie—Superius: 49, sharp on d' space in MS refers to f' in m. 50; 72, 1 f''-flat acc.

Gloria—Superius: 91, 2 f''-flat acc; 106, Fer; 113, Fer. Contratenor altus: 106, Fer. Tenor: 106, Fer. Contratenor bassus: 106, Fer.

Credo—Superius: 25, *Deum de Deo, lumen de lumine* lacking in all voices in MS; 73, *est* deleted after *passus* in MS; 140, comparison of Superius, CTA and CTB beginning here shows the triplet relationship of the blackened notes to the normal two-time flow of *tempus imperfectum*; 202, 1 two sm equal MS m. Contratenor altus: 59, 1 m and sb equal MS dotted sb; 73, *est* deleted after *passus*; 131-2, sb and br equal MS, dotted br; 170-80, *Et unam sanctam catholicam et apostolicam Ecclesiam* lacking in all voices in MS is inserted here as part of editorially added text ending at m. 230. Tenor: 1-5, b-flat om in sig; 202, 1 two sm equal MS m. Contratenor bassus: 25-9, *Deum de Deo, lumen de lumine*, lacking in all voices in MS, is inserted here as part of editorially added text beginning m. 13 and ending mm. 61-4; 43, 1 two sm equal MS m; 96, 2 b-flat acc; 165, 1 b-flat acc; 170-9, *Et unam sanctam . . . Ecclesiam* lacking in MS.

Sanctus—Superius: 42-4, *cae-* before *et* and *-li* before *terra*; 45, Fer; 89, 2 f''-flat acc. Contratenor bassus: 83, 2 b-flat acc.

Agnus Dei—Contratenor bassus: 43, 2 m d from TR 91, fol. 81, in place of e given in CS 51.

CONCORDANCE: TR 91, fols. 73v-82, Vincenet.

VARIANTS:

Kyrie, TR 91, fols. 73v-74—Superius: no flat in sig; 4, lig; 19, 1 sb d'', 4 sb a'; 20, 3 sb g', 5 m f'; 26, lig 3; 31, 2 sb a'; 41, lig 2d note bl; 42, 2 c'' bl; 44, lig; 45, 3 lig; 54, 3 lig; 69, lig 3; 73, 3 br d''; 74, 4 sb c''; 77, 1 lig; 80, 1 lig; 88, lig 3; 92, lig; 96, lig; 97, lig; 98, 3 lig; 105, br g'; 106, 4 sb f'. Contratenor altus: no flat in sig; 20, 2 dotted sb d'; 21, 1 lg d'; 24, *Christe tacet*; 70, lig; 71, 4 dotted sb g, and two sm a b; 86, sb, two m e', sb f', dotted sb d'; 88, 1 m b' and sb d'; 92-4, 3 lig; 95, 1 dotted m b, sm c', br d'; 98, lig; 101, 1 lig 2d note dotted; 104, 1 m d'; 106, 4 lig. Tenor: 2, lig; 4, 3 br g'; 5, 3 sb f'; 6-9, lig 4; 33, 3 sb g; 41-3, lig 4; 44, 1 lig; 49, 2 rare ligature semibreve-long g and a; 79, 1 lig; 80, 2 sb g'; 83, 2 m c'; 91, 1 lig 3; 96, lig; 97, 1 dotted sb d' and m e'; 98, 1 lig f' g'; 99, 2 lig; 101, 3 lig; 104, 3 lig. Contratenor bassus: 21, 1 lg d'; 28, lig; 52, 1 lig 3; 74, 3 dotted m a and sm g; 88, 1 sb d' dot om; 89, 1 m d'; 90, 1 dotted br d; 98, 3 lig; 99, 1 lig om.

Gloria, TR 91, fols. 74v-76—Superius: no flat in sig; 14, 1 sb f', 3 lig a' b' 2d note bl; 15, 2 bl m b', 18, 1 dotted sb a', 4 lig; 20, 2 sb b'; 21, 4 lig 2d note bl; 23, 2 dotted sb b'; 26, 1 sb b', 4 sb b'; 27, 1 sb g', 5 lig d'' and b'; 29, 2 sb a'; 35, 2 sb-rest, 3 sb g'; 36, 1 sb d' and m a'; 37, 2 lig a' and c''; 38, 2 dotted sb c''; 39, 2 dotted sb d''; 41, 2 sb a'; 42, 3 sb f'; 43, 4 lig; 45, 3 sb c''; 47, 3 lig g' and d'; 54, 3 lig; 56, 1 lig; *Qui tollis*, no flat in sig; 70, 1 dotted sb d'' and dotted sb e''; 71, lig c'' and d'' dotted; 74, 2 lig; 75, lig om; 80, 3 sb d''; 88, 2 m c''; 92, 2 sb e''; 94, 1 sb d'', 4 sb bl; 95, 2 m bl, 3 lig f' and a'; 97, 2 lig f' and a'; 101, 5 sb f'; 104, lg b'; 107, br-rest before m. 107; 108, br; 110, bl om; 118, br; 119, br; 124, lig; 129, lig; 130, lig; 137, 2 lig; 138, 2 lig; 143, 2 dot om; 146, 2 lig; 151, 3 sb bl; 152, 2 sm bl; 153, 3 br c''; 154, 4 sb b'; 156, 1 lig; 158, 2 b'-flat; 175, 1 sb g'; 186, 4 sm g'. Contratenor altus: no flat in sig; 1, 1 lig; 3, 2 dotted sb g'; 8, 1 lig d' and b; 11, 3 sb f', 5 lig; 17, 2 sb d', 4 sb e'; 20, 1 dotted sb; 21, 6 dotted sb; 22, 3 lig e' and c'; 25, 1 dotted sb; 27, 1 e'-flat, 4 bl sb and bl m; 30, 1 sb b, 3 bl sb and bl m; 33, 4 bl sb a' and bl m g'; 34, 3 m f'; 36, 2 bl sb and bl m; 37, 1 bl sb and bl m; 41, 2 bl sb and bl m, 5 bl sb and bl m; 42, 2 bl sb and bl m; 45, 2 lig; 48, 5 bl sb and bl m; 56, 3 lig; 71, 2 lig; 81, 1 sb g'; 107, br-rest before m. 107; 108, 1 br f'; 109, 3 bl sb and bl m; 112, 1 lg a; 117-20, lig 4; 122, lig; 123, lig; 136, lig; 146, lig e' and g'; 147-8, lig 3; 148, 1 br b; 151, 1 sb e', 4 dotted sb d'; 157, 4 sb f'; 159, 1 br d'; 160, 1 sb g' and sb e'; 160-1, 1 lig 3; 172, lig om; 173, 1 m g' and lig f' and a'; 175, lig; 176, 1 lig; 179, lig 3; 185, 1 dotted sb g'; 186, 3 lig d' and f'; 187, 2 dotted br d'; 189, 1 lg b. Tenor: 7, 3 sb c'; 12, 5 sb f'; 13, 5 sb d'; 14, 5 lig f and a; 15, 3 dotted sb c', 6 lig om; 19, 1 br d'; 21, 5 lig c' and g; 25, 1 lig c' and g'; 27, 1 sb b; 28, 1 sb g; 33, 3 sb d'; 36, 2 sb d'; 37, 1 sb d'; 42, 1 dotted sb d', 3 sb f', 5 m a'; 43, 1 sb d', followed by sb on a, m-rest, and sb on b'; 44, 2 sb a'; 45, 2 sb f'; 48, 4 sb c'; 51, 4 lig; 52, 2 lig; 53, 3 lig; 54, 2 lig; 55, 1 lig om; 56, 3 lig om; 58, 3 lig om; 89, lig; 91, 1 sb g'; 97, 1 sb d', 3 lig a and c'; 100, 1 sb e'; 107, br-rest before m. 107; 107, lig; 108, 1 br c'; 109, 2 lig; 110, 1 lig om; 111, lig g and b; 113, 1 lg a; 120, 1 br f'; 121, 1 br e'; 125, lig; 131, 2 lig om; 132, 1 lig; 134, 3 m b; 140, 1 lig e' and c', 3 lig om; 141, 3 sb d'; 153-6, lig 4; 164, bl notes om; 178, 1 sb b and sb c'; 187-92, lig 4. Contratenor bassus: 11, 1 sb g; 12, 1 sb a; 15, 1 dotted sb f; 17, 2 sb b, 3 sb g; 25, 1 bl sb and bl m; 27, 3 sb g; 45, 2 lig a and c'; 48, 5 sb f; 49, 4 sb e; 52, 5 lig om; 53, 2 sb c; 54, 3 lig; 58, 2 e-flat; 87, lig; 94, 4 bl sb g; 95, 2 bl m f; 99, 1 lig g and d; 101, 1 lig 3; 104, 1 lg g; 107, br-rest before m. 107; 107, 1 br b; 108, 1 br a; 110, 1 notes in 110-12 in lig 4 with Fer on last note; 120, 1 ligature *sine-sine* (br d and br a); 125, lig om; 127, 1 br g; 131, two imp lg d followed by sb d; 134, 1 lig; 139, lig om; 146, 1 lig c' and g; 156, 3 lig; 157, 1 lig om; 158, 3 lig; 159, 1 lig om; 160, 3 lig f and g and sb a; 175, 1 lig; 176, 2 lig; 179, 1 lig g and d; 180, 1 lig g and b; 183, 1 sb a, 3 bl sb and bl sm; 187, 1 lig 4.

Credo, TR 91, fols. 76v-78—Superius: no flat in sig; 8, 4 lig a' and c''; 9, 2 lig b' and a'; 13, 2 lig dotted d''; 16, 1 lig; 17, 4 sb c''; 29, 3 dotted m bl om; 30, 2 sm c'' not bl; 35, 5 lig f' and a'; 41, 3 sb f'; 43, 2 sb e'; 46, 1 imp br c''; 48, 2 sb b'; 49, 1 sb g'; 50, 1 lig; 65-79, *Crucifixus . . . est* om; *Et resurrexit*, no flat in sig before m. 80; 83, 2 m b'; 91, 2 m b', 4 sb c''; 97, 3 br a'; 106, 1 sm a', 2 sm g', 3 m f'; 108, 2 sm c''; 120, 3 br g'; 121, 5 m f'; 130, 2 ligature *sine-sine* (br e'' br d''); 132, 4 sb c''; 136, 3 m b'; 160, 2 sb g'; 168, 2 m g'; 170-80, *Et unam sanctam . . . Ecclesiam* om; 184-6, lig 4; 195, lig; 214, 2 m c''; 228, 2 m a', 3 m a'; 229, 5 sb f'. Contratenor altus: 2, 1 dotted sb d'; 4, 2 lig; 5, 2 sb a'; 7, 1 sb g', 4 sb d'; 8, 1 sb f'; 9, 5 br d'; 10, 4 lig g' and e'; 11, 4 dotted sb a'; 12, 3 sb g', 5 sb f'; 24, 1 per br d'; 25, 1 lig e' and f'; 26, 2 lig first note dotted b and c'; 28, 3 sb f'; 30, 1 lig g and c'; 31, 2 bl sb and bl m, 6 lig; 32, 2 sb a'; 33, 1 lig; 34, 2 lig f' and c'; 35, 3 dotted sb d' and sb d'; 36, 2 dotted sb d'; 41, 1 lig sb d' and bl sb f' and bl m g'; 43, 2 lig g' and f'; 44, 3 lig sb g' dotted sb a' and dotted sb d'; 45, 4 two sm c' and b followed by sb a; 46, 3 br g; 48, 1 lig sb d' and dotted sb b; 52, 3 lig b and d'; 54, 4 dotted sb f'; 59, 1 lig; 60, 1 per br d'; 65-79, *Crucifixus* om; 122, 3 sb g'; 123, 3 m e'; 137, 3 dotted m d' and sm c'; 144, 1 bl br d' and bl sb d'; 151, 3 lig 3; 155-6, 1 ligature *sine-sine* (br e' and br g'); 157, 2 m f'; 158, lig; 170-80, *Et unam sanctam . . . Ecclesiam* om; 171-2, 1 ligature *sine-sine* (br c' and br d'); 175, 3 lig; 186, 1 lig; 190, lig; 192, 3 lig; 194, 4 lig; 198, 1 dotted br a; 206, 1 dotted br a'; 210, 1 ligature *sine-sine* (lg d' and br f'); 213, 2 lig; 216, 2 dotted br d'; 224, 3 sb d'; 225, 3 sb a and two sm b and c'; 229, 1 lg d'. Tenor: no flat in sig; 1, 1 lg g'; 2, 2 sb f'; 5, 3 two sb e' and e'; 8, 1 lig; 12, 1 sb d', before 4 C¹ wrong clef (C³ correct), 4 lig; 13, 2 dotted sb f'; 16, 3 lig; 17, 4 sb e'; 24, before 1 C¹ wrong clef (C³ correct); 27, 1 sb e', 7 sb g'; 28, 6 sb g'; 29, 4 sb c'; 32, 1 per br; 33, 3 lig; 36, 1 dotted sb d'; 37, before 1 C¹ wrong clef (C³ correct), 2 dotted sb c'; 41, 1 imp br d'; 45, 1 imp br f', 5 dotted sb c'; 46, 2 dotted sb c' and m c'; 47, 1 lig e' and g'; 48, 3 sb d'; 49, 2 lig b and c'; 54, 2 lig; 55, 3 lig; 65-79, *Crucifixus* om; *Et resurrexit,* no flat in sig; 80, 1 lg; 82, 2 m d'; 87, 2 m e'; 88, 1 lg; 107, lig; 120-2, 1 lig 4; 170-80, *Et unam sanctam . . . Ecclesiam* om; 195, 2 br g'; 199, 1 lg f'; 205, 2 lig om; 206, 1 br d'; 207, 1 sb c'; 209, 1 lig. Contratenor bassus: 1, 1 lg; 2, 2 lg begun in m. 1 imp here by dotted m d and sm e identical to those given in edition; 6, before 3 C³ wrong clef (C⁴ correct); 7, 2 lig; 8, 1 lig om; 9, 4 lig om; 10, 1 lig d and a, 4 lig b and c'; 11, 2 lig d' and a; 13, 2 dotted sb d; 17, 1 lig d' and g, 4 sb a; 19, 1 sm d' marked as error in MS (the MS scribe marked his error, but did not correct it), from context should be m d', before 4 C³ wrong clef (C⁴ correct); 21, 4 lig 2d note bl and bl m; 25, 2 lig; 28, 3 lig; 33, before 3 C³ wrong clef (C⁴ correct); 35, 2 dotted sb d; 36, 4 two fu e and f; 37, 3 lig f and d; 38, 1 imp br b; 39, 6 sb f and sb f; 42, 1 dotted sb d; 44, 2 lig g and d; 45, 3 imp br; 46, before 3 C³ wrong clef (C⁴ correct), 3 imp br; 47, 1 dotted sb c'; 48, 5 lig 2d note bl followed by bl m; 49, 5 lig a and d; 50, 3 lig e and d; 57, before 3 C³ wrong clef (C⁴ correct); 58, 1 sb d; 59, 1 lig g and b, 4 lig; 61, 1 ligature *sine-cum* (lg g and lg d'); 65-79, *Crucifixus* om; 80, 1 br g; 82, 1 br d'; 84, 1 dotted sb b; 87, 1 br d; 88, 1 sb g; 92, 2 dotted sb g; 97, 1 lig 3; 98, 1 lig om; 99, 1 two sb d and d; 100, 1 br f; 101, lig; 103, 2 lig b and d'; 104, 2 lig; 108, 1 br d; 110, 1 two m d and f; 116, 1 br g; 118, 1 lig; 122, 1 lig; 123, 1 lig om; 124, 1 lig; 126, lig; 129, lig; 130, 2 lig; 131, 1 lig om; 135, 3 lig; 137, 2 lig 2d note bl; 149, rest om and lig begins at beginning of m. with bl br; 151, 3 lig om, 4 lig; 152, flat before 2; 162, 1 br f; 170, 1 lig 2d note dotted; 175, 3 lig; 185, 1 lig; 221, 1 lig, 2 lig om; 230, 1 ligature *sine-cum* (lg g and lg d').

Sanctus, TR 91, fols. 78ᵛ-80 —Superius, no flat in sig; 4, lig; 10, 3 br a' dotted; 40, 2 sm a'; 41, 6 m b' and m g'; 42, 1 sm a', 2 sm g', 3 sm f', 4 sm e'; 44, 6 sb g', 9 m f'; *Gloria tua* tacet; *Hosanna,* no flat in sig; 71, 1 br; after 82 four m. om and introduced after m. 101; 90, 3 sm bl c''; 92, after 5 C³ wrong clef (C¹ correct); 96, 4 lig a' and g'; following m. 101 four m. inserted supplying om notes from mm. 83-6, no change except C³ should be C¹; *Benedictus,* no flat in sig; 103, 3 br d'; 104, 4 sb c''; 111, 2 lig; 123, lig; 128, 2 lig; 139, 2 sign here may be a sharp. Contratenor altus: 1, 3 sm g; 7, 3 sm c'; 11, lig; 26, 1 dotted sb a; 29, 2 sm e' and sb dotted d'; 30, 2 sm c'; *Pleni* tacet; 50, 2 sb e'; 51, 1 sb d'; 75, sb c' in place of sb-rest; 97, 3 dotted sb d'; 98, 1 lg d'; 119-20, 1 ligature (br g and bl br d') and bl sb e'; 121, lig; 131, 3 m b and two sm a and g; 133-5, 1 ligature (lg a and br g); 138, 2 m-rest and sb d' and two m c' and b. Tenor: 22, 2 lig; 26, 1 sb f' and two m f' and e'; 66, 1 lig; 70, 1 lig 3, 1 lig 4 om; 75, 3 lig om; 76, 1 lig 4; 86, 1 lig 4; 91, lig; 92, 2 m c'; 95, 2 lig. Contratenor bassus: 9, 2 sb g; 10, 3 sb f; 20, 1 lig b and a, 2 lig om; 25, 1 sb c', 3 lig sb a and dotted sb f; 27, 1 sb f; 30, 1 lg g; 81, 1 lig f and a; 86, 1 ligature *sine-sine* (lg d and br a); 97, 3 rare ligature sb d and lg g.

Agnus Dei, TR 91, fols. 80ᵛ-82 —Superius: no flat in sig; 5-9, lig 4; 28, lig; 29, 1 lig; 55, no flat in sig; 70, 4 sb a'; 71, 2 dotted m g'; 72, 2 lig e'; 76, lig; 91, 1 m d'', 2 sb b'; 97, 4 lig; 103, no flat in sig; 111, 2 dotted m b' followed by sm c''; 121, 5 m b'; 122, 2 dotted sb c''; 123, 2 sm a'; 125, br a'; 126, 1 sb-rest added and g' om. Contratenor altus: 7, 1 lig om; 8-10, 1 ligature *sine-sine* (lg d' and br g); 20, 1 lig om; 21-3, 1 ligature *sine-sine* (lg d' and br c'); 47, lig; 50, 1 dotted m f' and sm e', lig om; 55, no flat in sig, 2 sb b; 58, lig (dotted sb g and sb d') follows sb at beginning of measure 58; 61, 1 lig, 2 sb d'; 86, 1 sb g'; 89, 4 dotted m b and sm a; 96, 4 sb g'; 103, no flat in sig, 1 lig om; 105-7, 1 ligature *sine-sine* (lg f' and br d'); 110, 4 lig; 114, 2 sm b. Tenor: 1, 1 lig 4; 49, 1 lig 3, 1 lig 4 om. Contratenor bassus: 3, 1 lig (sb d and bl sb f) and bl m; 10, 1 bl br d' and bl sb c'; 11, 1 lig 5; 21, 1 lig 3 om; 22, 1 lig; 26, 1 lig 3; 29, lig; 38, 1 lig c' and d'; 44, 2 lig 3; 152, *Et sic est finis huius misse.*

[5] *Villancico—La pena sin ser sabida, a 4*

TRANSCRIPTION: *MEL*, fols. 57ᵛ-59 (*olim* pp. 112-15), Vincenet, (t) (i) (i) (i), *unicum*. Superius: 8-15, b-flat in sig; 11, 5 modern usage *bien*; 29, 2 Nu 3; 38, Fer; text underlay limited to *estribillo* and *mudanza*, text for telescoped *vuelta* and *estribillo* given separately on fol. 57ᵛ. Contratenor [altus]: 38 Fer. Tenor: 8-16, b-flat in sig; before 8, clef C⁴ to C³; before 17, clef C³ to C⁴.

[6] *Rondeau—Triste qui spero morendo, a 4*

TRANSCRIPTION: *MEL*, fols. 56ᵛ-57 (*olim* pp. 110-11), Vincenet, (t) (-) (i) (i), *unicum*. Superius: modern text usage is as follows: 2, 2 *chi*; 3, *spera*; 14, 1 *chi*; 29, 2 *chi*; 32, 2 *Ha*; 34, 5 *servito*; text underlay limited to refrain (no supplemental text given). Contratenor [altus]: Rubric: *Si placet alius*. [Contratenor] bassus: 9, 1 e-flat acc.

[7] *Rondeau—Ou doy je secours querir, a 3*

TRANSCRIPTION: *MEL*, fols. 31ᵛ-32 (*olim* pp. 60-1), Vincenet, (t)(i)(i). Superius: 1-10, no flat in sig; 11-26, b'-flat in sig; 23, 1 b'-flat acc; 27-41, b'-flat and e'-flat in sig; 41-54, e'-flat in sig; 44, 1 f'-sharp by a later hand; text underlay limited to refrain, stanza given separately on fol. 31ᵛ. Tenor: underlay of complete text ed added.

CONCORDANCE: *PIX*, fols. 168ᵛ-169, Anon., (t) (i) (i), *Ou doy ge seccours*.

MODERN EDITION: Opening given by Manfred F. Bukofzer, "An Unknown Chansonnier of the 15th Century (The *Mellon Chansonnier*)," *MQ* 28 (1942): 22. See also, idem, "The Mellon Chansonnier," *The Yale University Library Gazette* 15 (1940): 25.

VARIANTS: *PIX*, fols. 168ᵛ-169—Superius: ¢; 1-13, no flat in sig; 14-28, b'-flat in sig; 29-45, no flat in sig; 46-54, e''-flat in sig; 4,1 b'-flat acc; 21, 2 two sm b'-flat and a'; 24, 1 b'-flat acc; 25, 3 dotted sb g' and m f'; 26, 2 two m f' and e'; 46, before 1 G-clef; 52, 1 lg c''. Tenor: ¢; b-flat as sig throughout; 9, 1 e'-flat acc; 17, sharp om; 20, 2 e'-flat acc; 22, lig om; 40, 1 e'-flat acc; 42, 1 e'-flat acc; 46, 1 lig; 47, 1 bl br f' and bl sb g'. Contratenor: ¢; 5, lig 3; 7, 1 bl br f; 16, lig; 17, 1 lg g; 23-4, lig om; 40, 2 a-flat om.

[8] *Rondeau—Fortune, par ta cruaulté, a 3*

TRANSCRIPTION: *MEL*, fols. 23ᵛ-24 (*olim* pp. 44-5), Vincenet, (t) (t) (i). Superius: 22, 1 e''-flat acc; 37, 1 e''-flat acc; 48, 1 e''-flat acc; text underlay limited to refrain in S and T, stanza from *CORD* (fols. 34ᵛ-36). The refrain in *CORD* differs in spelling in m. 16, *deul*; mm. 24-7, *douleur*; mm. 28-31, *m'avanches*; and mm. 49-54, *laschete*. Contra [tenor]: 12, 3 B-flat acc; 48, 2 B-flat acc.

CONCORDANCES: *BU*, 596, H H, 2¹⁻⁴; Anon., (i) (i) (i), T and CT in tablature with superius in mensural notation, *fortuna vincinecta*; *BUX*, fol. 66ᵛ, Anon., organ tablature; *CG*, fols. 33ᵛ-34, Vincinet, (i) (-) (-); *Fortuna par te cruelte*; *CORD*, fols 34ᵛ-36, Anon.; (t) (t) (t), with supplementary text, fols. 35 and 36; *CT Grey*, fol. 121 (*olim* fol. 138), Contrafactum with text: *Nihil est opertum quod non reveletur et occultum quod non sciatur*, Matt. 10:26; S and T given, CT lacking; *F229*, fols. 50ᵛ-51, Anon., (t) (i) (i), *Fortune per ta crualte*; *FPn*, fols. 36ᵛ-37, Anon., lute tablature, *Fortuna per te crudele*; *GLO*, Discantus l11ᵛ, Tenores m7ᵛ, Kontratenores m12ᵛ, Anon., (-) (-) (-); *ODA*, 65ᵛ-66, Vincinet, (i) (i) (i), *Fortuna per ta crudelte*; *PER*, fols. 94ᵛ-95, Anon., (i) (-) (-); *Fortuna vincinecta*; *PIX*, fols. 166ᵛ-167, Anon., (t) (i) (i); *Q16*, fols. 116ᵛ-117, Anon., (i) (i) (i), added *altus* transcribed below in variants, and printed in facsimile by Helen Hewitt (see Editions, below); *Q18*, fols. 37ᵛ-38, Vincinet (added ascription); (i) (-) (-) (-), added *altus* of instrumental character (different from that of *Q16*) with rubric: *Per diateseron intensa*; *SEG*, fol. 105 (*olim* 112), Eloy, (i) (i), *Fortuna vincineta*, two-voice instrumental arrangement based on the S and T voices of *Fortune*; *SEV*, fols. 61ᵛ-62, Anon., (i) (i) (i), *Fortuna per te crudele*; *VER*, fols. 66ᵛ-67, Anon., (-) (-) (-).

MODERN EDITIONS: *FPn* variant: a transcription of the lute tablature printed by F. Spinacino can be seen with a transcript of the *ODA* variant in: Benvenuto Disertori, *Le frottole per canto e liuto intabulate da Franciscus Bossinensis*, IMAMI, nuova serie, 3 (Milano, 1964): 180-3; *GLO* variant: H. Ringmann and J. Klapper, eds., *Das Glogauer Liederbuch, Erster Teil: Deutsche Lieder u. Spielstücke*, Das Erbe Deutscher Musik, Reichsdenkmale 4 (Kassel: 1936): 68, No. 275; *ODA* variant: Helen Hewitt, ed., *Harmonice musices Odhecaton A* (Cambridge, Mass.: 1942), p. 347, No. 60 (see also p. 200 for facsimile of added *altus* in *Q16*); a facsimile of the Treviso, Biblioteca Capitolare, copy of the 1501 print of *ODA* [RISM I 1501] has been issued, *Harmonice . . .A*, Collezione di trattati e musiche antiche edite in facsimile (Milano: 1932), as well as a facsimile of the 1504 printing [RISM I 1504²] (New York: 1973); *SEV* variant: a reproduction of the Sevilla manuscript appears in *Facsimile Reproduction of the Manuscripts Sevilla 5-I-43 and Paris N. A. Fr. 4379 (Pt. 1)*, intro. Dragan Plamenac, Publication of Mediaeval Musical Manuscripts, No. 8 (Brooklyn, N. Y.: 1962).

VARIANTS:

CG, fols. 33ᵛ-34—Superius: 29, 2 dotted bl sb and bl m g'; 37-8, ligature *cum-sine*; 40, f''-flat acc; 42, 3 lig; 48, 1 e''-flat acc. Contratenor: clef C⁵; 7, 1 a-flat acc om; 16, 2 a-flat acc om; 28, 2 two sb b-flat a; 31, 3 a-flat acc om; 33, 3 dotted br c; 39-40, ligature *cum-sine*; 45, 1 a-flat acc om; 47, 3, lig om; 48, 2 lig om; 51, 1 a-flat acc om.

CT Grey, fol. 121 (*olim* 138)—Superius: sig e'-flat, b'-flat, e''-flat; 5, b-natural om; 13, 2 two m f' and e'-flat (error—should be two sm); 42, 2 two sm c'' and b'-flat; 43, lig om; 48, 1 e''-flat acc om; 53, Fer. Tenor: 6, two sb d' and d'; 20, 3 lig om; 44, 4 two sm e'-flat and d'; 45, 1 bl sm and bl m c' and b-flat, 2 dotted sb c'; 46, 2 two sm b'-flat and a; 53, Fer. Contratenor is lacking.

CORD, fols. 34v-36—Superius: 1-21, b'-flat alone as sig; 5, b-natural acc om; 12, 1 e'-flat acc; 18, lig om; 19, 3 lig om; 48, 1 e''-flat acc. Tenor: 19, lig om; 35, sharp as acc before b'-flat; 41, 2 bl om, dotted m d' and sm e'-flat; 52, lig. Contra[tenor]: 7, 2 bl m g and f; 8, bl br and sb e-flat and f; 12, 3 B-flat acc; 13, 1 bl om, dotted m e-flat and sm f; 16, 2 a-flat om; 24, lig; 26, lig; 31, 3 a-flat acc om; 33, 1 dotted m and sm e-flat and d, 3 dotted sb c and dotted sb c.

F229, fols. 50v-51—Superius: ₵ 2; 13, 2 two sm f' and e'; 23, lig; 29, 2 m and sm b' and g'; 43, lig om; 47, lig; 48, 3 bl om, dotted m and sm; 51, bl om, dotted m and sm. Tenor: ₵ 2; 12, 4 lig om; 20, 3 lig om; 23, 1 lig; 25, lig; 35, sharp as acc before b'-flat; 38-9, ligature *cum-sine*; 41, 2 bl om, dotted m and sm; 42, 3 lig; 48, lig; 49, 2 bl om, dotted m and sm; 52, lig. Contratenor: ₵ 2; clef C5; 1, lig om; 3, lig om; 7, 2 two sm g and f; 12, 3 B-flat acc; 16, 2 a-flat om; 24, 2 lig; 26, lig; 28, 1 dotted m and sm c' and b-flat; 30, 2 bl om, dotted m and sm; 31, 3 a-flat acc om; 33, 1 dotted m and sm e-flat and d, 3 dotted br c; 39-40, ligature *cum-sine*; 43, lig; 47, bl om, dotted m and sm; 48, 2 B-flat acc; 50, 1 bl om, dotted m and sm; 52, lig.

GLO, Discantus 111v, Tenores m7v, Kontratenores m12v—Superius: ₵ 2; 2, 1 dotted sb c'' and two sm b'-flat and a', bl om; 8, 1 dotted sb g' and two sm f' e', bl om; 18, lig om; 23, lig; 24, lig 2d note dotted; 25, 2 lig; 26, 3 dotted m and sm c'' and b'-flat, bl om; 29, 2 dotted m and sm b'-flat and a'; 37-9, lig 3; 46, 1 lig; 47, 2 lig; 48, 2 dotted m and sm f'' and e''-flat, bl om; 51, 1 dotted m and sm c'' and a', bl om; 53, Fer. Tenor: ₵ 2; 10, dotted sb c' and two sm b-flat and a, bl om; 27, 2 m b-flat; 45, 3 dotted m and sm c' and b-flat; 49, 2 dotted m and sm f' and e'-flat, bl om; 53, Fer. Contratenor: ₵ ; 5-6, lg; 7, sb a-flat and two sm g and f, bl om; 13, 1 dotted m and sm e-flat and f, bl om; 15, e-flat acc; 24, lig; 25, 1 m-rest and three m g a c'; 26, lig; 30, 1 half bl c.o.p. sb d and dotted bl sb e-flat; 31, 3 m, a-flat om; 33, 1 dotted m e-flat and sm d, 3 sb c; 34, 1 m c sb c and m c; 39-40, ligature *cum-sine*; 43, lig; 47, 1 dotted m c' and sm b-flat, bl om; 50, 1 dotted m c and sm b-flat, bl om; 51, 1 a-flat om; 52, lig; 53, Fer.

ODA, fols. 65v-66—Superius: sig e'-flat, b'-flat, e''-flat; 2, bl om, dotted sb and two sm; 3, lig om; 5, sharp as acc before b'-flat; 8, bl om, dotted sb and two sm; 9, 1 two sb d' and d'; 10, lig om; 18, lig om; 19, 3 lig om; 26, 3 bl om, dotted m and sm; 30, 3 bl om, dotted m and sm; 38, 1 two sb d'' and d''; 39-40, ligature *cum-sine*; 42, 2 two sm c'' and b'-flat; 43, lig om; 48, 2 bl om, dotted m and sm; 51, 1 bl om, dotted m and sm. Tenor: 1-3, lig om; 6, 1 two sb d' and d'; 7, lig om; 10, 1 dotted sb and two sm, bl om; 12, 4 lig om; 19, 1 lig om; 20, 3 lig om; 41, 2 dotted m and sm, bl om; 49, 2 dotted m and sm, bl om. Contratenor: clef F3; 3, lig om; 5-6, lg; 7, 1 br a-flat, bl om; 8, 1 br c; 9, 1 two m e-flat and f and sb g; 13, 1 dotted m and sm, bl om; 16, 1 lig; 17, 1 br; 22, 1 lig om; 30, 2 dotted m and sm, bl om; 31, 3 m, a-flat acc om; 47, 1 dotted m and sm, bl om, 3 lig om; 48, 2 lig om; 50, 1 dotted m and sm, bl om, 3 m g and m-rest; 51, 1 a-flat acc om.

PER, fols. 94v-95—Superius: b'-flat in sig; 2, dotted sb c'' and two sm b'-flat and a, bl om; 8, dotted sb g' and two sm f' and e', bl om; 12, 3 bl br g' and two bl m f' and e'; 17,1 b'-flat acc; 26, 3 dotted m and sm, bl om; 29, 2 dotted m b'-flat and sm g'; 35, Fer; 43, lig om; 51, 1 dotted m c'' and sm a', bl om. Tenor: 9, 2 two sm b-flat and a, 3 sb b-flat; 29, 2 dot after sb d' is an error in MS; 35, Fer; 41, 1 br c' (error—should be sb); 42, 3 br e' (error—should be sb). Contratenor: e'-flat in sig, mm. 1-46; b-flat in sig, mm. 47-54; 4, 1 m g (error—should be sb); 9, br f; 13, 1 dotted m e-flat and sm f, bl om; 34, 2 sb c lacking; 35, Fer; 47, bl om 1 dotted m c' and sm b-flat; 51, 1 a-flat acc om.

PIX, fols. 166v-167—Superius: 8, dotted sb g' and two sm f' and e', bl om; 13, 2 two sm f' and e'; 22, 1 e''-flat acc; 29, 2 dotted bl sb b' and bl m g'; 30, 4 sm e'; 43, lig om; 44, before sb c'' sig e'-flat, b'-flat, e''-flat, clef G. Tenor: 10, dotted sb c' and two sm b-flat and a, bl om. Contratenor: 16, 2 a-flat acc om; 33, 3 dotted br c.

Q 16, fols. 116v-117—[Superius]: 5, sharp om; 13, 2 two sm f' and e'; 22, 1 e''-flat acc; 26, 3 m c'' and two sm b'-flat and a', bl om; 29, 2 dotted m b'-flat and sm g'; 30, 3 m g' and two sm f' e', bl om; 35, Fer; 37, e''-flat acc; 50, 1 e''-flat acc; 51, 1 dotted m c'' and sm a', bl om. Added Contratenor altus: clef C3; ₵; sig b-flat and e'-flat; fol. 117:

Tenor: 35, Fer; 41, 2 dotted m d' and sm e', bl om; 46, 2 two sm b-flat and a; 49, 2 dotted m f' and sm e', bl om. Contratenor: 7, 2 bl sm g and f; 13, 1 dotted m e-flat and sm f; 16, 2 a-flat acc om; 30, 2 dotted m e-flat and sm f, bl om; 33, 3 dotted br c; 45, 4 sb c; 47, 1 dotted m c' and sm b-flat; 50, 1 dotted m c' and sm b-flat; 51, 1 a-flat acc om.

Q 18, fols. 37ᵛ-38—Superius: 5, sharp om; 8, dotted sb and two sm, bl om; 18, lig om; 19, 3 lig om; 30, 3 dotted m and sm, bl om; 33, 3 bl sb c' and bl m d'; 42, 2 two sm c'' and b'-flat; 43, lig om; 51, 1 dotted m and sm, bl om. Added CTA, instrumental in character with the rubric: *Per diateseron intensa*. Tenor: 7, lig om; 9, 2 two sm b'-flat and a', 3 sb b'-flat; 20, 3 lig om; 41, 2 dotted m and sm, bl om; 49, 3 dotted m and sm, bl om. Contratenor: 5-6, lg; 7-8, lg c; 13, 1 dotted m and sm, bl om; 16, lig om; 21, lig om; 24, 2 lig; 26, lig; 29, 1 bl sb g and bl m f; 30, 2 dotted m and sm, bl om; 33, 3 dotted br c; 47, 1 dotted m and sm, bl om, 3 lig om; 50, 1 dotted m and sm, bl om, 3 m g and m-rest; 52, lig.

SEV, fols. 61ᵛ-62—Superius: sig b-flat, e'-flat, b'-flat; 8, dotted sb g' and two sm f'c', bl om; 19, 3 lig om; 26, 3 dotted m c'' and sm b'-flat; 29, 2 lig; 30, 3 dotted m g' and sm f', bl om; 41, 1 dotted m e'' and sm d'', 2 dotted sb d'' and two sm c'' and b'-flat; 51, 1 dotted m c'' and sm a', bl om. Tenor: 6, 1 two sb d' and d'; 10, dotted sb c' and two sm b'-flat and a', bl om; 20, 3 lig om; 33, 1 bl sb c' and bl m d'; 40, 1 dotted m d' and sm e'-flat, bl om; 44, 4 two sm e'-flat and d'; 45, 1 two m c' and b-flat, 3 dotted sb c'. Contratenor: 3, 1 lig om, 2 lig; 7, br a-flat, bl om; 8, br c; 9, two sm e f and sb g; 16, 2 a-flat acc om; 21, lig om; 29, 1 bl sb g and bl m f; 31, 3 a-flat acc om; 45, 2 m g, 3 m a, 4 m f; 46, 1 m c; 47, 1 dotted m c' and sm b-flat, bl om, 3, lig om; 48, 1 lig, 2 lig om; 50, 1 dotted m c' and sm b-flat, bl om, 3 m g and m-rest; 51, 1 a-flat acc om.

VER, fols. 66ᵛ-67—Superius: sig. e'-flat, b'-flat, e''-flat; 8, dotted sb and two sm, bl om; 9, 1 two sb d' and d'; 10, lig om; 13, 2 two sm f' and e'; 19, 3 lig om; 26, 3 m a' and two sm g' f', bl om; 28, 3 two sm c'' and b'-flat; 29, 2 dotted m b'-flat and sm a'; 30, 3 m g' and two sm f' e', bl om; 42, 2 two sm c'' and b'-flat; 43, lig om; 45, 2 two sm b'-flat and a'; 48, 2 m f'' and two sm e'' and d''; 51, 1 two m c'' and a'. Tenor: 6, 1 two sb d' and d'; 7, lig om; 10, dotted sb c' and two sm b-flat and a', bl om; 12, 4 lig om; 19, lig om; 20, 3 lig om; 41, 2 dotted m d' and sm e', bl om; 44, 4 two sm e' d'; 45, 1 two m c' and b-flat, 2 dotted sb c'; 46, 2 two sm b-flat and a; 49, 2 dotted m f' and sm e', bl om. Contratenor: 1-2, lig om; 3, lig om; 7, 1 two sb a-flat and c, bl om; 13, 1 two m e and f, bl om; 14-15, lig om; 16-17, lig om; 18-19, lig om; 21, lig om; 22, 1 lig om; 24, 2 lig; 31, 3 a-flat acc om; 45, 1 dotted m a and sm g (a-flat acc om), 3 two m a and f; 46, m c in place of m-rest; 47, 1 m c' and two sm b-flat and a, bl om, 3 lig om; 48, 2 lig om; 50, 1 m c' and two sm b-flat and a, bl om; 3 m g and m-rest.

Variants are not listed for the tablatures *BU, BUX*, and *FPn*, or for the added parts which are instrumental in character, the CTA in *Q18* and the two-part arrangement in *SEG*. The instrumental arrangements of *Fortune* are the subject of an article now in preparation by the editor.

Rondeau—Entrepris suis par grant lyesse, a 3

TRANSCRIPTION: *OC*, fol. 39ᵛ, Bartholomeus Bruolo, (t) (i) (i). Superius: 1 (verse 3), 3 *lavoyel* in MS; 14 (verse 3), 2 *ge* in MS; 28 (verse 3), 1 *pris que* in MS; 29, *coeur* in lines 3 and 5 added ed in place of heart-shaped sign in MS; 41 (verse 6), 2 *is le* in MS (the word *is* may be a reflexive with the meaning "itself"); Text underlay limited to refrain; stanza given as supplemental text on fol. 39ᵛ. Contratenor: 19, 2 sb on c lacking in *OC* added ed from *Q16*, fol. 80, staff 2.

REFERENCE LIST OF VARIANT COPIES: *BUX*, fol. 59ᵛ, *Entrepris, a 2*; *GLO*, *Discantus* e6ᵛ, *Tenores* e7ᵛ, *Kontratenores* e10ᵛ, *Der entrepris*; *MNS*, fols. 13ᵛ-15, *Entre prison*; *Q16*, fols. 79ᵛ-80.

MODERN EDITIONS: A facsimile ed. of *BUX* has been issued by Bertha Antonia Wallner, ed., *Das Buxheimer Orgelbuch*, Documenta musicologica, Zweite Reihe (Kassel: 1955), No. 106; for the *MNS* variant see: Robert Eitner, "Das Walter'sche Liederbuch," *Beilage MfMg* 6, No. 10 (1874): 159; for a comparison of the variant copies in *MNS* and *GLO* see: R. Eitner, "Taenze des 15. bis 17. Jahrhunderts," *Beilage MfMg* 7, No. 4 (1875): 74-5; for the *GLO* variant see: H. Ringmann and J. Klapper, eds., *Das Glogauer Liederbuch, Erster Teil: Deutsche Lieder und Spielstücke*, Das Erbe Deutscher Musik, Reichsdenkmale 4 (Kassel: 1936): 80, No. 102.

Song-motet O gloriosa regina mundi, a 3

TRANSCRIPTION: *PIX*, fols. 3ᵛ-4, Anon., (t) (i) (i). Superius: 18-21, *pia* lacking in *PIX* (fol. 3ᵛ, staff 2) added ed from *TR 91* (fol. 178ᵛ, staff 1); 25-32, *clamamus* in *PIX* (fol. 3ᵛ, staff 2) deleted, *clamantibus* added ed from *TR 91* (fol. 178ᵛ, staff 2); 34, 3 *tu* lacking in *PIX* (fol. 3ᵛ, staff 2), added from *TR 91* (fol. 178ᵛ, staff 2), two m and one sb equal MS br; 46, *in* lacking in *PIX* (fol. 3ᵛ, staff 3), added from *TR 91* (fol. 178ᵛ, staff 3); 66, 1 flat as acc before f''; 79-83, *salvatorem* in *PIX* (fol. 3ᵛ, staff 4) deleted, *salutem* added from *TR 91* (fol. 178ᵛ, staff 4); 84-9, *salutem* ed repeated. Tenor: 14-102, text completed ed; 36, 1 two m equal MS sb; 75, two sb equal MS br; 85-9, *salutem* ed repeated. Contratenor: 17, 2 dot following g deleted (*PIX*, fol. 4, staff 1) in accordance with the reading in *FR* (fol. 30, staff 1), 2 lig om following *FR*.

REFERENCE LIST OF VARIANT COPIES: *CAS*, fols. 63ᵛ-65, Jo. Touront; *FP*, fols. 53ᵛ-54; *FR*, fols. 29ᵛ-30; *P676*, fols. 32ᵛ-33; *PER*, fols. 58ᵛ-59, Caecus; *PIX*, fols. 3ᵛ-4; *PRA*, fols. 182ᵛ-183; *Q 16*, fols. 141ᵛ-142 (CXXV bisᵛ-CXXVI "O gloriosa domina"); *SEV*, fols. 88ᵛ-89; *TR 91*, fol. 178ᵛ; *VER*, fols. 18ᵛ-19.

MODERN EDITIONS: A. J. H. Vincent, "Note sur la modalité du chant ecclésiastique," *Revue archéologique* 14 (1857): 675-9 (*PIX* variant); H. Besseler, ed., *Capella*, Meisterwerke mittelalterlicher Musik (Kassel, 1950) 1:7-8 (*TR 91* variant); G. Adler and O. Koller, eds. *Sechs Trienter Codices, Erste Auswahl*, DTOe (Vienna, 1900) Jg 7:219; an Italian version of the text, "O gloriosa regina del mondo," is item No. 87 in *Laude Spirituali di Feo Belcari* (Florence: Molini e Cecchi, 1863), p. 43 with the comment *"cantasi come O gloriosa Regina mundi succurre nobis."* The text is from a 1480 print, see ibid., p. iv. The *SEV* variant may be seen in *Facsimile Reproduction of the Manuscripts Sevilla 5-I-43 and Paris N. A. Fr. 4379 (Pt. I)*, intro. Dragan Plamenac, Publication of Mediaeval Musical Manuscripts, No. 8 (Brooklyn, N. Y.: 1962), p. 68.

Performance

The compositions in this edition should be thought of as accompanied vocal works since instruments and voices were used together in the performance of polyphony in the fifteenth century. The term "accompanied" here refers to the doubling of all the individual voice parts by melodic instruments. In order to have all melodic lines sounding in performance, instruments must be assigned to voice parts when text is completely lacking (this often happens in the lowest voice of works in the present edition). Further, the melodies provided with text should also be doubled by instruments since textless passages occur from time to time in these parts. Although instruments could simply double voice parts in textless passages, an instrumental doubling of the entire part seems preferable in view of possible interpretations of performance descriptions from the period and of fifteenth-century iconographic evidence showing instrumentalists and singers performing together.

Further, a solo singer might improvise a setting of the text in places where particular voice parts are lacking text in the edition (basing the improvisation on the words given in those voice parts provided with text). The number of singers and/or instrumentalists assigned to particular voice parts could have varied in different fifteenth-century performances of the same composition, but in general the use of a chamber group would be preferable to a larger ensemble. We know there were seldom more than ten or twelve singers in the Papal chapel during the fifteenth century, and, in Florence, a performance using three treble singers, one alto, one tenor, and one bass would have been appropriate during the third quarter of the century.[75] We also know that "choral" polyphony was an innovation in the fifteenth century, and the performance of complex polyphonic settings may still have been reserved for soloists as in earlier times. In this regard, the use of soloists is clearly intended in the Mass sections marked *duo*. As an alternative to performance of the secular songs using several voices with instrumental participation, it would be appropriate to sing them as solo songs with an accompaniment for lute fashioned from the music given in the edition (paralleling the treatment given the *rondeau Fortune, par ta cruaulté* in two lute tablatures from the period—see Critical Notes, p. xxv).

As stated above, in sections where the modern metric signs 3/2 or 2/2 are used, the half-note is the unit of time at a tempo of 75 to 85 counts per minute. Where the signs 2/4 or 3/4 occur, the quarter-note is the unit at a relatively faster tempo, ca. 100 M.M. The 2/4 and 3/4 sections could be realized as strict diminutions by taking the half-note as the unit of time at the tempo adopted in the 2/2 and 3/2 sections, and thus equating the notated breve in the passages written in *diminutio dupla* with the semibreve in *integer valor* (i.e., *alla breve*); however, this alternative is not recommended since the resulting tempo seems too fast for an appropriate realization of rhythmic values as small as the semiminim and *fusa*.

Acknowledgments

It is a pleasant duty to acknowledge the contributions made by colleagues in the preparation of this edition, and it is appropriate in this regard to acknowledge a special debt to the late Glen Haydon whose friendship and criticism were an unfailing source of inspiration during the early years of my work with Vincenet's music. I am also indebted to specialists in linguistics for their help with translations and for criticism related to the texts; these specialists include Robert White Linker (who first transcribed the secular texts) at The University of North Carolina at Chapel Hill, David Griffin and Mark P.O. Morford at The Ohio State University, and Juan Gamez and George Preda at East Texas State University. I thank Dragan Plamenac for making photographs available of two manuscript copies of *Fortune* which I was unable to obtain and for providing data on the little-known manuscript collection

Bologna, Biblioteca Universitaria, MS 596, Busta H H, 2¹⁻⁴.

I am grateful also to the following authorities and institutions for permission to publish folios of particular manuscripts in facsimile: Marjorie G. Wynne, Research Librarian, The Beinecke Rare Book and Manuscript Library, Yale University; Father Alfonso Raes, S. J., Prefect of the Vatican Library; Professor Dr. N. Rasmo, Superintendent of Art Treasures for the provinces of Trento and Bolzano; and Dr. Pietro Puliatti, Director, Biblioteca Estense, Modena. Thanks are expressed also to Wade Weiler at the University of Texas Music Library at Austin; to Diane Saucier at the James Gilliam Gee Library, East Texas State University; to Dottoressa Luigia Risoldi at the Biblioteca Universitaria in Bologna; to P. W. Philby, Research Librarian at the Peabody Institute in Baltimore; and to A. M. Lewin Robinson, Director of the South African Library at Cape Town for help with special materials in their libraries. I am indebted also to Elizabeth Hunt Davis for critical reading of the final draft of the Preface and for numerous helpful suggestions in this regard.

The history of the edition would be incomplete without recognition of the encouragement and understanding of my wife, Betty Hunt, and of the helpfulness and support supplied in generous quantities over the years by Elizabeth and Sally.

Bertran E. Davis
East Texas State University
Commerce, Texas

July 1978

Notes

1. Bertran E. Davis and Peter Gülke, "Vincenet," *MGG* 13 (1966): cols. 1652-3.

2. Gustave Reese, *Music in the Renaissance* (New York: W. W. Norton, 1954), p. 137, n. 188.

3. Manfred Schuler, "Zur Geschichte der Kapelle Papst Martin V.," *AfMw* 25 (January 1968): 45.

4. Manfred F. Bukofzer, "An Unknown Chansonnier of the 15th Century (The *Mellon Chansonnier*)," *MQ* 28 (January 1942): 29.

5. Giuseppe Baini, *Memorie storico-critiche della vita e delle opere de Giovanni Pierluigi da Palestrina*, 2 vols. (Rome: Società tipografica, 1828; reprint ed., Hildesheim: Georg Olms, 1966), 2:403-4.

6. Bukofzer, "An Unknown Chansonnier," p. 29. Cf., Higinio Anglès, "Johannes Cornago," *MGG* 2 (1949): col. 1679.

7. Noel Dupire, ed., *Les fuictz et dictz de Jean Molinet*, 3 vols. (Paris: Société des anciens textes français, 1937-9), 2:789. It seems equally probable that the *Vincenet* mentioned in the poem is the soldier *Vincenet de Lannoy* whose name occurs in two prose works of Molinet called prognostications since the name *Vincenet* and others cited in the sixth stanza of the poem *Lettres missives* . . . (Rosimbois, Ripaupé, and Pinche Aigret) are listed as *capitaines* in the prognostications, ibid., p. 895, lines 78-81; p. 903, lines 42-6.

8. H. Colin Slim, *A Gift of Madrigals and Motets*, 2 vols. (Chicago: Published for the Newberry Library by The University of Chicago Press, 1972), 1:45.

9. Karl August Fink, comp., "Verzeichnis der in den Registern und Kameralakten Martins V. vorkommenden Personen, Kirchen, und Orte des Deutschen Reiches, seiner Diözesen und Territorien, 1417-1431," hrsg. vom Deutschen Historischen Institut in Rom, *Repertorium Germanicum* 4 (1958): pt. 3 (L-Z), cols. 2517-18.

10. Schuler, "Zur Geschichte," pp. 30-45.

11. Archivio di Stato di Roma, under the signature Camerale I, vol. 1711, fol. 93 (the quotation below follows the original except for the addition of punctuation and the realization of *sigla*):

> Anno domini MCCCCXXV, Indictione III, pontificatus Sanctissimi in Christo Patris et domini nostri domini Martini divina providentia Pape Quinti, Anno eius Nono, honorabilis vir Johannes Vincinetti presbitero Tullensis, Die XXIII mensis Decembris receptus est in Cantorum Capelle domini nostri Papae. Juravit in manibus domini Benedicti, locumtenens Camerarius officii pontificalis, Reverendi in Christo Patri domino Antonio Episcopo Sencii et domino Johannie Aezel, Clerico Camerae apostolicae. Visum L. Robring

The volume cited above is described by Oscar Freiherrn von Mitis in an article entitled "Curiale Eidregister," in Mittheilungen des Instituts für österreichische Geschichtsforschung, Ergänzungsband 6 (Innsbruck: Verlag der Wagner'schen Universitäts-Buchhandlung, 1901): 417-18. Cf., Schuler, "Zur Geschichte," p. 30.

12. Archivio Segreto Vaticano, Rome. *Registra Lateranensia:* Vol. 246, fol. 292ᵛ-293 (April 25, 1424); Vol. 260, fol. 151ᵛ. *Diversa Cameralia:* Vol. 11, fol. 207ᵛ. *Registra Supplicationum:* Vol. 207, fol. 46ᵛ, and fol. 298; Vol. 209, fol. 278; Vol. 210, fol. 235ᵛ and fol. 292; Vol. 213, fol. 226; Vol. 220, fol. 10ᵛ; Vol. 224, fol. 98; Vol. 225, fol. 160; Vol. 235, fol. 7ᵛ-8 (Jan. 23, 1429). Cf. Fink, "Verzeichnis," cols. 2517-18.

13. Franz Xaver Haberl, "Wilhelm du Fay," *VfMw* 1 (1885): 455.

14. Archivio Segreto Vaticano, Rome. *Introitus et Exitus:* Vol. 383, fols. 67 (January 7, 1426), 70, 74ᵛ, 77ᵛ; Vol. 385, fols. 116ᵛ, 118, 121, 124, 126, 129, 131, 134, 136ᵛ, 138, 141, 143ᵛ, 146, 148, 151, 153, 156, 158ᵛ, 160, 164, 167, 170ᵛ; Vol. 387, fols. 70ᵛ, 72ᵛ, 75, 77, 79ᵛ, 83ᵛ, 86ᵛ, 88ᵛ, 91, 94, 96 (May 11, 1429).

15. Archivio Segreto Vaticano, Rome. *Introitus et Exitus:* Vol. 387, fol. 83ᵛ (*olim* 114ᵛ), cf., Haberl, "Wilhelm du Fay," p. 456.

16. Archivio Segreto Vaticano, Rome. *Introitus et Exitus:* Vol. 387, fol. 96 (*olim* 127). The quotation, below, follows the original except for the addition of punctuation and the realization of *sigla*.

Exitus mensis Maii MCCCCXXVIIII, Rome

Pro Cantoribus domini nostri Papae. Docuit, Johannes de Reate.

Die undecima dicti Mensis, praefatus dominus Oddo[de Vacis], thesaurarius, solvi fecit infrascriptis domini nostri Papae Cantoribus pro eorum salario mensis Junii proximi futuri, videlicet: Egidio L'infant, Johanni Delesme, Toussano de Ruella, Philippo Foliot, Johanni Vincenot, quinque; Johanni Dupassage, sex; Bartholomeo Poignare, Guillelmo Dufay, Galtero Liberti, quatour; et Jacobo Robaille, duos florenos auri de camera. In totum florenos similes Quadraginta quinque. F[lorenos] xlv.

The weight, quality and nomenclature of fifteenth-century gold coinage vary greatly. Since Florentine gold coins were relatively consistent as to weight and quality in the period and since Florence was close to the lands controlled by the Papacy, the value of the Florentine *fiorino largo d'oro* offers one type of comparison with the *florenos auri de camera* mentioned in the pay record. The *fiorino largo d'oro* was twenty-four carats and weighed seventy-two grains. Since 437.5 grains equals one ounce, about six of the Florentine coins would equal one ounce of gold. The salaries quoted above in *florenos auri de camera* may have had symbolic value only with payment being made in coin of other kinds. In the middle of the century, a gold florin of Florence was equal to twenty silver florins. The above salaries would have been in addition to the benefices given singers as rewards for their services to the Pope and in addition to other benefits accruing to members of the Roman Curia.

17. Haberl, "Wilhelm du Fay," p. 498, see *Beilage 1* for the document (pp. 511-14), and see remarks on *Beilage 1* under *Archivio della Cappella pontificio* (p. 450).

18. André Pirro, review of Ch. van den Borren, *Guillaume Dufay* (Brussels, 1925) in RMI 7 (1926): 323.

19. Most of the account books of the Royal Treasury (about 700 volumes) were destroyed during bombings of Naples during World War II, and nothing pertaining to Vincenet survived the bombings. Riccardo Filangieri, Superintendent, *Archivio di Stato di Napoli*, and President, International Council on Archives, to Bertran E. Davis, Chapel Hill, North Carolina, July 16, 1958.

20. Edmond van der Straeten, *La Musique aux Pays-Bas avant le XIXe siècle*, 8 vols. (Bruxelles, G. A. van Trigt, 1867-8), 4:31.

21. Charles van den Borren, "A Light of the Fifteenth Century: Guillaume Dufay," MQ 21 (July 1935): 284.

22. Nino Pirrotta, "Music and Cultural Tendencies in 15th-Century Italy," JAMS 19 (Summer 1966): 129, n. 7.

23. Schuler, "Zur Geschichte," see references to the singers Johannes Carnin, p. 38, and Richard Bellengues, pp. 43-4.

24. Phillipe Charles Delhaye, "Celibacy, History of," *New Catholic Encyclopedia* (c. 1967), 3:373. See also Fink, "Verzeichnis," p. vii, who provides abbreviations for use in describing facts related to the birth of those listed in his index. Among these abbreviations is the term *def. nat. (p. c.)* meaning *defectus natalium, de presbytero genitus et coniugata* (defect of birth, begotten of a priest and a married woman).

25. The Church frowned upon the "easy morality" of the fifteenth century, but such matters did not necessarily prohibit the holding of ecclesiastical offices. This is the age of the Borgia Popes, and we know, for example, that Cardinal Rodrigo Borgia had numerous children and that as Pope Alexander VI he arranged a marriage between his natural daughter Lucrezia and Don Alfonso (Duke of Bisceglie) the natural son of King Alfonso II in order to improve relationships between the Papacy and Naples. The youthful Don Alfonso was the grandson of Ferrante who was himself the natural son of Alfonso I, King of Naples *(el Magnanimo)*. In a moral climate such as this, it is possible that Ferrante would choose to provide money for a female dependent of his late cantor even if the latter were a priest.

26. Bianca Becherini, "Relazioni di musici fiamminghi con la Corte dei Medici," *La Rinascita* 4 (January 1941): 96-101.

27. Frank A. D'Accone, "The Singers of San Giovanni in Florence during the 15th Century," JAMS 14 (Fall 1961): 321. Cf., Becherini, "Relazioni," p. 96.

28. Alfonso was King of Aragon as Alfonso V (1416-58) and King of Naples as Alfonso I (1443-58).

29. Becherini, "Relazioni," p. 101. Cf., D'Accone, "The Singers," p. 323, n. 44.

30. D'Accone, "The Singers," p. 324. Cf. Becherini, "Relazioni," p. 99.

31. Charles Warren Fox, "Non-Quartal Harmony in the Renaissance," MQ 31 (January 1945): 35-6. Cf. Reese, *Music in the Renaissance*, pp. 103-4.

32. For a comparison of the regular form of the *villancico* and the telescoped type mentioned above, see Reese, *Music in the Renaissance*, pp. 581-2. See also Isabel Pope, "Musical and Metrical Form of the Villancico," AnM 2 (1954): 193-6.

33. *Graduale sacrosanctae Romanae ecclesiae de tempore et de sanctis* (Rome and Paris: Desclée, 1924), p. 141*. The Solesmes version of the chant is cited here for general comparison since the exact fifteenth-century source is unknown.

34. Franz Xaver Haberl, "Bibliographischer und thematischer Musikkatalog des päpstlichen Kapellarchives im Vatican zu Rom," *Beilage MfMg* 19-20 (1887-8): 21.

35. G. Adler and O. Koller, eds., *Sechs Trienter Codices, Erste Auswahl*, DTOe, Jg 7 (Vienna: Österreichischer Bundesverlag, 1900): xvi, xx.

36. Haberl, "Wilhelm du Fay," pp. 468-9. Cf., Haberl, "Musikkatalog," pp. 6-7.

37. Haberl, "Wilhelm du Fay," pp. 446, 470. Cf. Heinrich Besseler, *Bourdon und Fauxbourdon* (Leipzig: Breitkopf und Härtel, 1950), p. 144. See also Jules Houdoy, *Histoire artistique de la cathédrale de Cambrai* (Paris: D. Morgand et Ch. Fatout, 1880), p. 194.

38. Guglielmi Dufay, *Opera omnia*, ed. H. Besseler, vol. 3: *Missarum pars altera*, CMM 1 (Rome: American Institute of Musicology, 1951): iv, vii.

39. Associazione dei musicologi italiani, *Catalogo delle opere musicali: Città di Modena, R. Biblioteca Estense*, comp. Pio Lodi, Bolletino dell' Associazione, serie 8 (Parma: Fresching, 1916), p. 17.

40. Guglielmi Dufay, *Opera omnia*, ed. H. Besseler, vol. 2: *Missarum pars prior*, CMM 1 (Rome: American Institute of Musicology, 1960): ix. Cf., Manfred F. Bukofzer, *Studies in Medieval and Renaissance Music* (New York: W. W. Norton, 1950), p. 181.

41. Dufay, *Opera omnia*, 3: vii. Cf. Besseler, *Bourdon*, p. 225.

42. Haberl, "Musikkatalog," p. 21.

43. Bukofzer, "Unknown Chansonnier," p. 18. See also idem, "The Mellon Chansonnier," *The Yale University Library Gazette* 15 (1940): 25.

44. Heribert Ringmann, "Das Glogauer Liederbuch (um 1480)," ZfMw 15 (1923): 52.

45. Luigi Torchi, "I Monumenti dell'antica Musica francese a Bologna," *RMI* 13 (1906): 499.

46. Edward L. Kottick, ed., *The Unica in the Chansonnier Cordiforme*, CMM 42 (n.p.: American Institute of Musicology, 1967): x. See also *Catalogue des livres composant la bibliothèque de feu Monsieur le baron James de Rothschild*, comp. Émile Picot, 5 vols. (Paris: D. Morgand, 1912), 4:314.

47. Dragan Plamenac, "A Reconstruction of the French Chansonnier in the Biblioteca Columbina, Seville," *MQ* 37 (October 1951): 501.

48. Paris, Bibliothèque nationale, *Catalogue général des manuscrits français: ancien Supplement française*, ed. Henri Omont, 3 vols. (Paris: Ernest Leroux, 1895-6), 3:319.

49. Plamenac, "Reconstruction," p. 502.

50. *Inventari dei manoscritti delle biblioteche d'Italia, V, Perugia: Biblioteca Comunale*, comp. Alessandro Belluci (Forli: Luigi Bordandini, 1895), pp. 130-1.

51. Found on flyleaves from a copy of the incunabulum: Pietro Borghi, *Aritmetica mercantile* (Venice: E. Ratdolt, 1484).

52. Giulio Cattin, "Nuova Fonte Italiana della Polifonia intorno al 1500," *AM* 45 (July-December 1973): 185.

53. Knud Jeppesen, *Der Kopenhagener Chansonnier* (Copenhagen: Levin and Munksgaard, 1927), p. lxxii.

54. Helen Hewitt, ed., *Harmonice musices Odhecaton A* (Cambridge, Mass.: Mediaeval Academy of America, 1942), pp. 6, 9. RISM I, 1501.

55. Ibid., p. 156. See also Albert Smijers, "Vijftiende en zestiende eeuwsche muziekhandschriften in Italie met werken van Nederlandsche componisten," *TVNM* 14 (1935): 178.

56. Jeppesen, *Der Kopenhagener Chansonnier*, p. lxxiii.

57. Torchi, "I Monumenti," pp. 502-3.

58. *Intabulatura de Luuto, Libro primo* (Venice: O. Petrucci, 1507). RISM I, 1507⁵.

59. Bertha Antonia Wallner, ed., *Das Buxheimer Orgelbuch*, Documenta musicologica, Zweite Reihe (Kassel: Bärenreiter, 1955), p. vii.

60. Julius Joseph Maier, *Die musikalischen Handschriften der königlichen Hof und Staatsbibliothek in München, Erster Theil: Die Handschriften bis zum Ende des XVII. Jahrhunderts* (Munich: In commission der Palm'schen hofbuchhandlung, 1879), p. 125.

61. J. F. R. Stainer and C. Stainer, eds., *Dufay and His Contemporaries* (London: Novello, 1898), p. xviii.

62. Gilbert Reaney, "The Manuscript Oxford, Bodleian Library, Canonici Misc. 213," *MD* 9 (1955): 75.

63. Stainer, *Dufay*, p. xviii.

64. Dragan Plamenac, "The 'Second' Chansonnier of the Biblioteca Riccardiana (Codex 2356)," *AnM* 2 (1954): 107.

65. Nanie Bridgman, "Un manuscrit italien du début du XVIe siècle à la Bibliothèque nationale, Department de la musique, Rés. Vm⁷ 676," *AnM* 1 (1953): 179.

66. Dragan Plamenac, "Postscript to the 'Second' Chansonnier of the Biblioteca Riccardiana (Codex 2356)," *AnM* 4 (1956): 264.

67. Albert Seay, "The Proportionale Musices of Johannes Tinctoris," *JMT* 1 (March 1957): 22.

68. Edmond de Coussemaker, ed., *Scriptorum de musica medii aevi, nova series*, 4 vols. (Paris: A. Durand, 1864-76), 4:156ᵇ. Cf. Seay, "The Proportionale Musices," p. 29.

69. Coussemaker, *Scriptorum*, 4:171ᵃ. Cf., Seay, "The Proportionale Musices," p. 41.

70. Coussemaker, *Scriptorum*, 4:171ᵇ. Cf., Seay, "The Proportionale Musices," p. 41.

71. Besseler, *Bourdon*, pp. 171-3.

72. See below, p. 43, m. 210, superius; p. 48, m. 81, altus; p. 64, m. 142, superius and altus; p. 66, m. 174, superius and altus; p. 71, m. 75, superius, and m. 76, altus; p. 74, m. 155, superius, and m. 156, altus; and p. 128, mm. 111-12, tenor.

73. "A Treatise on Text Underlay by a German Disciple of Francisco de Salinas," *Festschrift Heinrich Besseler (zum sechzigsten Geburtstag)*, hrsg. vom Institut für Musikwissenschaft der Karl-Marx-Universität (Leipzig: VEB Deutscher Verlag für Musik, 1961), pp. 243, 245.

74. Ibid., p. 237. See below, p. 115, m. 21, bassus; p. 116, m. 56, superius; p. 119, m. 107, bassus; p. 125, m. 59, tenor and bassus, and m. 60, altus.

75. D'Accone, p. 324. Cf. Pirrotta, p. 129, n. 7.

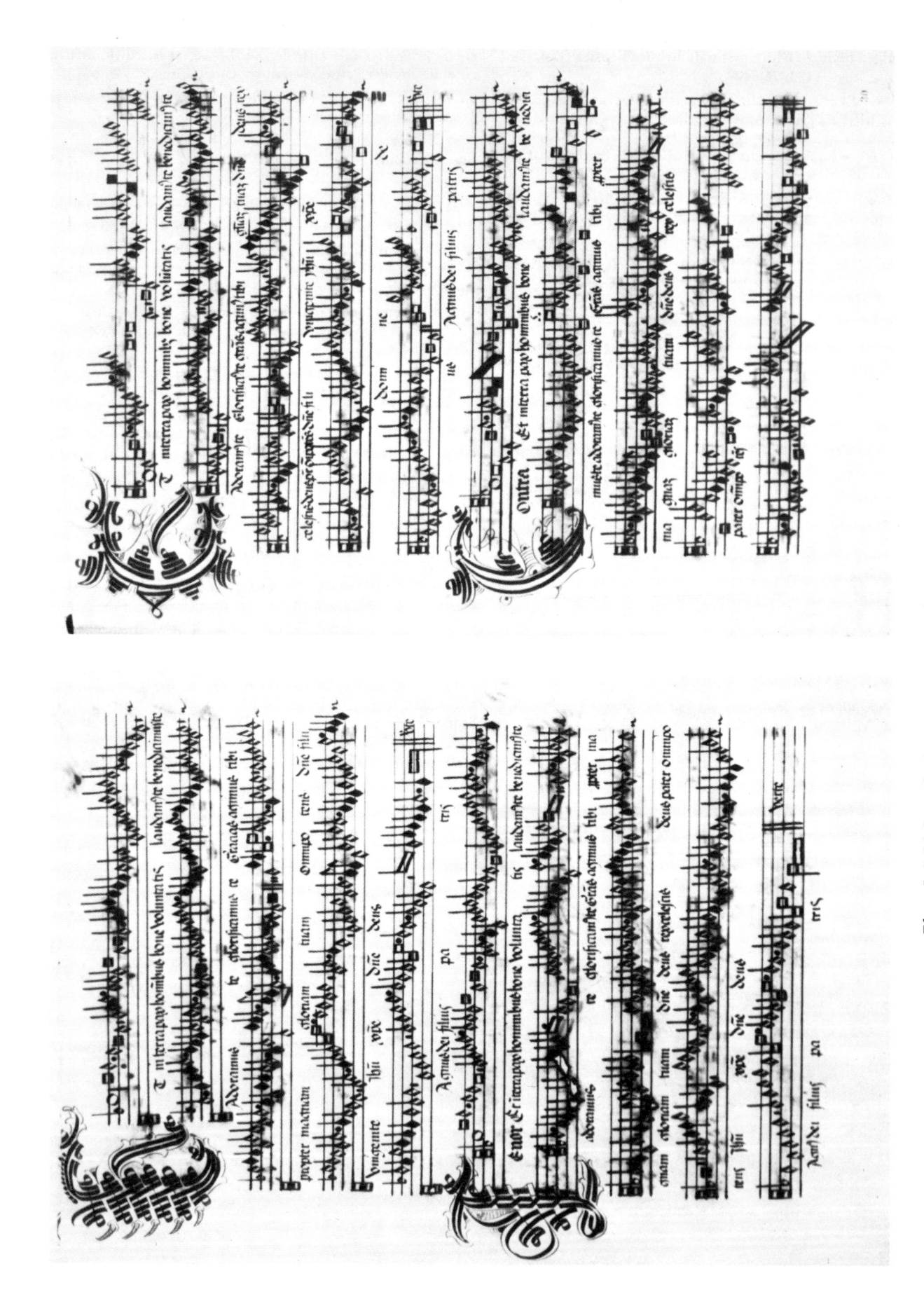

Plate I. [4] Mass *O gloriosa regina mundi*, "Et in terra," pp. 119-25. Biblioteca Apostolica Vaticana, MS Cappella Sistina 51, fols. 29ᵛ-30.

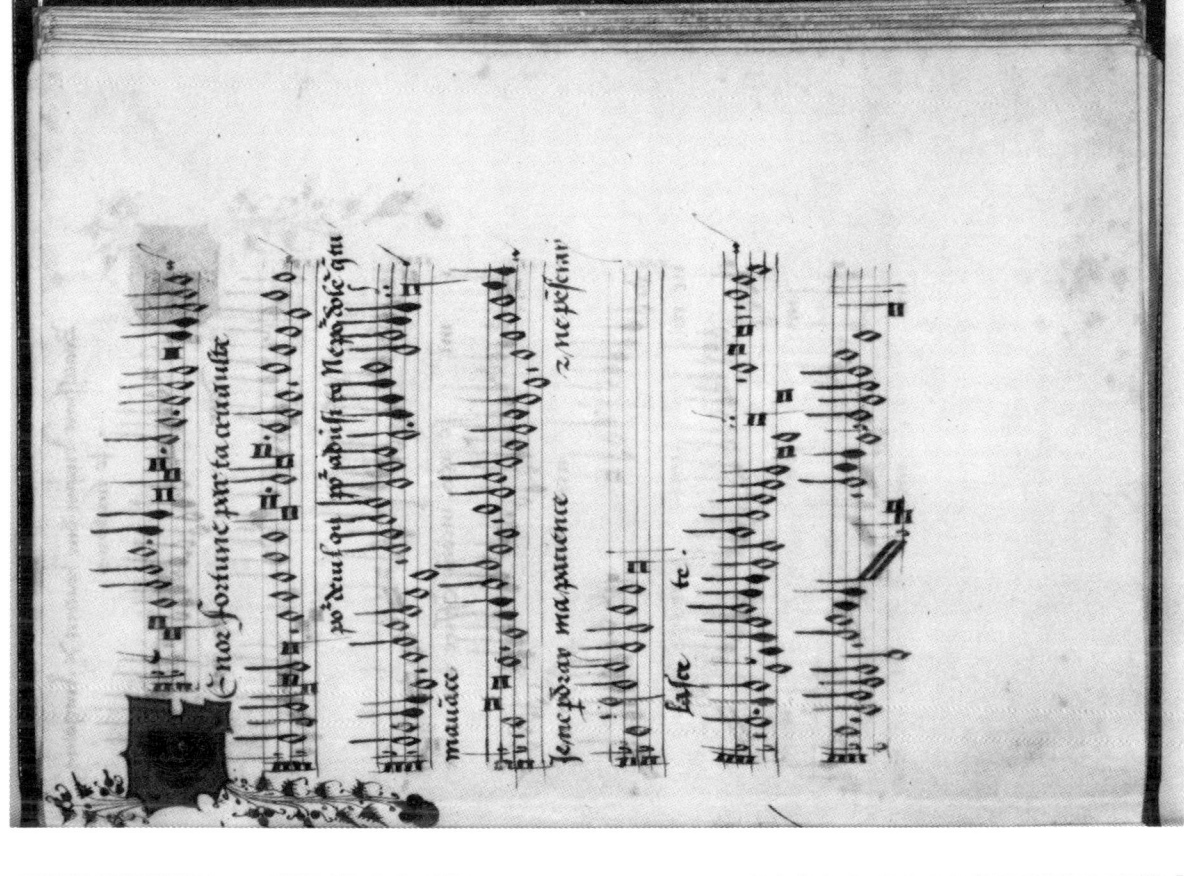

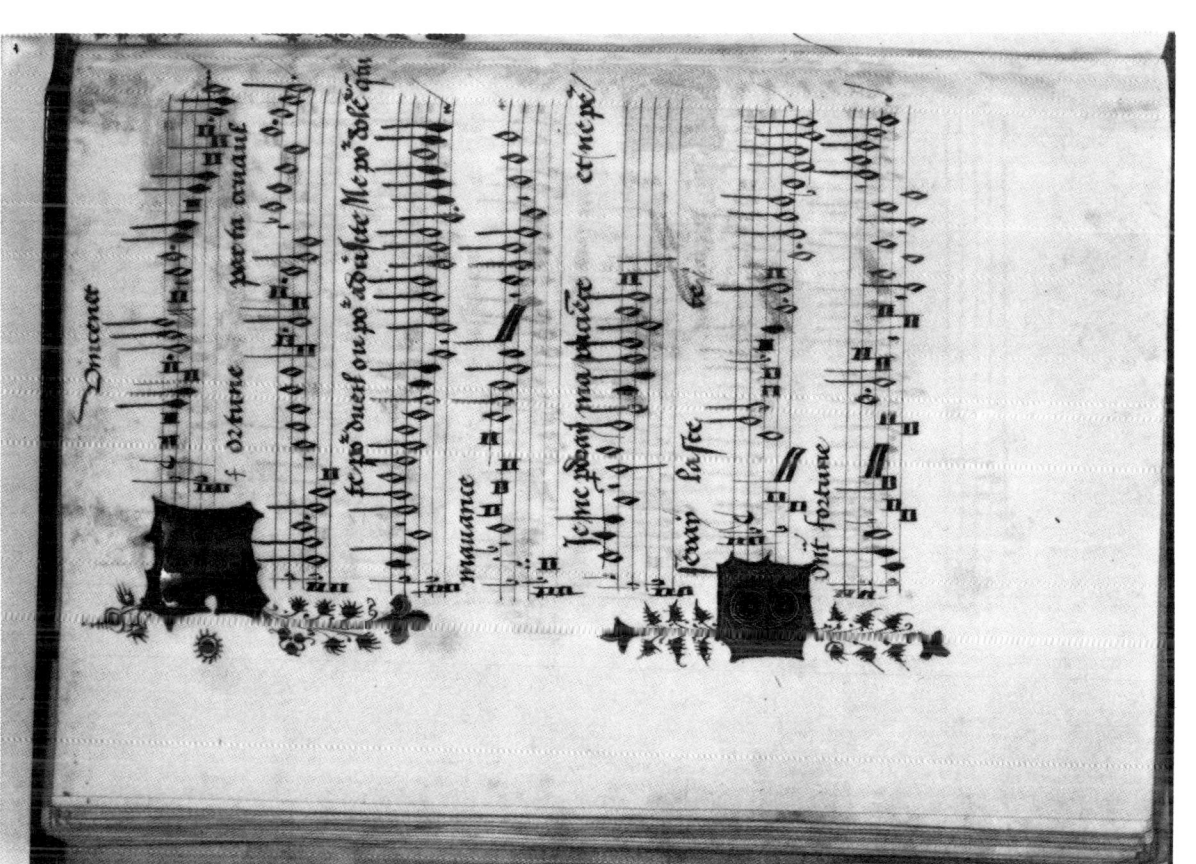

Plate II. [3] Rondeau *Fortune, par ta cruaulté*, pp. 167-9.
Yale University Library, Mellon Chansonnier, fols. 23v-24 (*olim* pp. 44-5).
(Courtesy, Beinecke Rare Book and Manuscript Library)

THE COLLECTED WORKS OF VINCENET

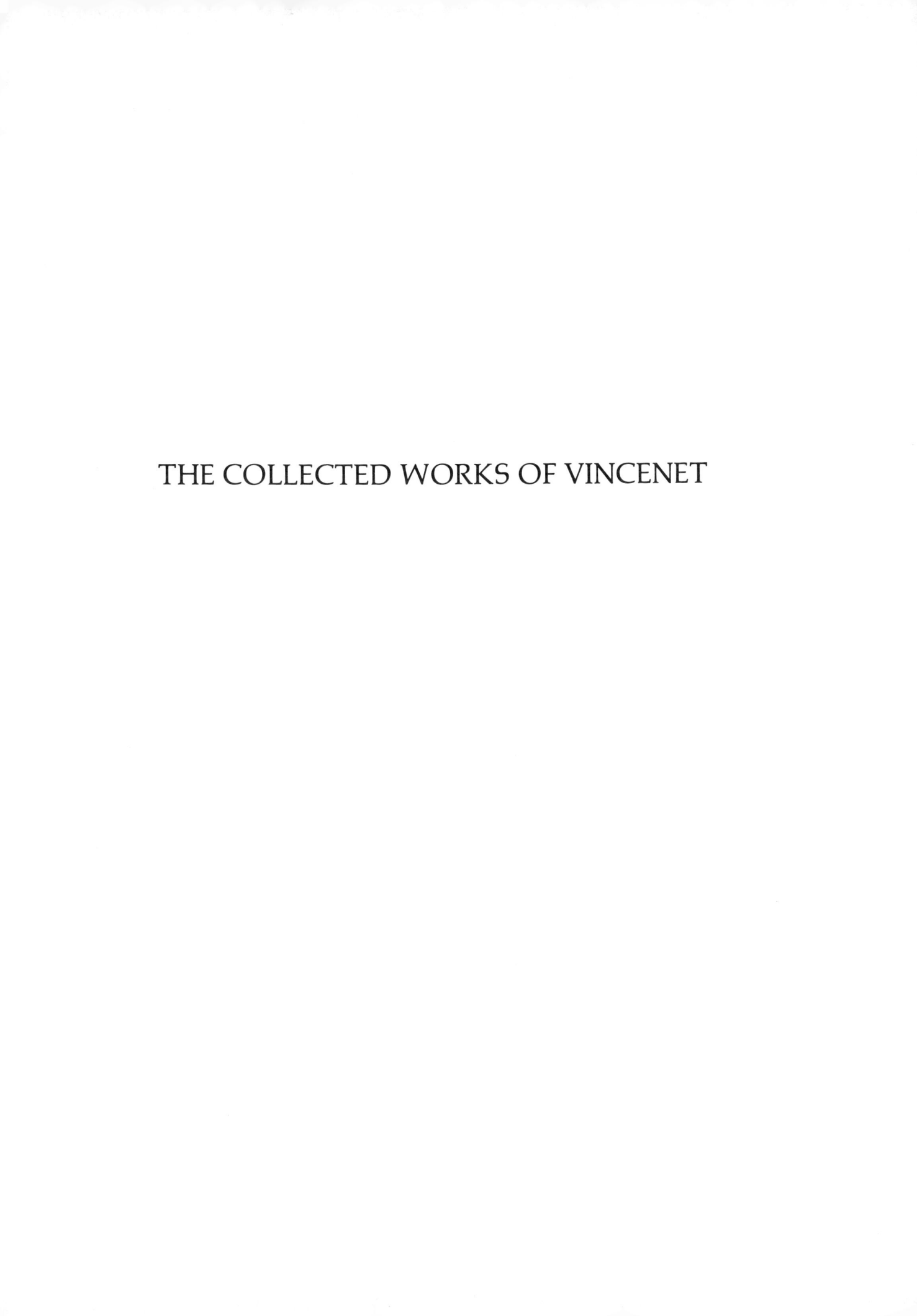

[1] Mass: [sine nomine]

Kyrie

Ky- ri- e] e- - - lei - son.
- son. Ky- ri- e e- - lei - son.]
[Superius]
[Tenor]
[Contratenor]
Chri - - - ste [e- - lei- -
Christe
Christe
- son. Chri - ste e-
- lei - son. Chri - - - ste]

3

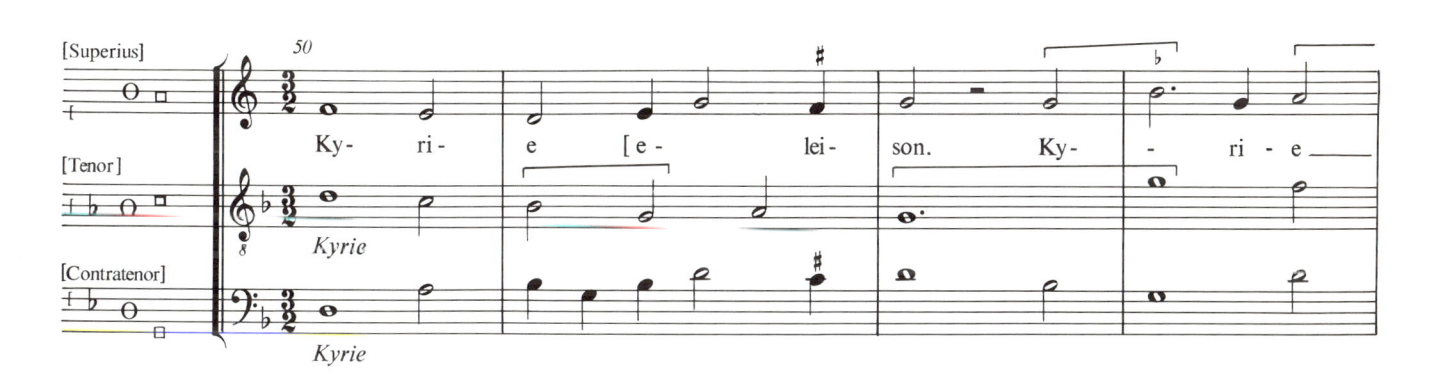

Gloria in excelsis Deo

20
Lau- da- mus te. Be - ne - di - ci- mus te. A- do- ra- mus
Glo- ri- fi-
.S.
- mus [te. Be- ne- di- ci- mus te. A- do- ra- mus te.] Glo-
25
te. Glo- ri- fi- ca- mus te. Gra- ti- as a- gi- mus ti- bi
- ca- - mus [te.] Gratias
- ri- fi- ca- - mus te.
30
pro- pter ma- - gnam glo- - ri- - am
35
40
tu- - - - am. Do- mi- ne
Do-

45
Deus, Rex caele- stis, De-
mi- ne Deus, Rex caele- stis, [De- us
50
-us Pa- ter o- mni- po- tens. Do- mi- ne
Pa- ter o- mni- po- tens.]
55
Fi- li u- ni- ge- ni- te Je- su Chri-
[Je- su
60
ste. Do- mi- ne De- us, A- gnus De-
Chri- ste. Do- mi- ne De- us,

7

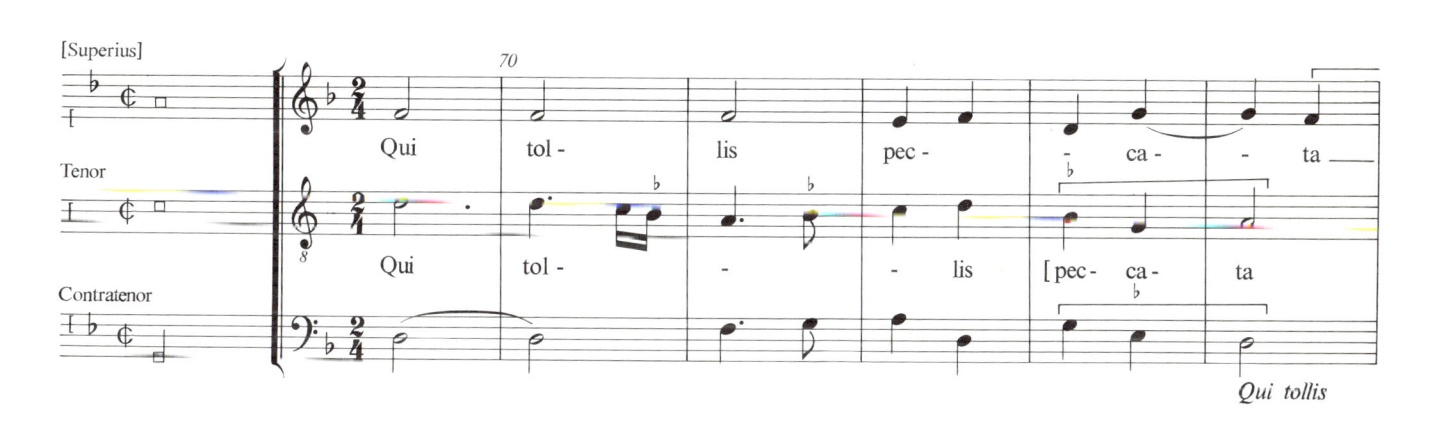

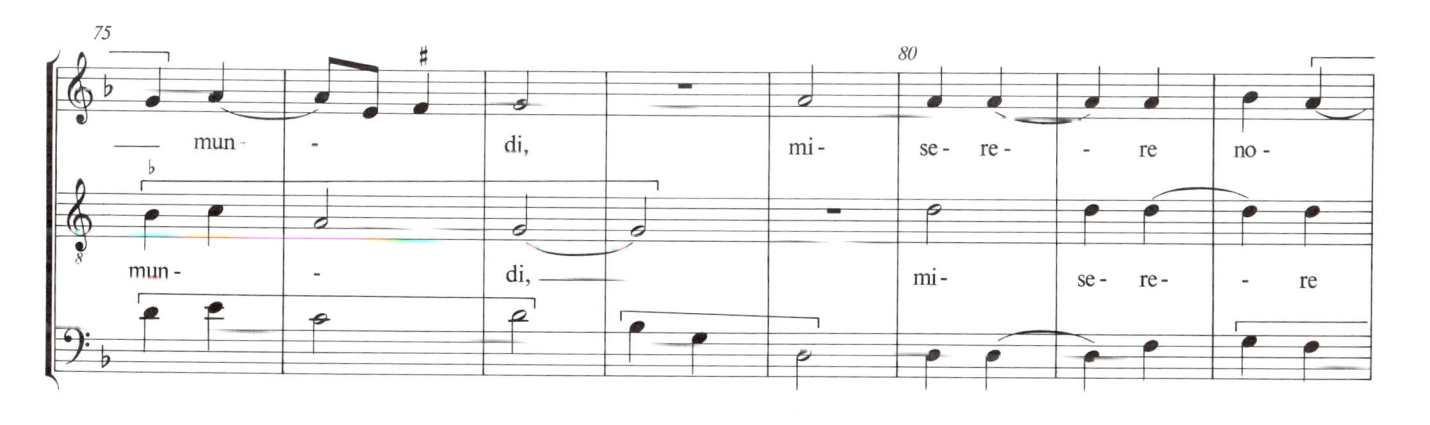

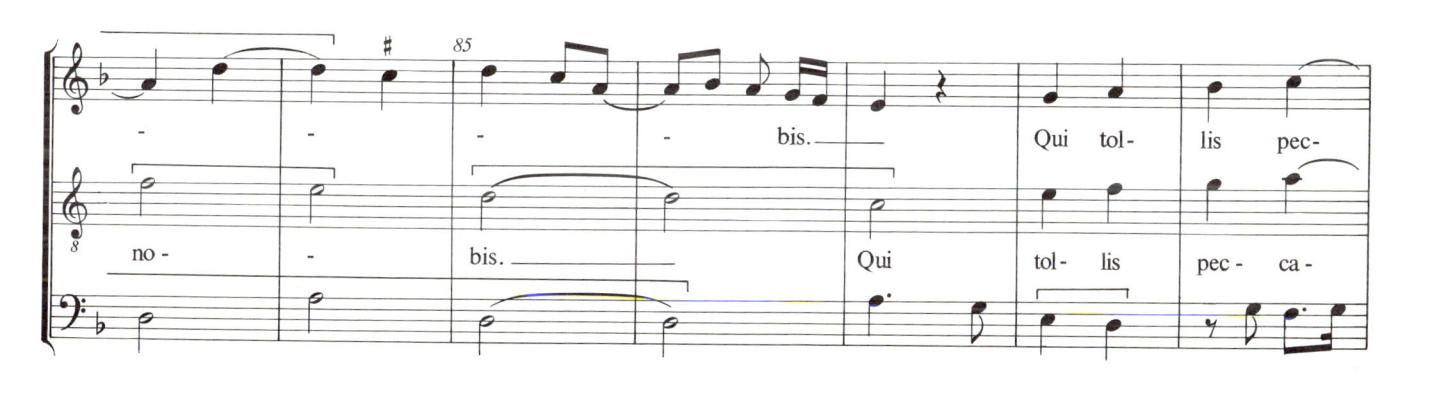

- ca- - ta mun- di, su- sci- pe
- ta mun- - di,] su-
suscipe
de- pre- ca- ti- o- nem [no- - stram] no-
- sci- pe [de- - pre- ca- ti- o- - nem
- - - stram. Qui se- des ad
no- - - - stram.] Qui sedes
dex- te- ram Pa- tris, mi- se- re- re
Qui sedes

115
120
no- bis. Quo- ni- am tu so- lus san- -
Quo- - ni- am tu so-
Quo- - ni- am tu so- -
125
- ctus. Tu so-
- lus [san- - - ctus.] Tu
lus [san- - - ctus.]
130
- - lus Do- - mi- nus. Tu so-
so- - - lus Do- - mi- nus. Tu so-
135
140
-lus Al- tis- si- mus, Je- - su Chri- -
- lus Al- tis- si- mus, [Je- - su Chri-

145
.S.
- - ste. Cum San- cto Spi- ri-
.S.
ste.] Cum San- - cto
Cum San- - cto [Spi- ri- tu,
150
155
tu, in glo- ri- a De- - i
[Spi- ri- tu, in glo- ri- a De- - i
in glo- ri- a De- i Pa- -
160
Pa- - - - tris. A- -
Pa - - - - - tris. A-
- - - tris. A- - -
165
170
- - - - - - men.
- - - - men.]
- - - - men.]

Credo in unum Deum

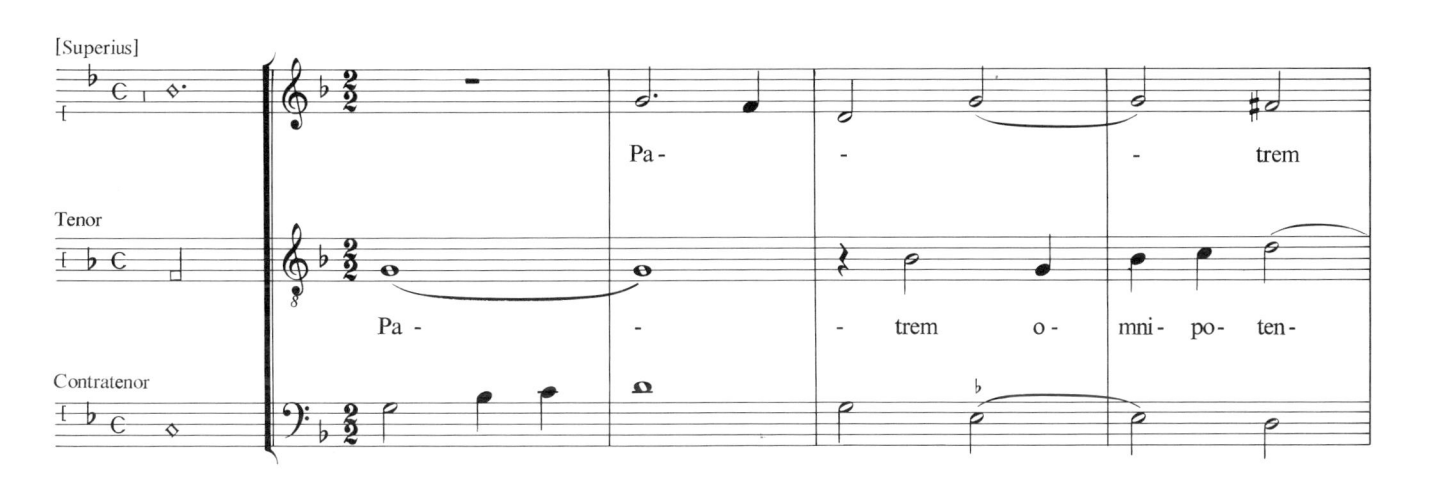

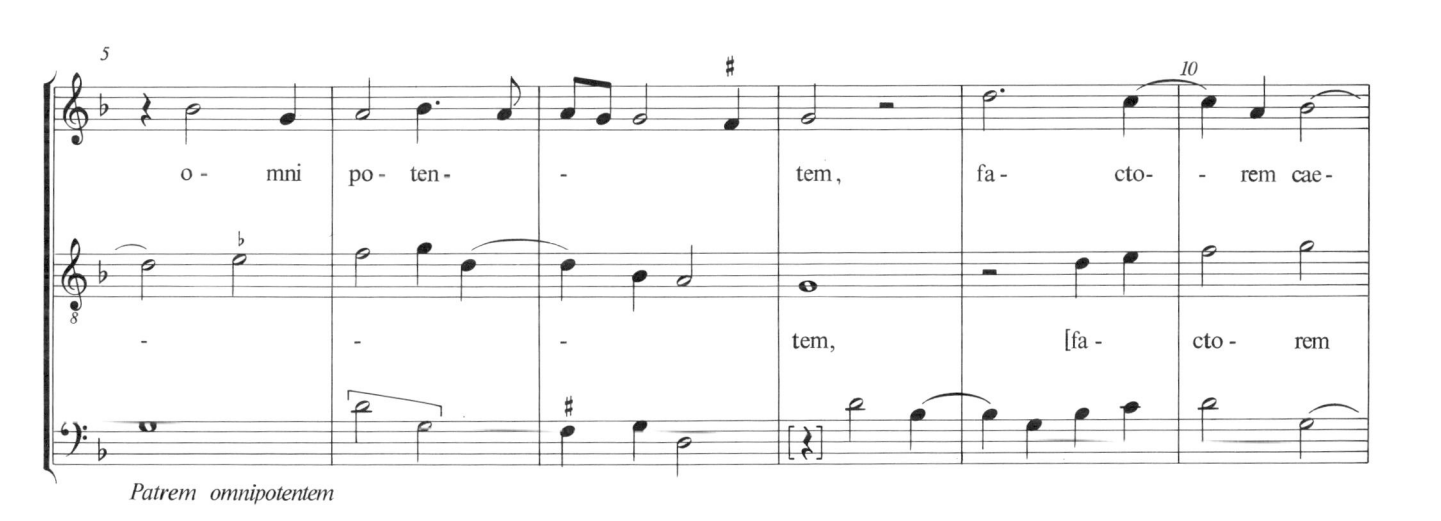

12

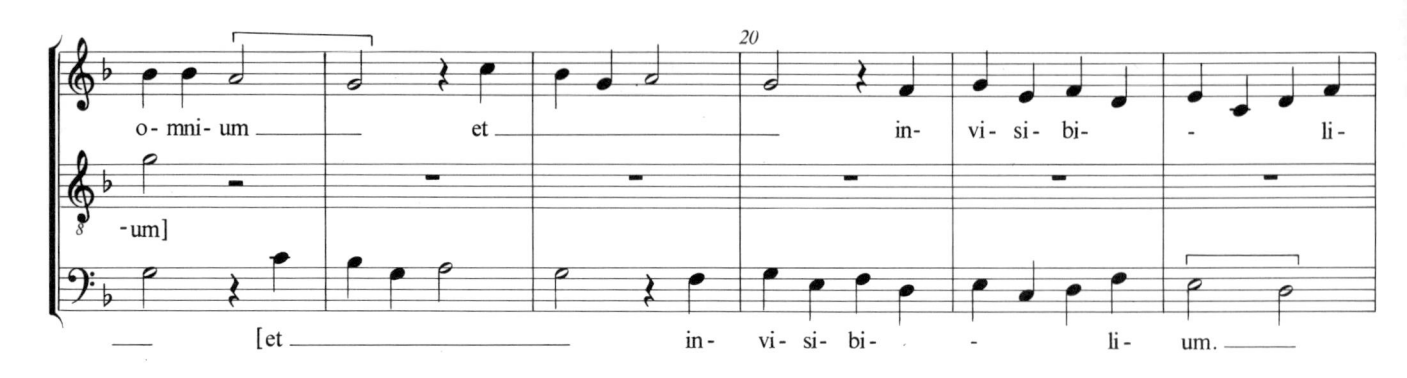

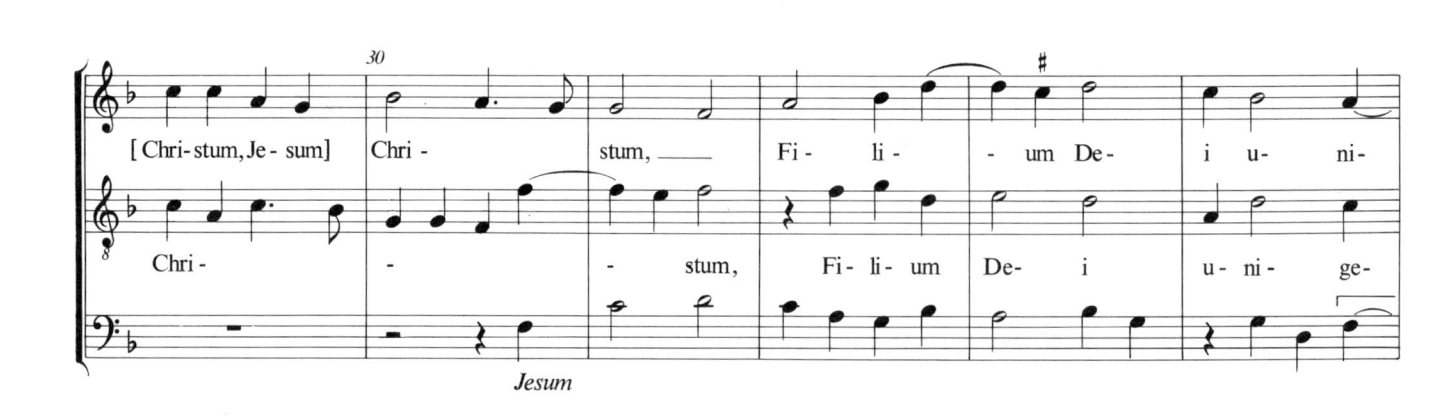

13

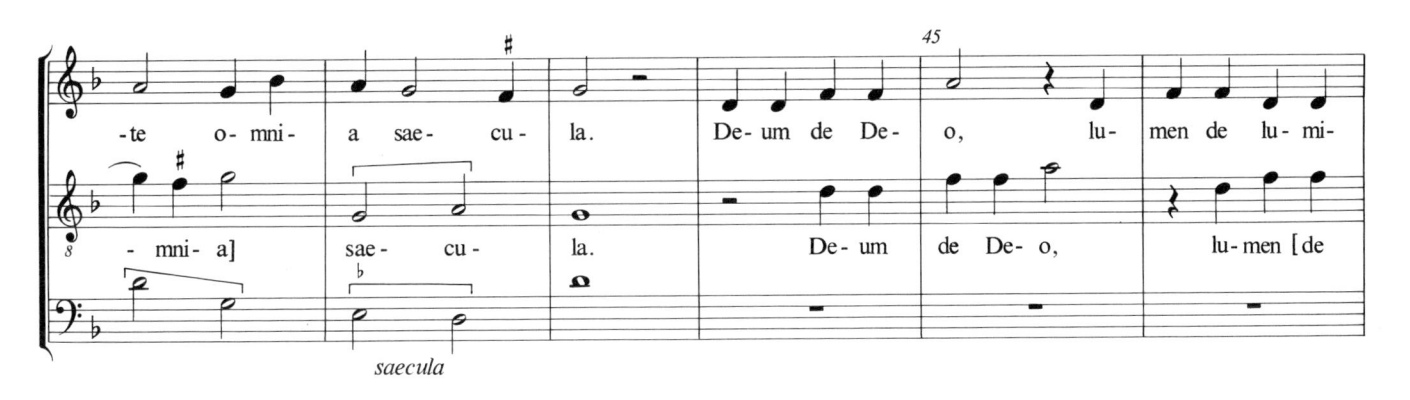

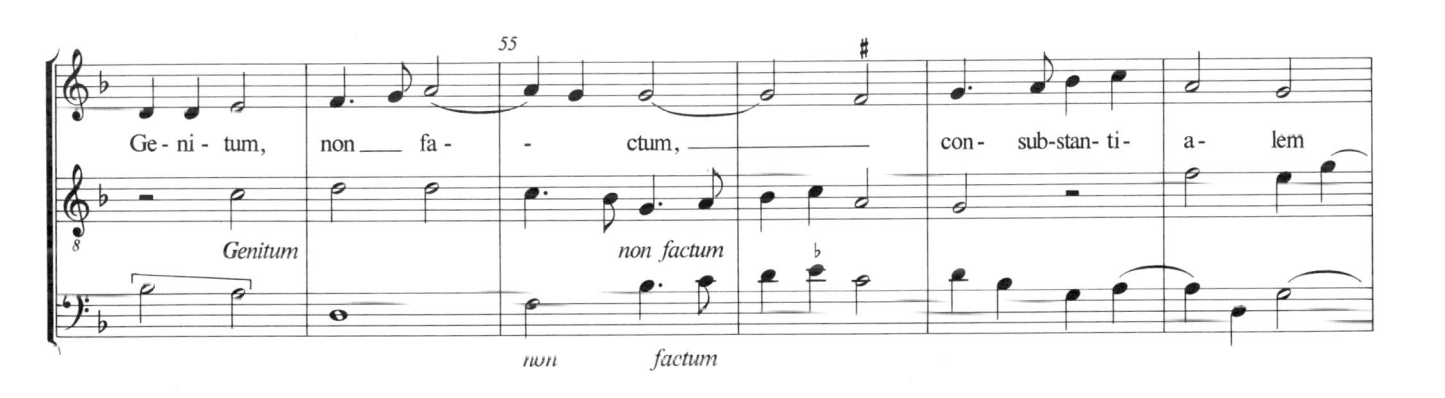

- - cta sunt. Qui pro- - pter nos ho- mi-
Qui pro- - pter nos
Qui propter
- nes,
ho- mi- nes, [et pro- pter no- stram sa- lu- tem de-
Et in- car - na - tus
.S.
- scen - - dit de cae - lis.] Et in- car - na- tus est
Et in- car- na- tus est
est de Spi- ri- tu San - - - cto ex
[de Spi- - ri- tu San- - - cto] ex
[Et in- car- na- tus est de Spi- ri- tu San- cto]
ex Maria

90
Ma- ri- a Virgi- ne: et ho-
Ma- ri- a Vir- gi- ne: [et ho- mo- fa-
95
- mo fa- ctus est. Cru- ci- fix- us e- ti- am
- ctus est.] Cru- ci- fix- us [e- ti- am
Cru- ci- fix- us e- ti- am pro
100
pro no- bis: sub Pon- ti- o Pi- la- to pas-
pro no- bis:]
no- bis:
105
- sus, et se- pul- - tus est.

[Superius]
Tenor
Contratenor
Et re- sur- re- xit ter- ti- a di- e, se- cun- dum Scri- ptu- ras. [se- cun- dum Scri- ptu- ras.] Et a- scen- dit in cae- lum: se- det ad dex-
Et resurre- xit
Et resurrexit
Et a- scen- dit [in cae- lum:] se- det [ad
Et ascendit

145
- te - ram Pa - tris. Et i - te -
dex - te - - ram Pa - tris.] Et i - - te - rum [ven - tu - rus
150
- rum ven - tu - rus est cum glo - ri - a,
est cum glo - ri - a,] ju -
cum gloria
155
160
ju - di - ca - re vi - vos et
- di - ca - re vi - - vos et mor - - tu - os:
judicare
165
mor - tu - os: cu - - jus re - - gni non e
cu - jus re - gni

170
175
rit fi- - - nis. Et in Spi- - ri- tum
[non e- - rit fi- - - - nis.]
180
San- ctum, Do- mi- num, et vi- vi-
[Et in Spi- ri- tum San- ctam, Do- mi- num,
185
190
- fi - can- - - tem: qui ex Pa-
et vi- vi- - fi- can- tem:] qui ex Pa- tre
qui ex
195
- tre Fi- li- o- - que pro- ce- - dit. Qui
[Fi- li- o- - que pro- ce- - dit.]
Pa- - tre [Fi- li- o- que pro- ce- dit.]

19

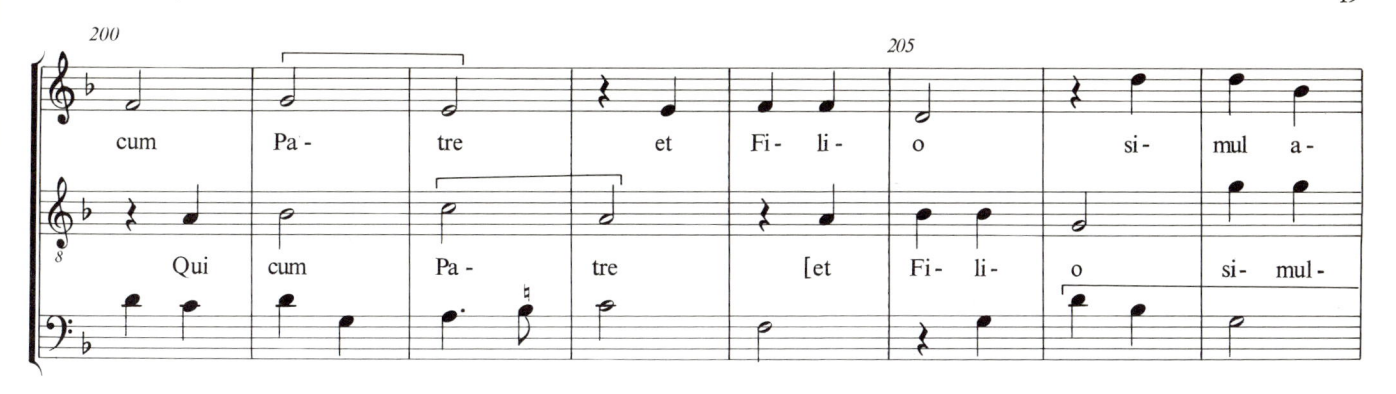

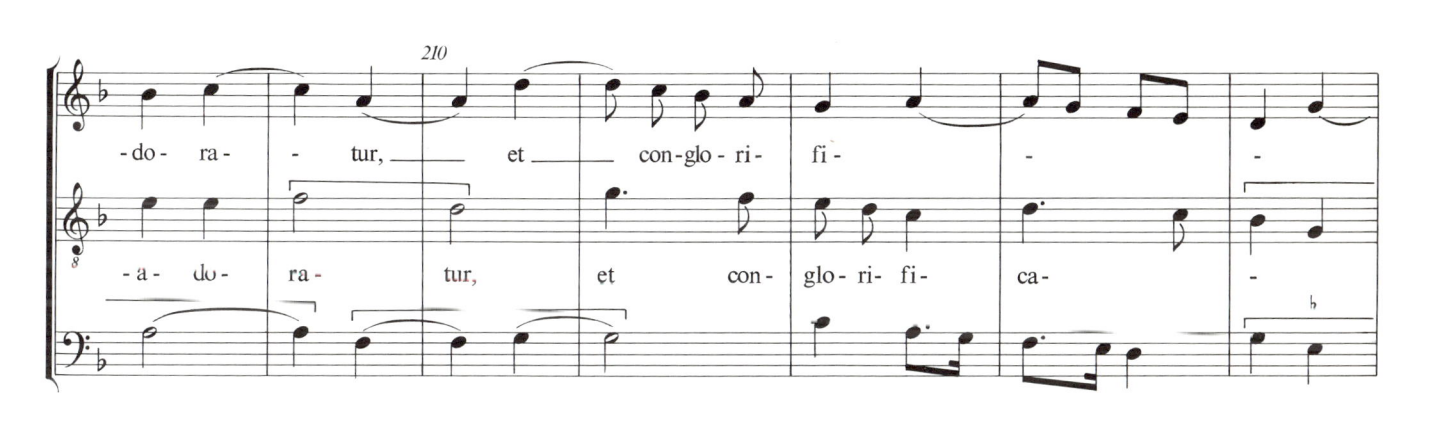

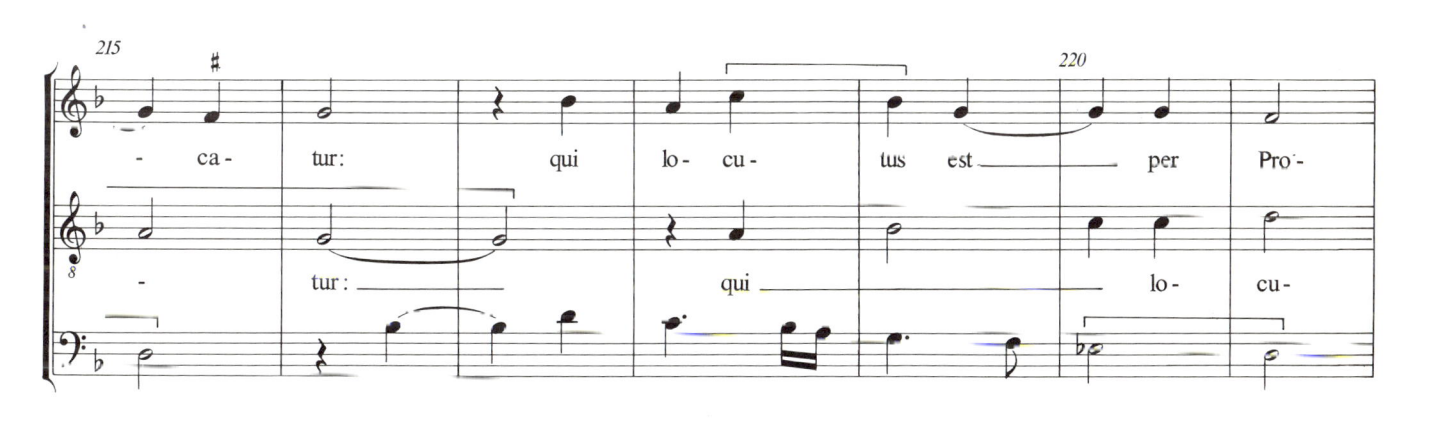

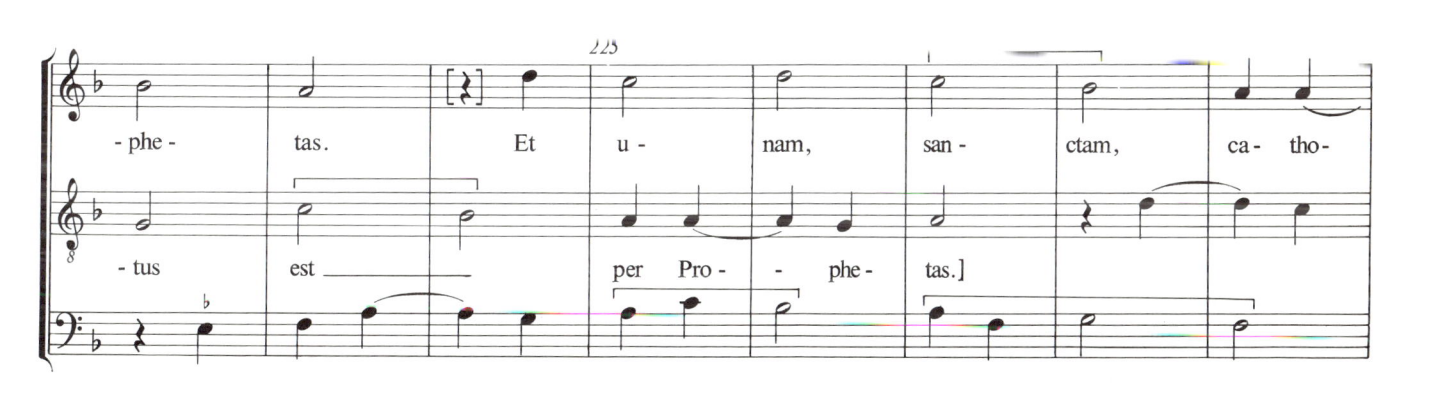

230
235
-li- cam et a- po- sto- li- cam Ec- cle-
240
-si- am. Con- fi- te- or u- num bap-
Con- fi- te- or [u- num bap-
245
250
-tis- ma in re- mis- si- o- -nem pec-
-tis- ma in re- mis- - si- o- -
255
260
-ca- to- - rum. Et ex- spe- cto re- - sur- re- cti- o-
- - - nem.]
Et ex- spe- - cto re- sur-

265
nem mor- tu- o- rum. Et
Et
re- cti- o- nem mor- tu- o-
270
vi- tam ven- tu- ri
vi- tam [ven- tu- ri se- cu-
rum.
275
280
se- cu- li. A-
-li. A-
285
men.
men.]

Sanctus

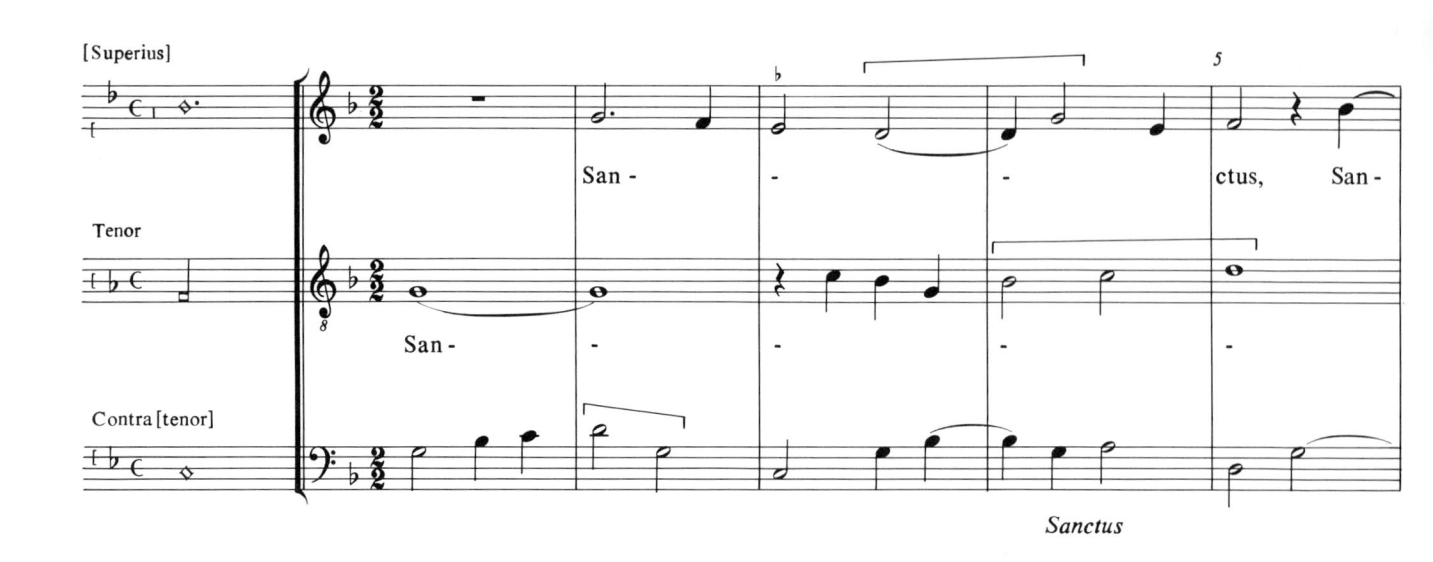

20
Do - mi - - nus De - - -
- ctus Do - mi - - nus De -
25
- us Sa - - - -
- - us Sa - - - -
30
- - - - ba - oth.
- - - - ba - oth.]
Pleni tacet
[Superius]
duo
35
Ple - - - - -
[Tenor]
duo
Ple - - - - -

24

25

90
[in ex- cel-
95
cel- sis.
sis.]
[Benedictus tacet]
[Superius]
duo
[Tenor]
duo
100
Be- ne-
Be- ne-
105
di-
di-
110
115

Hosanna ut supra
[mm. 76 - 95]

[2] Mass: Eterne rex altissime

Kyrie

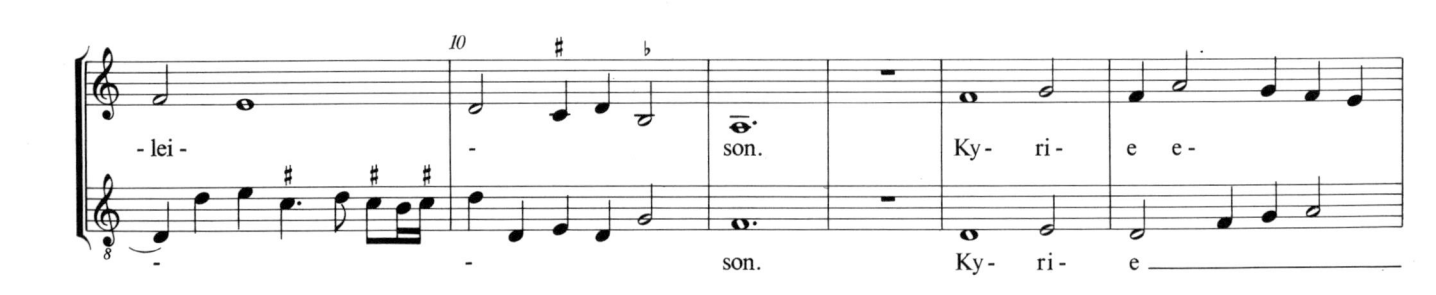

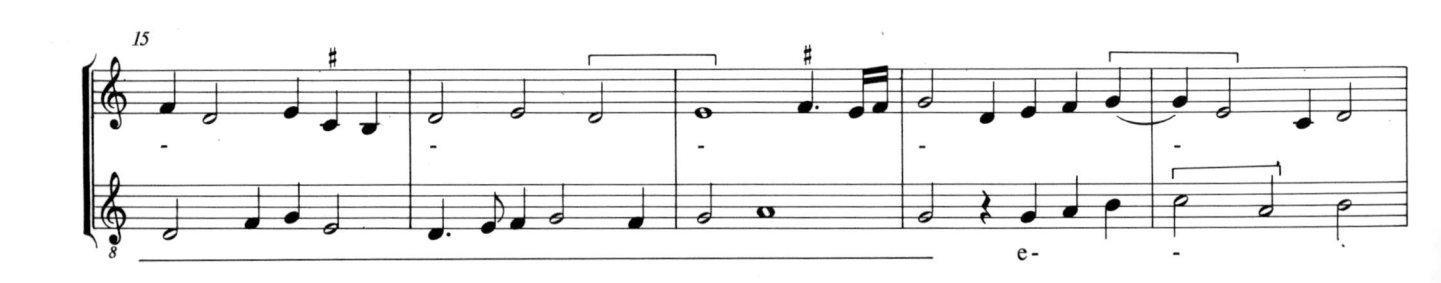

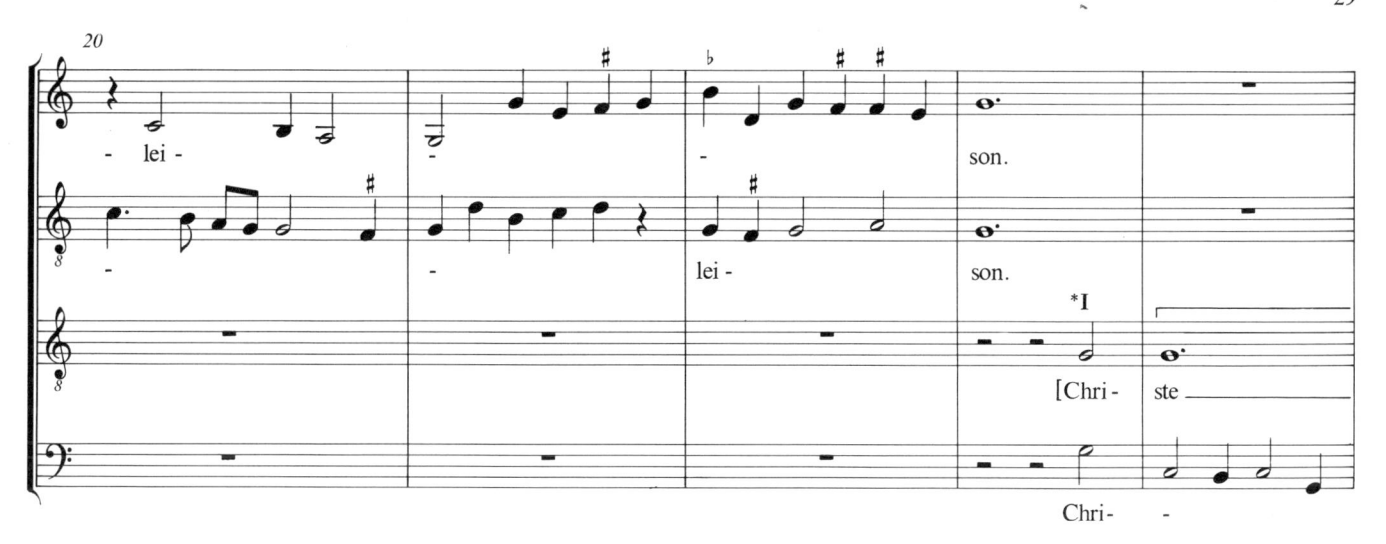

*Roman numerals identify the different incises of the *cantus prius factus*.

35
- son. Chri - - ste
[Chri - - ste] e - lei -
II
Chri - - ste
Chri - - - ste
40
e - - lei - son. Chri - ste
- son. Chri - ste e -
e - lei - -
e - lei - - -
45
e - - lei - son. Ky -
- lei - - - son. Ky - - ri -
III
- son. [Ky - -
- son. Ky - -

31

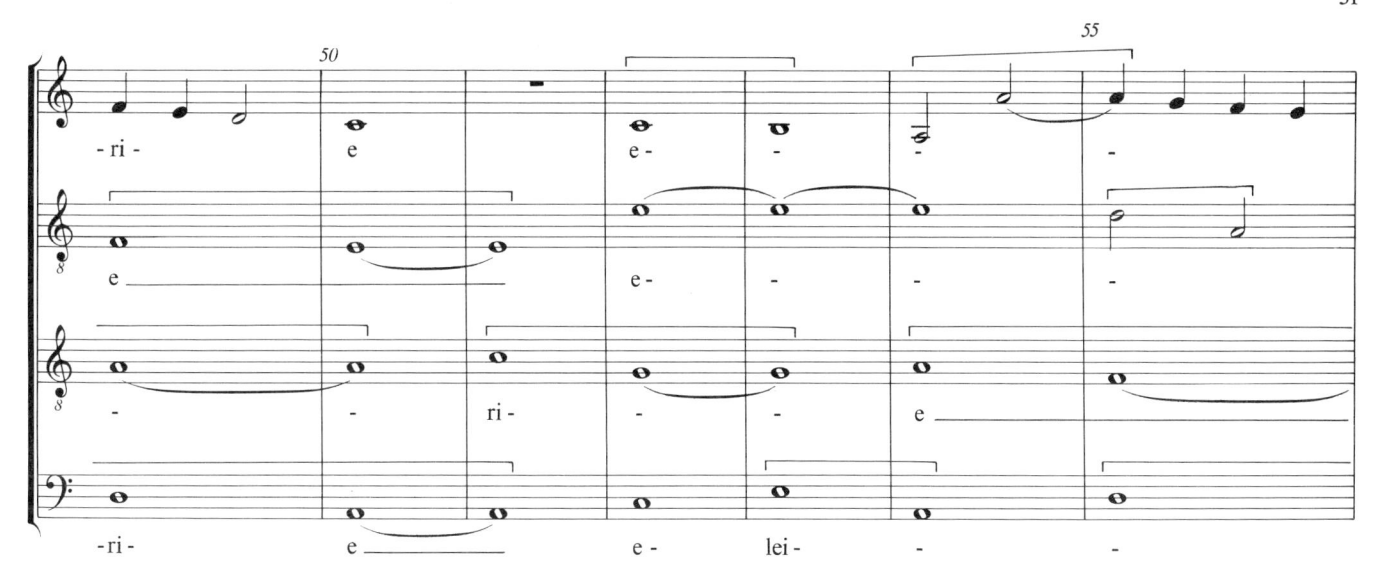

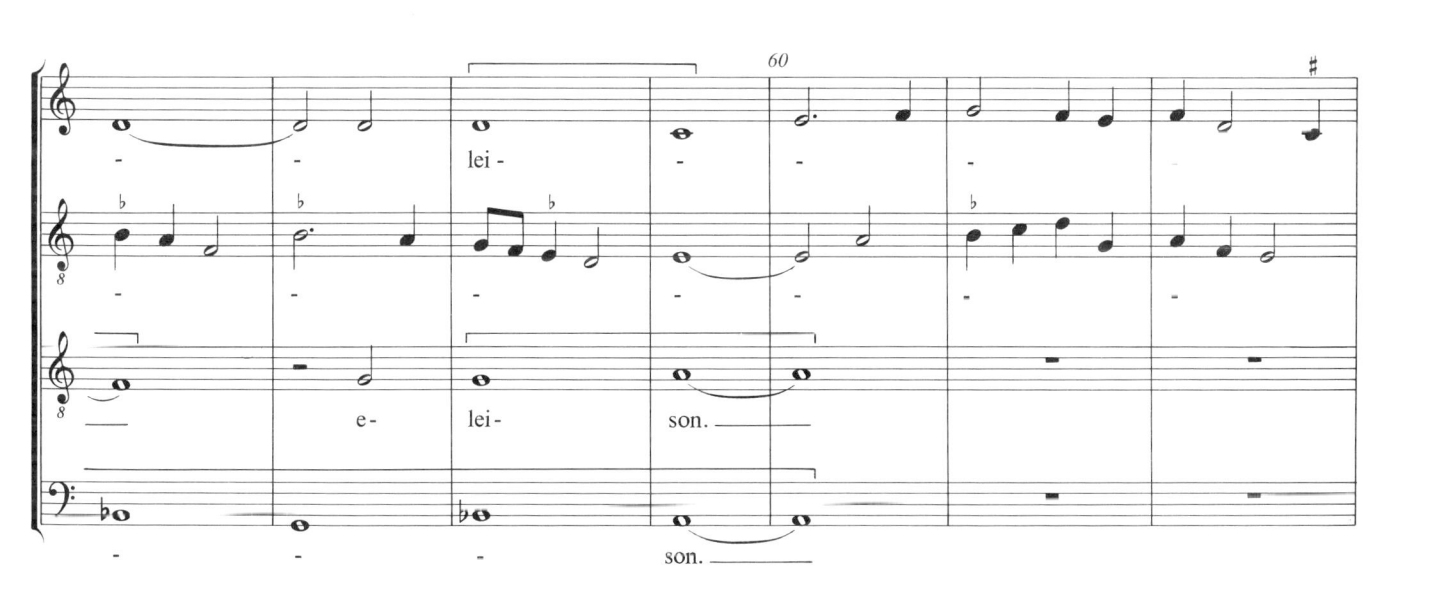

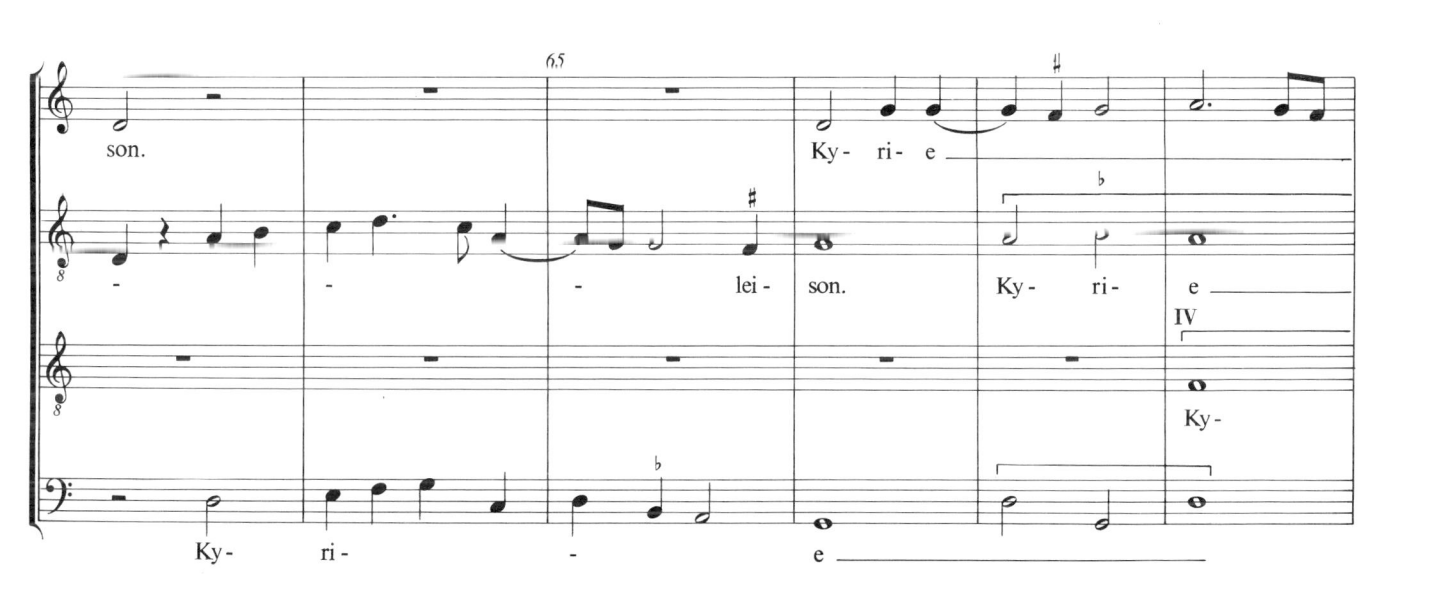

70
75
[e- lei- son. Ky- - ri-
[e- - lei- - -
- - ri- - e
e- - - - - -
80
- e]
- son. Ky- ri- - - e]
e- - - - - - lei-
- - - - - - -
85
90
e- - - lei- son.
e- - lei- - son.
- - son.]
-lei- - - - son.

Gloria in excelsis Deo

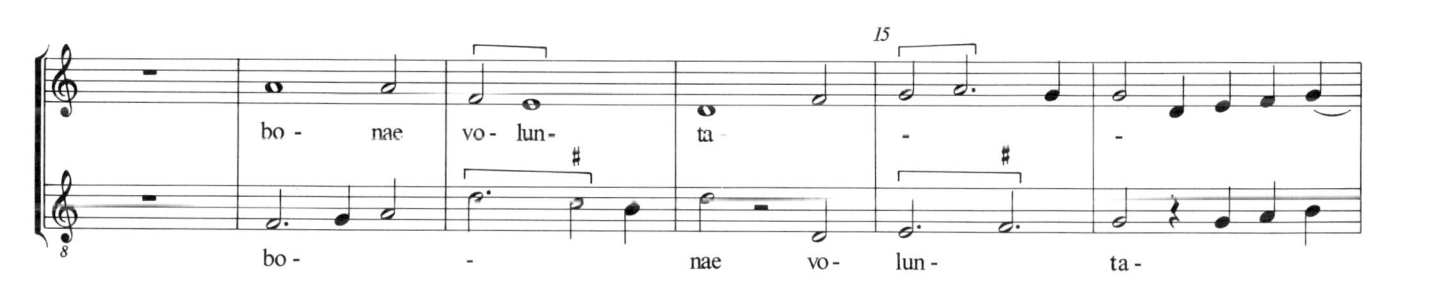

25
te.
te.
I
Benedicimus
te.
Laudamus
30
Be-
ne-
Be-
ne- di-
ci- mus
Adoramus
te.
te.
35
- di -
-
-
ci- mus
te.
A-
[te.]
A-
do-
ra-
-
II
Glorifi
camus

40
- do- - ra- - - mus
- mus te. Glo- ri- fi- ca-
te. Gratias agimus
45
te. Glo- - ri- fi- ca- mus
- - - mus te. Gra- ti-
50
te. Gra- ti- as a- gi- mus ti- bi pro-
- as a- gi- mus ti- bi pro- pter
III
propter

55
-pter ma- gnam glo- ri- am tu-
ma- gnam glo- - ri- am tu- am. Do-
magnam
60
-am. Do- - mi- ne De-
-mi- ne De- - - IV
Deus
Domine Deus
65
- us, Rex cae- le- stis [Rex cae- le-
- us, Rex cae- le- -
Pater
Rex caelestis

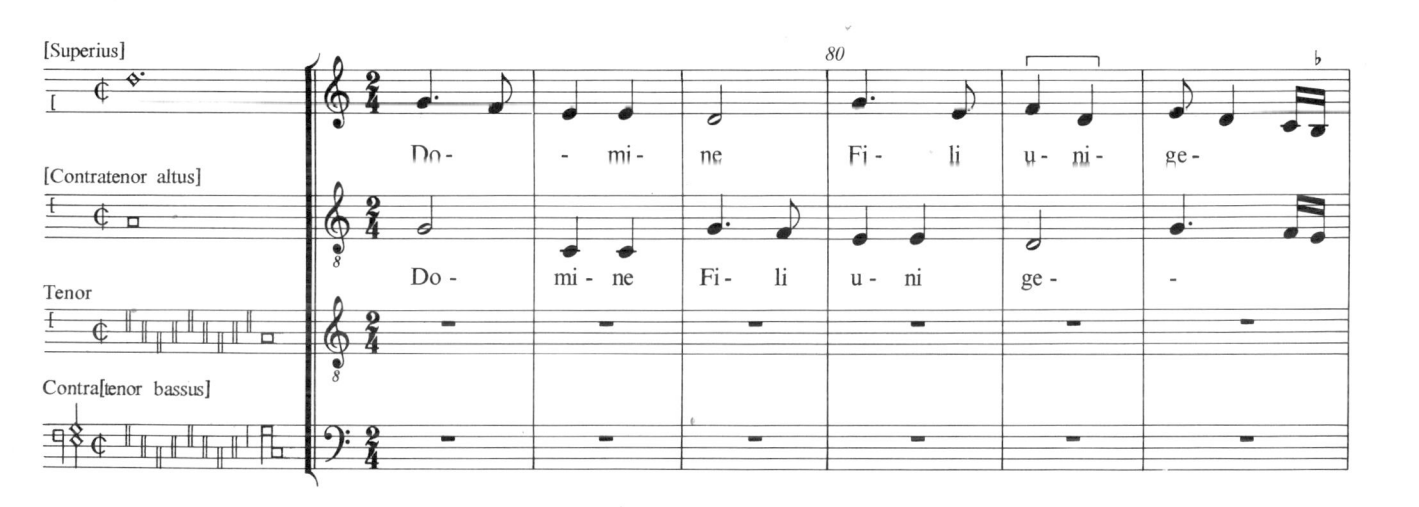

37

[Superius]

[Contratenor altus]

Tenor

Contra[tenor bassus]

38

120
-re- - re no- bis. Qui tol- lis pec-
-ta mun- di, mi- se-
mundi mise- rere
mundi miserere
125
130
-ca- - ta mun- di,
-re- re no- bis.
nobis Qui
nobis Qui tollis peccata
135
su- sci- pe de- pre-ca- ti- - o- - nem
tollis peccata
mundi, suscipe deprecationem

140
145
su- sci- pe de- pre- ca- ti- o- nem
no- stram. Qui se- des
II
nostram
Qui
150
no- stram. Qui se- des ad dex-
ad dex- te- ram Pa- tris, mi- se-
sedes
ad
dexteram
Patris,
155
160
-te- ram Pa- tris, mi- se- re-
-re- re no-

165
-re no- - - bis. Quo- ni- am
-bis. Quo- - ni- am tu so- lus san- ctus.
III
170
tu so- lus san- - ctus.
Tu so- lus Do- mi- nus.
175
180
Tu so- lus Do- mi- nus. Tu so- lus Al-
Tu so- lus Al- tis- si- mus,

42

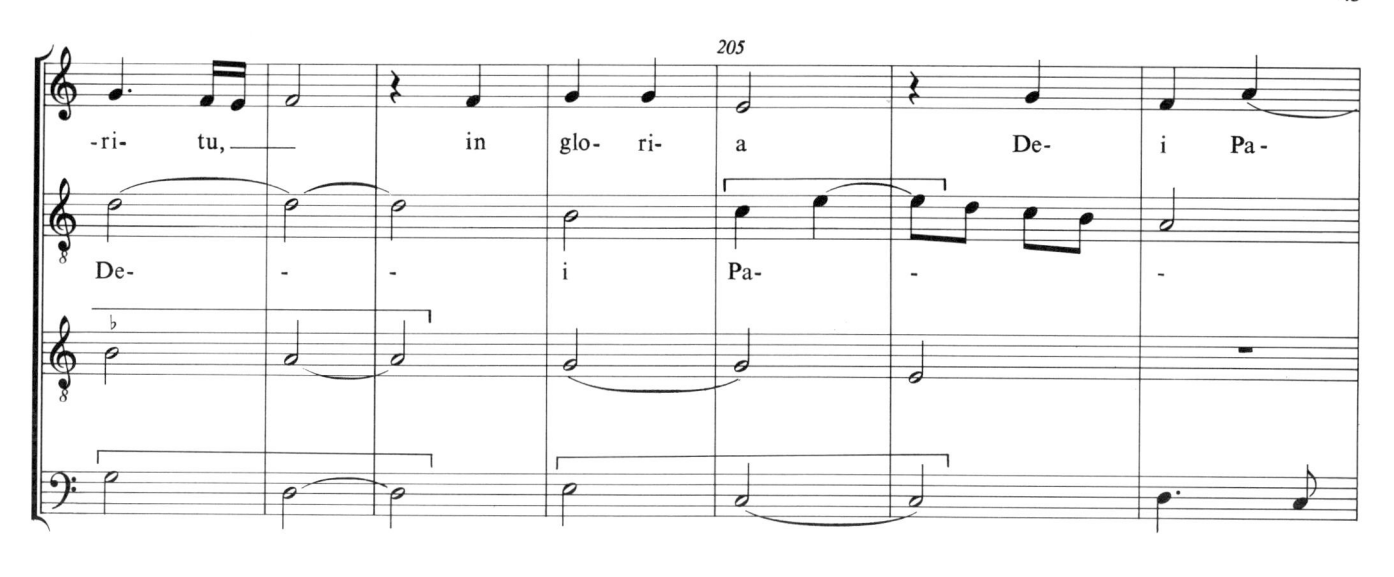

Credo in unum Deum

44

30
-sum Chri- - stum, Fi- li- um De-
Chri- stum, Fi- li- um De- i u- ni- ge- ni- tum. Et ex Pa- tre na-
Christum, Filium Dei unigenitum.
Filium Dei unige-
35
-i u- ni- ge- - - ni- tum.
-tum ante o- mni- a
-nitum.
40
Et ex Pa- - tre na- tum an- te o- mni-
sae- cu- la. De- um de De- o,

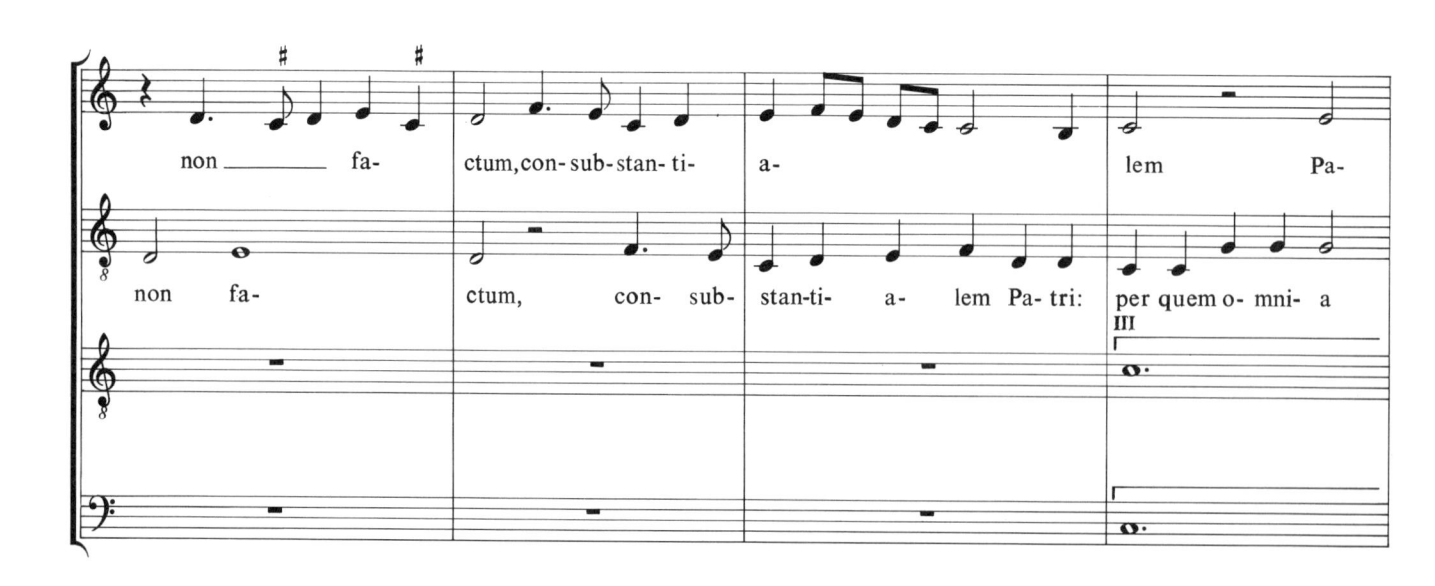

-a ___ saecu-la. De-um de De-o, lu-
[lu- men ___ de lu- mi- ne, De-
-men de lu- mi- ne, De- um ve- rum de De- o ve- ro. Ge- ni- tum,
-um ve- rum de De- o ve- ro. Ge- ni- tum,
non ___ fa- ctum, con-sub-stan-ti- a- lem Pa-
non fa- ctum, con- sub- stan-ti- a- lem Pa- tri: per quem o- mni- a

Et incarnatus

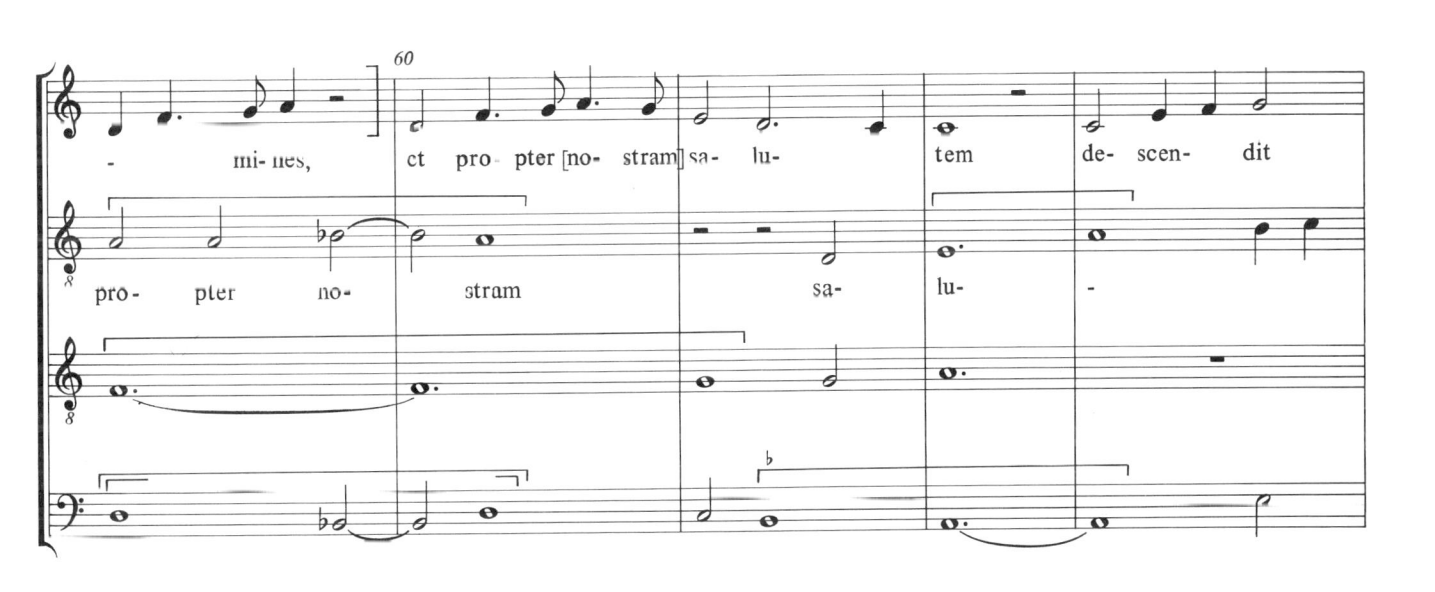

70
- tus est de Spi- ri- tu San- -cto ex
-car- na- - tus est [de Spi- ri-
est
75
Ma- ri- a Vir- gi- -ne: et ho-
-tu San- cto ex Ma- ri- a Vir- gi-
80
- mo fa- ctus est.
-ne: et ho- mo fa- ctus est.]

[Superius]
[Contratenor altus]
[Tenor]
[Contratenor bassus]
85
Cru- ci- fix- us e- ti- am pro
Cru- ci- fix- - us e- ti- am pro
90
95
no- bis: sub Pon- ti- o Pi- - la- to
no- - - bis: sub Pon-ti- o Pi- la-
100
pas- sus, et se- pul- - - tus est. Et re- sur-
- to pas- sus, et se - pul- - tus est. Et
105
110
- re- - - xit ter- ti- a di- e,
re- sur- re - - xit ter- - ti- a di- e,
115
se- cun- - dum Scri- ptu- ras, Et a-
se- cun- dum Scri- ptu- ras. Et a-

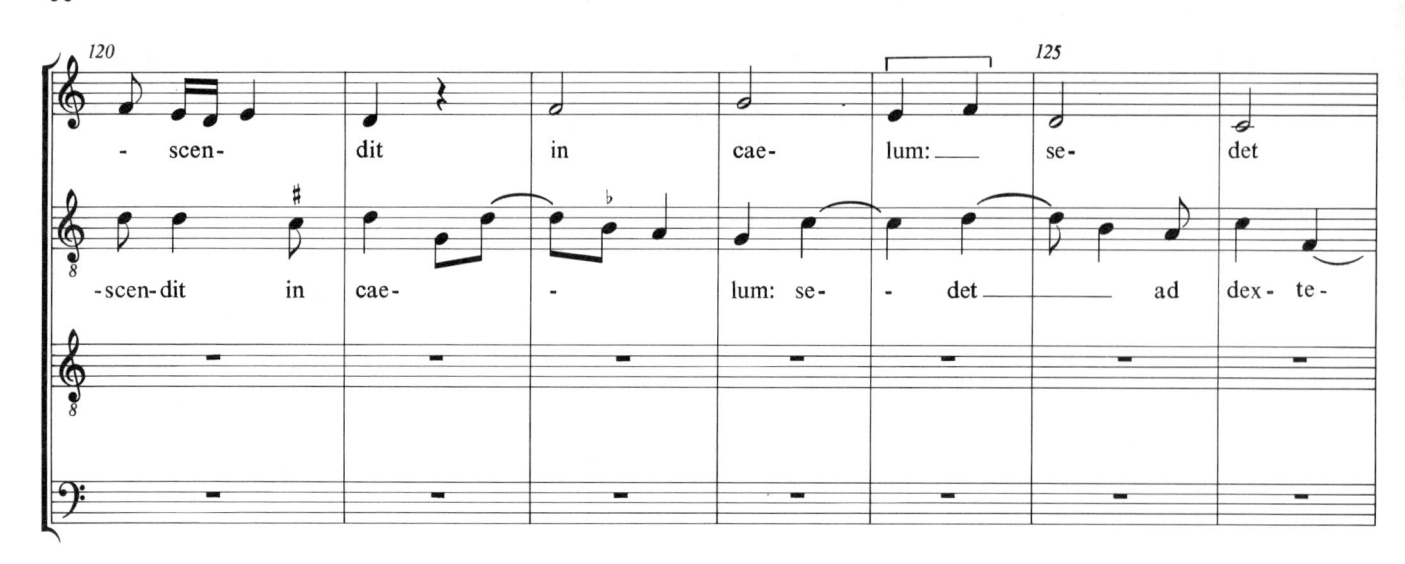

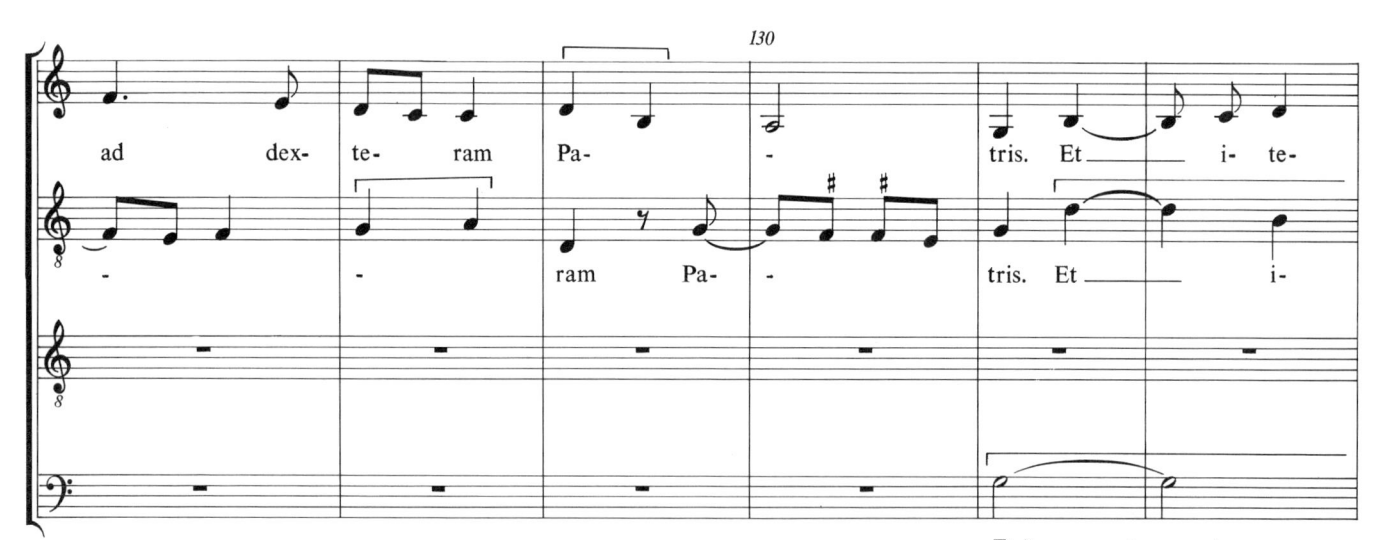

Et iterum venturus est

Et ascendit in caelum
.S.

51

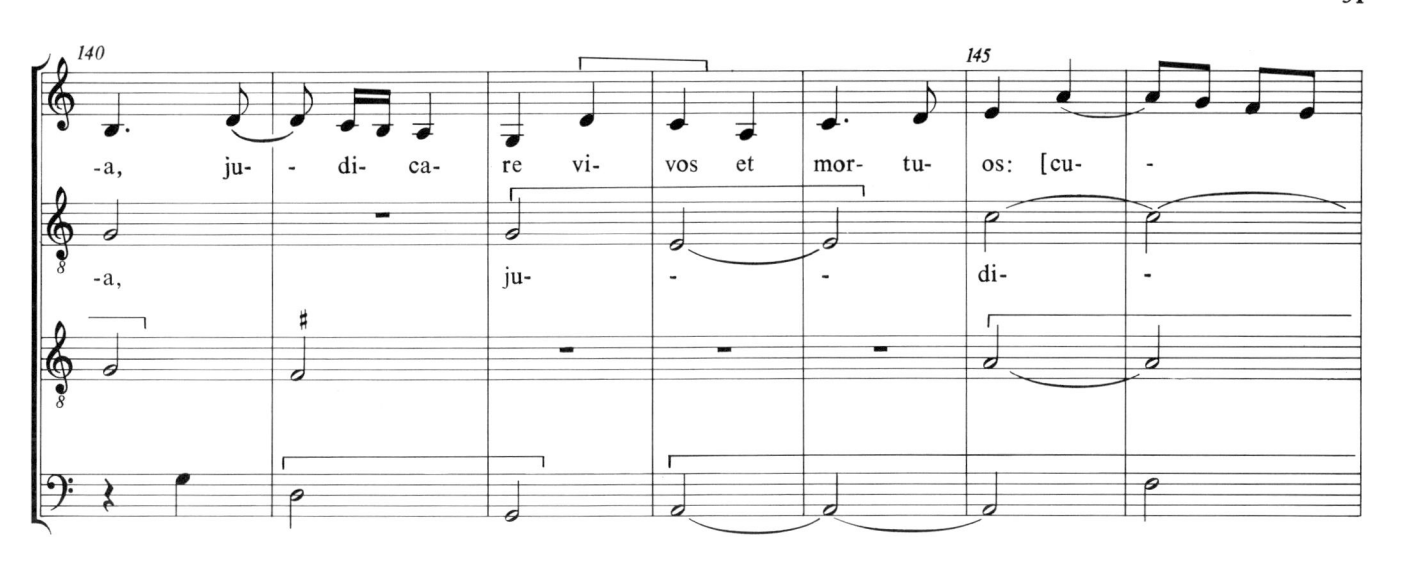

52

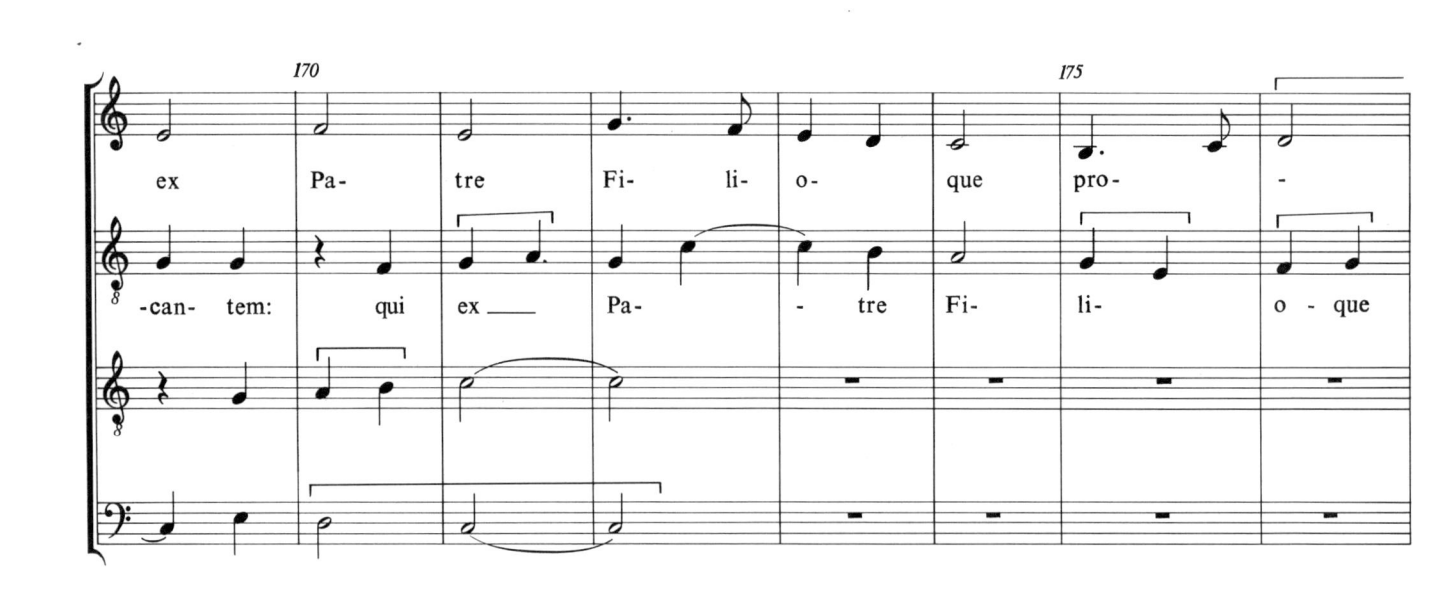

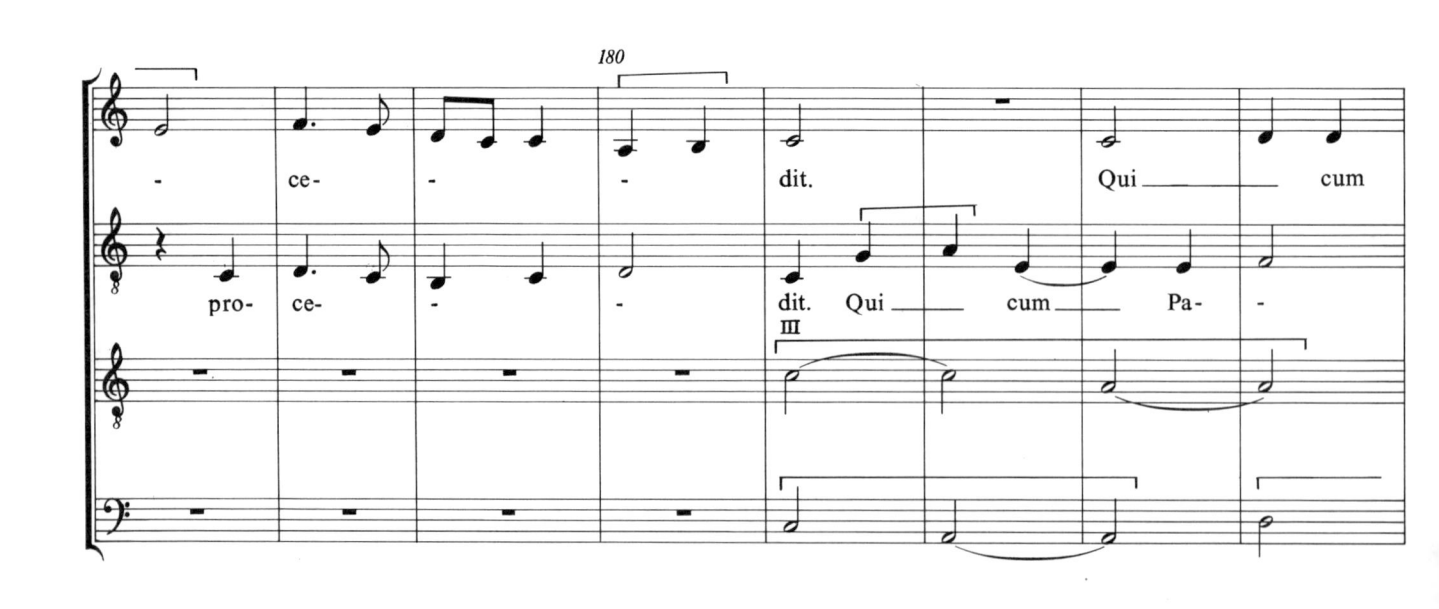

185
190
Pa- tre et Fi- li- o si- - mul a- do- ra- tur, et con - glo-
- tre et Fi- li- o si- mul a- do-
195
- ri- fi- ca- - tur: [qui lo- cu- tus est
-ra- - tur, et con - glo- - - ri- fi- -
200
205
per Pro - phe- tas.]
- ca- tur: Et u- nam, san- -

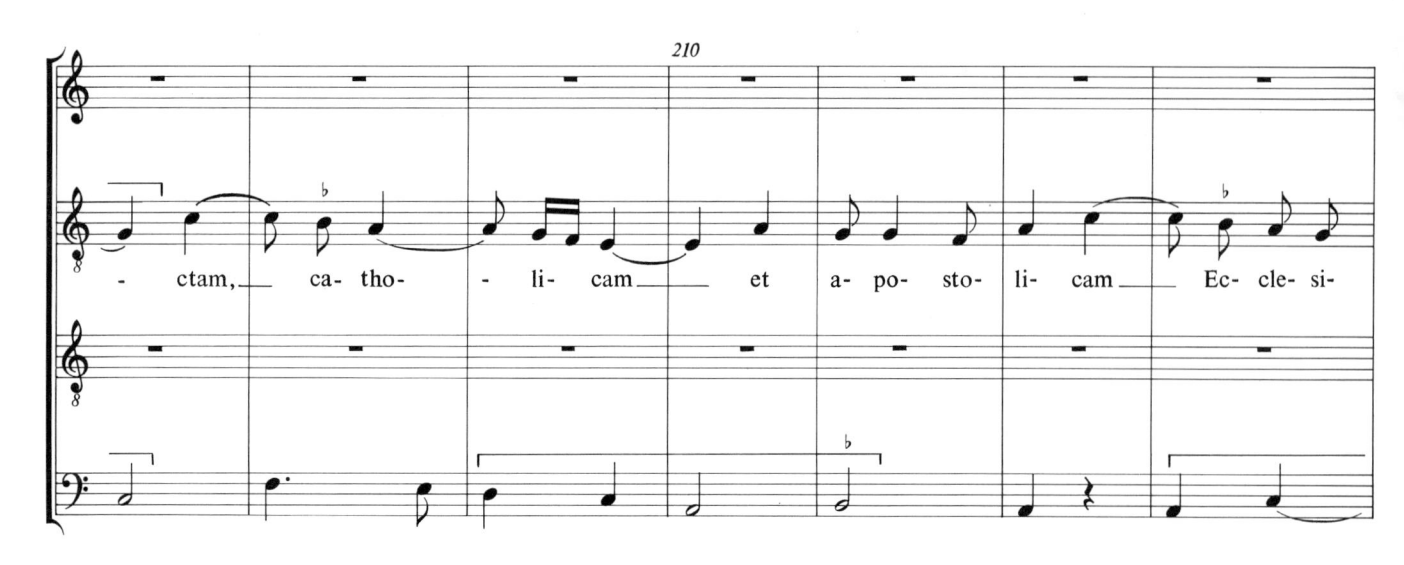

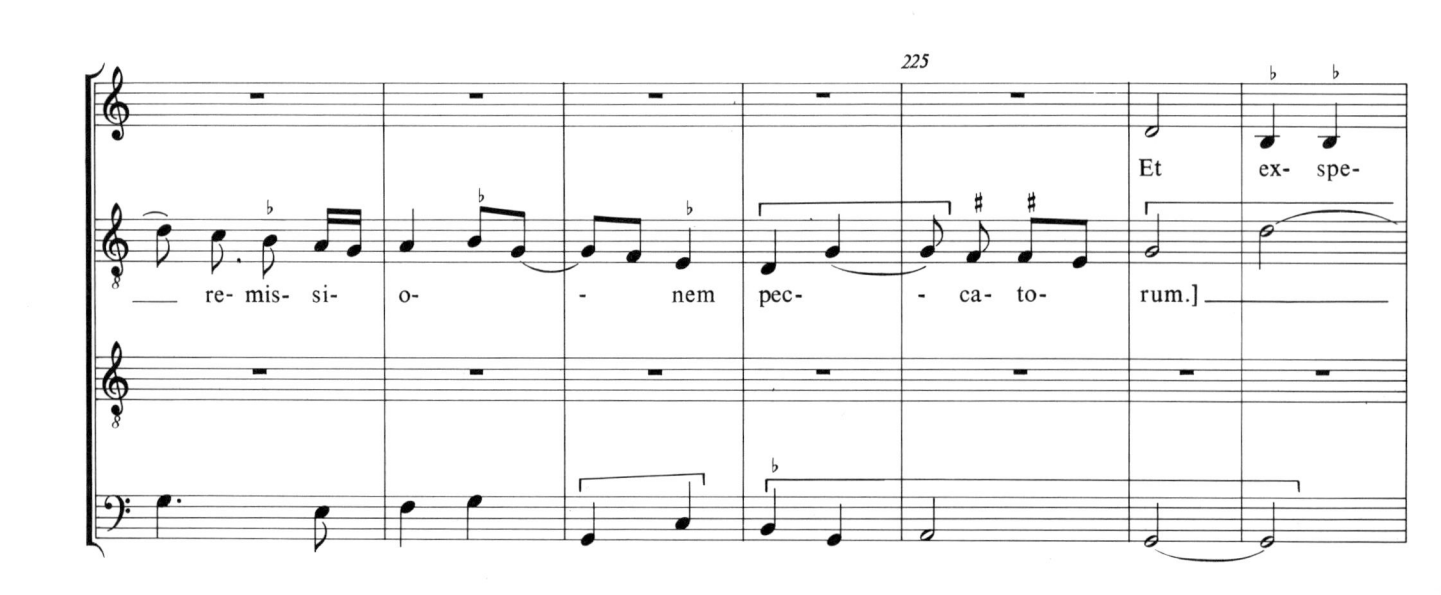

-ctam, catholicam et apostolicam Ecclesi-am. Confiteor unum baptisma in remissionem peccatorum.] Et exspe-

230
-cto re- sur- re- cti- o- - - nem mor-
IV
235
240
tu- - o- - rum. Et vi- tam ven- tu- - ri
Amen
245
250
sae- cu- li. A- - men.

Sanctus

57

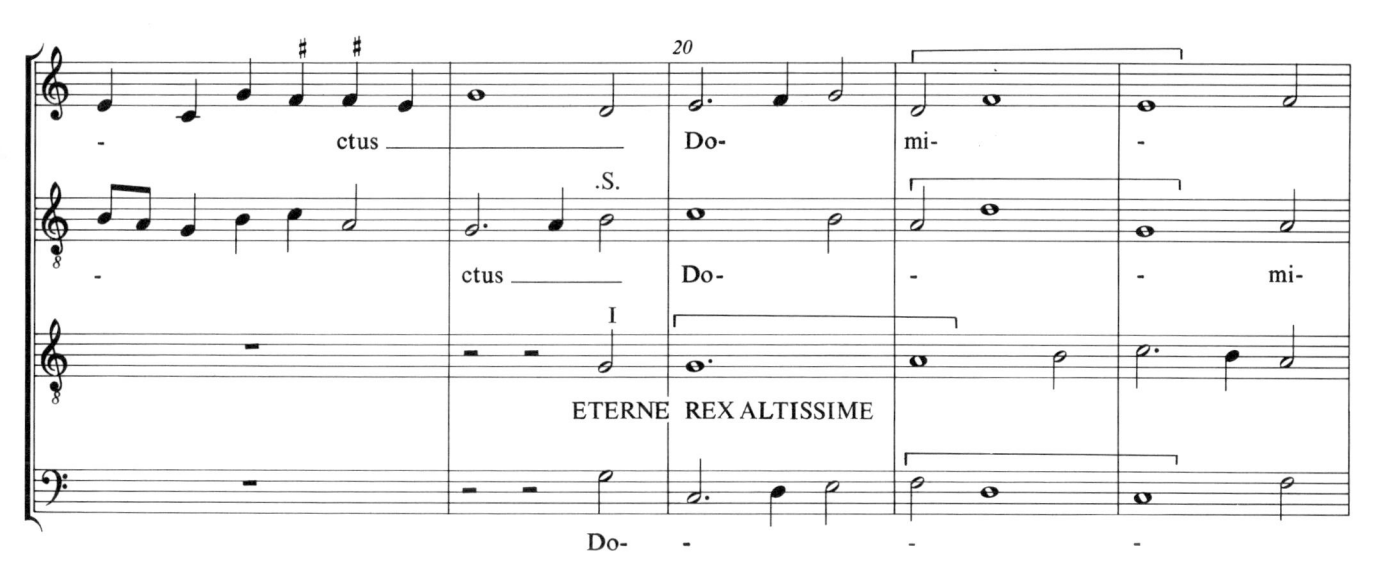

35
-ni sunt cae- -
- - - - ni sunt
-ni sunt cae- li [et
40
- li et ter- - -
cae- - li et ter- - -
ter- - - - ra]
45
- - ra glo- - ri-
- - ra glo- - ri- a

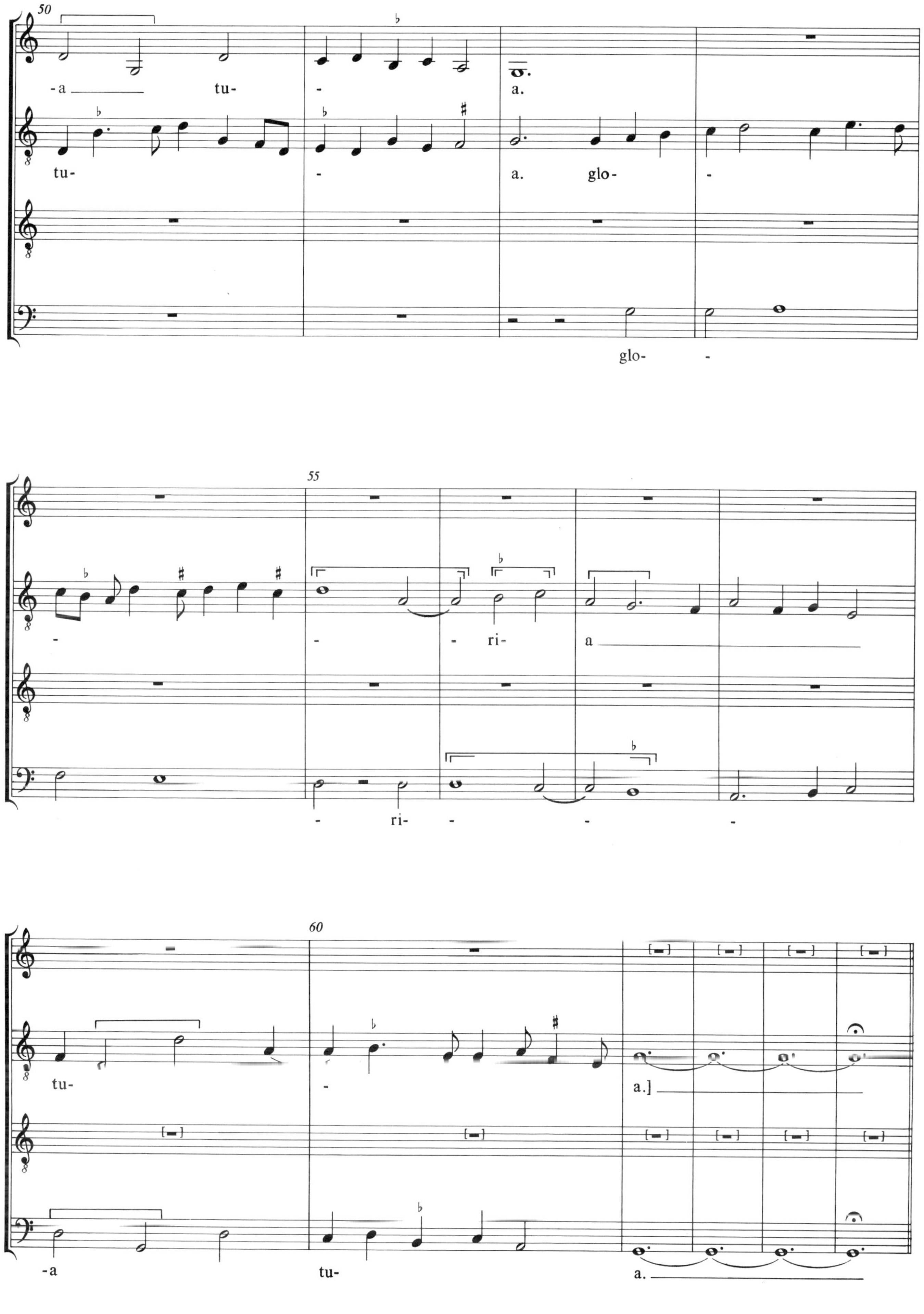
50
-a tu- - a.
tu- - a. glo- -
glo- -
55
- - - ri- a
- ri- - - -
60
tu- - a.]
-a tu- a.

[Superius]
[Contratenor altus]
[Tenor]
[Contratenor bassus]
65
Ho-
III
san-
70
san-
75
na
in
IV

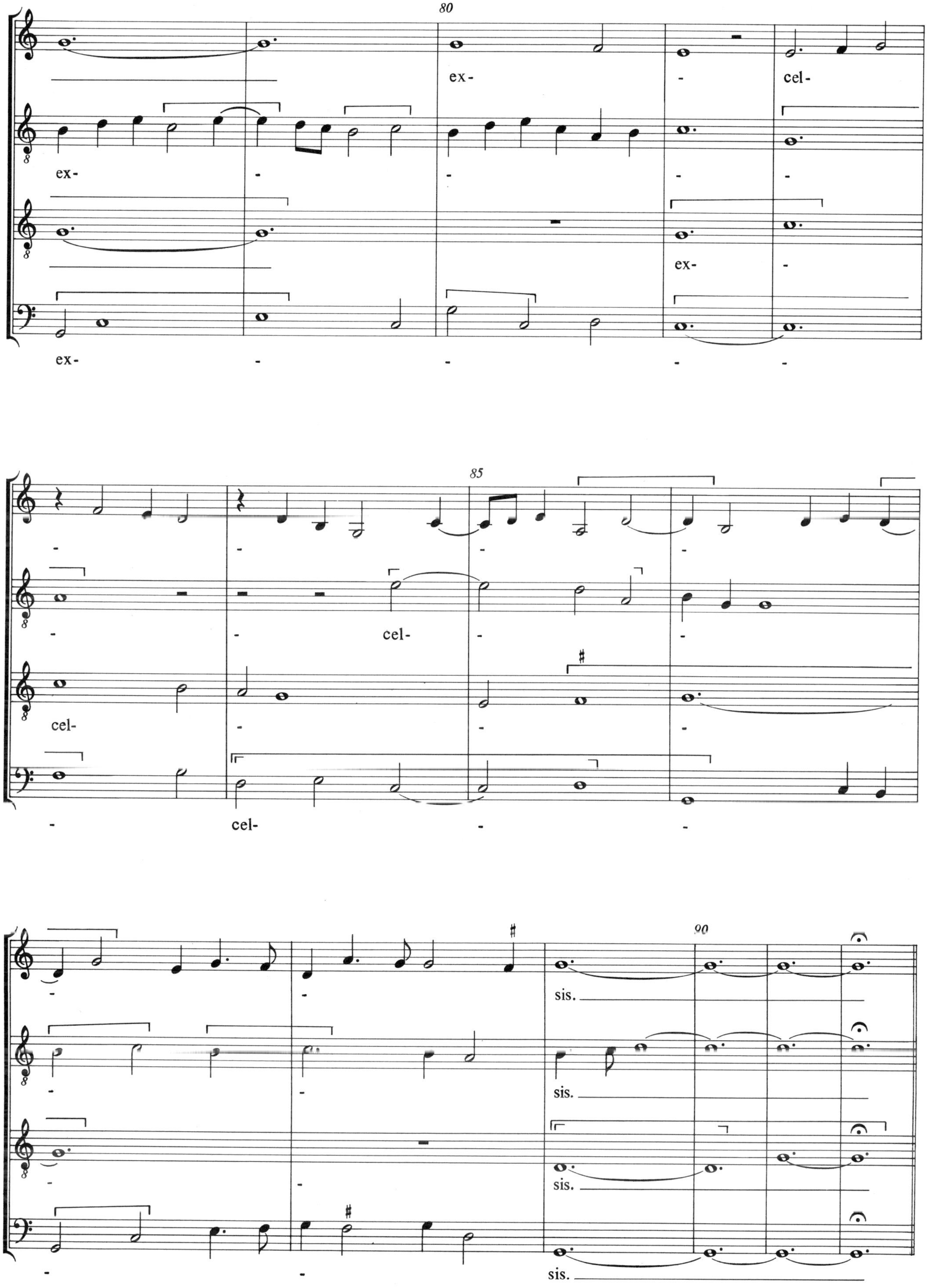
80
ex- - cel-
ex- - - - -
ex- -
ex- - - - -
85
- - - - cel- - -
cel- - - -
- cel- - -
90
- - sis.
- - sis.
- - sis.
- - sis.

62

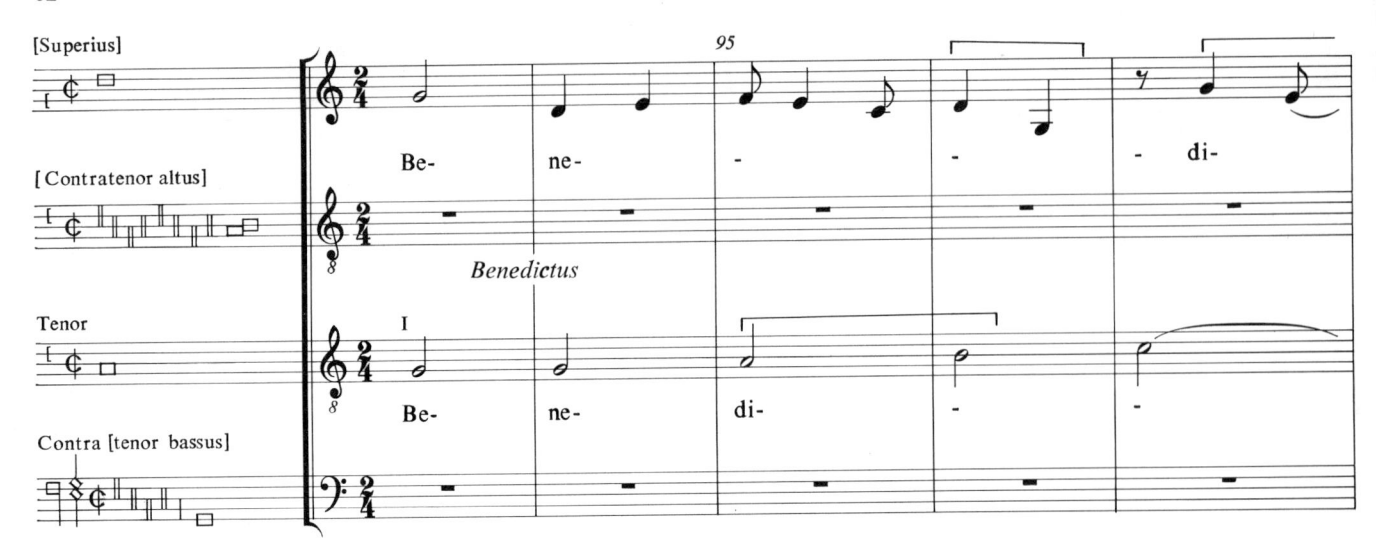

115
nit
II
in
no-
mi-
qui ve-
120
ne
nit
in
no-
125
130
in no- mi- ne
in no- mi- ne
III
Do-
-mi- ne
Do-

135
Do-
Do-
mi
mi-
140
mi-
ni.
ni.
ni.
-mi-
ni.
[Superius]
[Contratenor altus]
[Tenor]
[Contratenor bassus]
145
150
Ho-
san-
Ho-
san-

155
Ho - san -
IV
Ho -
na
160
na in
na
san - na in
in ex - cel -
165
170
ex - cel -
in ex - cel-
ex - cel -
sis.

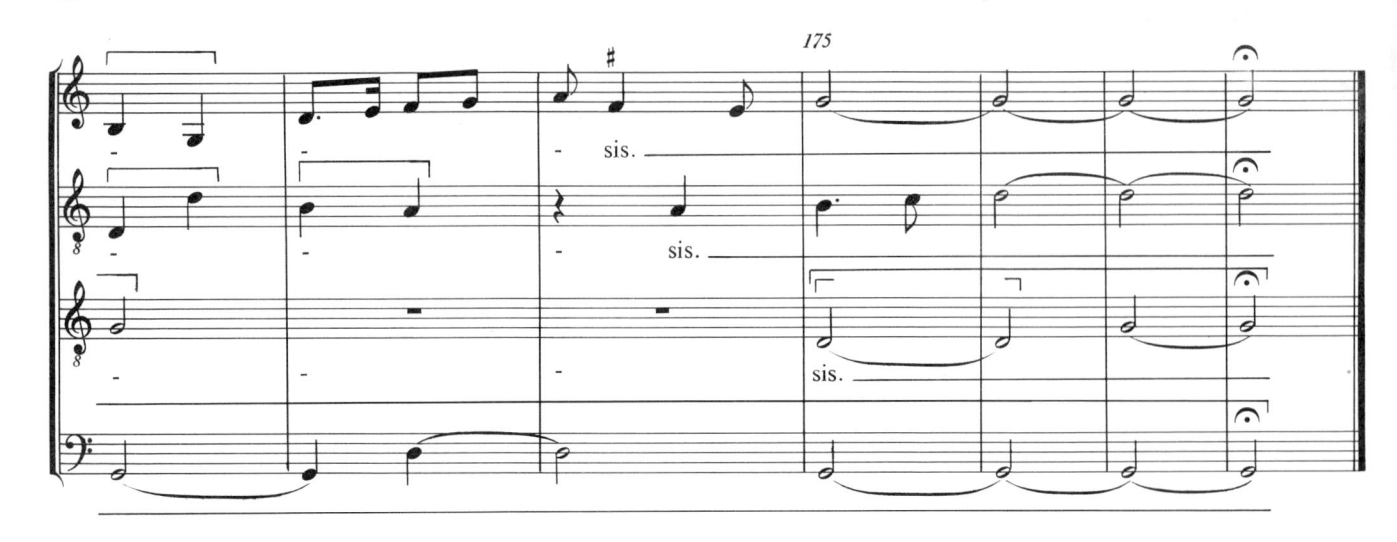

Agnus Dei

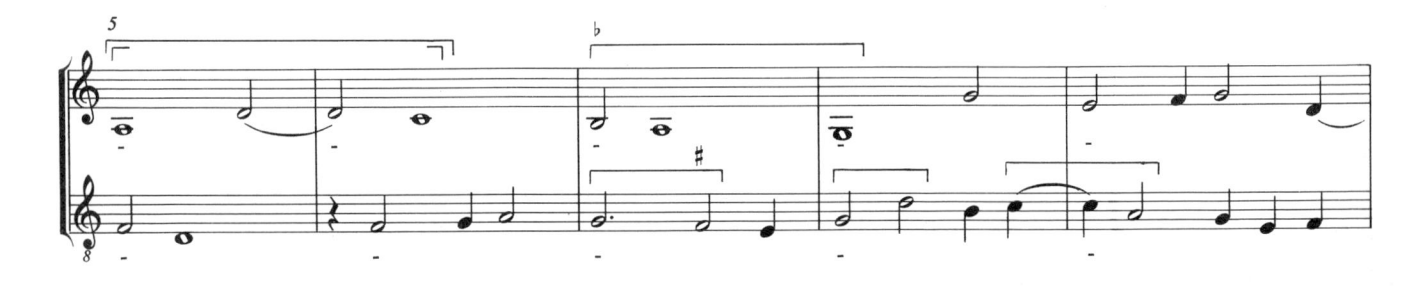

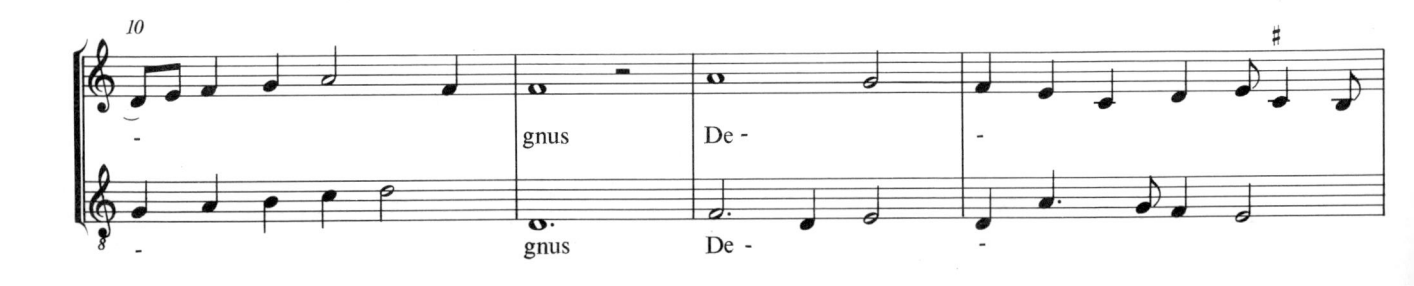

15
i, qui tol - - - - lis
S.
- - - - i, [qui tol -
I
qui tollis
pe- ca -
20
pec - - ca - ta mun -
- - lis pec - ca - - ta
peccata mundi:
- - - - ta
25
- - - di: mi - -
mun - di :
mun - - - - -

30
se -
mi -
se -
re -
II
miserere
- di :
mi -
se -
re -
35
re-
re
re
no -
re
40
45
no -
bis.
bis.]
no -
bis.

[Superius]
[Contratenor altus]
[Tenor]
[Contratenor bassus]
A - - - gnus De - - - - - i, - -
A - - - - -gnus De - - i, qui
III
Agnus
Dei,
A - - - gnus De - - i,
50
55
tol - lis pec - ca -
qui tol - - -

60
- lis pe -
65
qui tol - lis pec - ca - ta mun -
- ta mun -
IV
ca - ta mun - di:
70
- di: mi - se - re - re no -
- di: mi - se - re -
mi - se - re - re no -

75
bis.
re
no-
bis.
bis.
[Superius]
[Contratenor altus]
Tenor
Contra[tenor bassus]
80
85
Agnus
Dei,
A-
gnus
De-
90
A-
qui
tollis
i,

95
De -
gnus De - i,
II
100
i, qui tol -
peccata
mun -
105
- lis
[qui tol - lis]
qui tol -
III
110
[qui tol - lis

115
120
pec - - - - - - - ca
- lis pec - ca - - - - ta
pe - - ca - - - ta
125
- - - ta mun - - - -
mun - - - di : [pe - ca -
di
mun - - - - di :
130
135
- - di : do -
- ta mun - - di :] do - - - -
do - - - - -

74

[3] Mass: Entrepris suis par grant lyesse

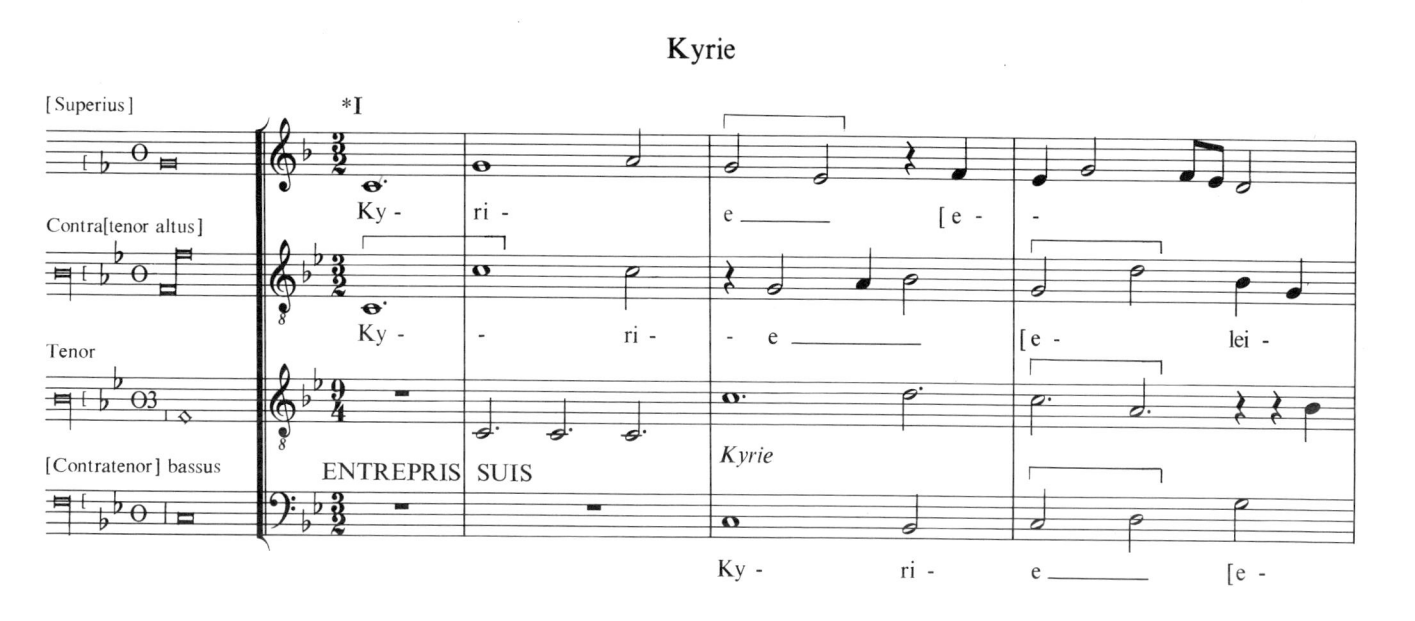

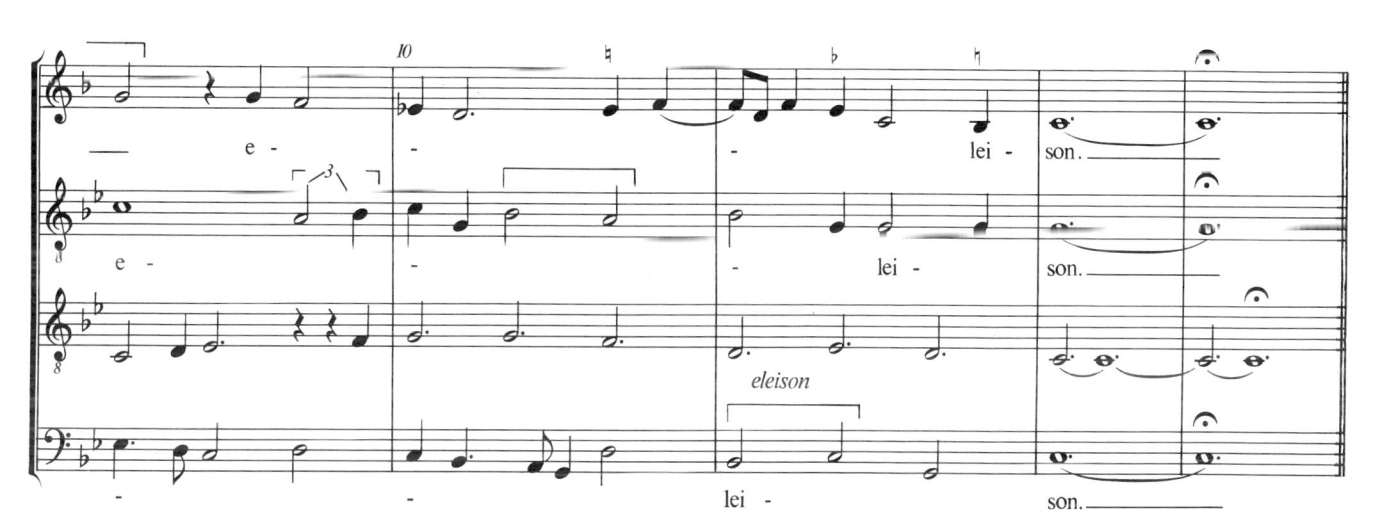

Kyrie

*Roman numerals refer to sections of the rondeau *Entrepris suis* (cf., pp. 173-176) and show where portions of these sections are used in the Mass.

[Superius]
[Contratenor altus]
[Tenor]
[Contratenor bassus]
II
15
Chri - ste [e - lei - son. Chri -
Chri -
ste [e -
Christe
Chri - ste
[e -
20
- ste e -
lei - son.
Chri -

77

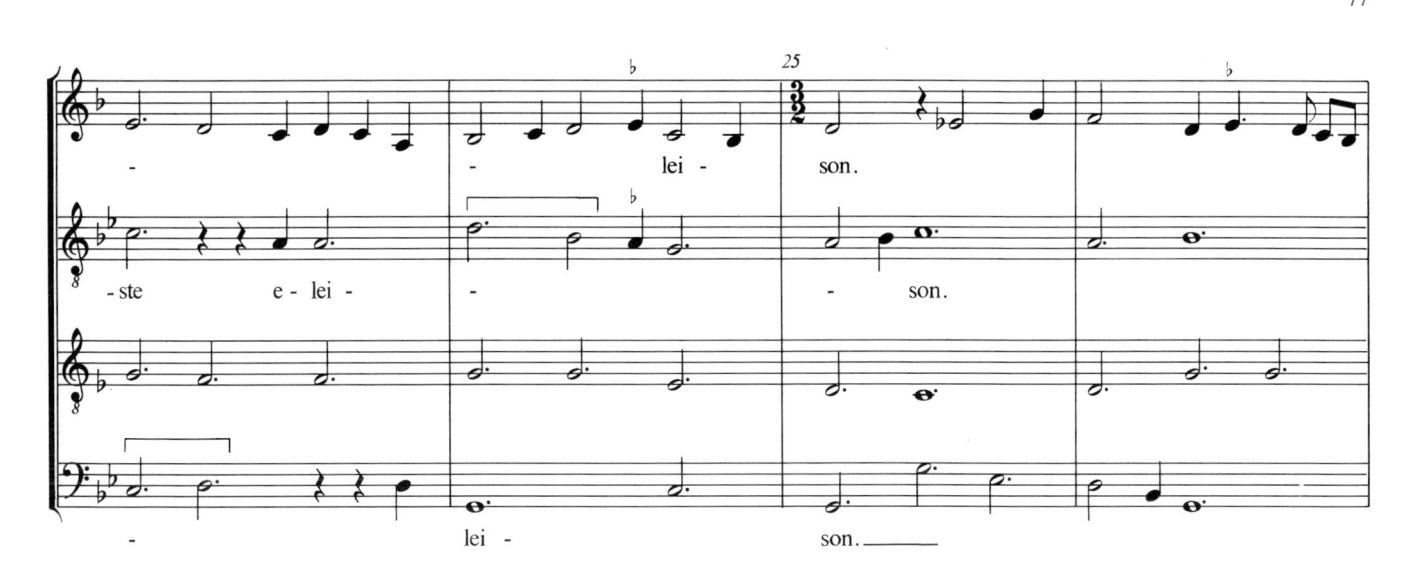

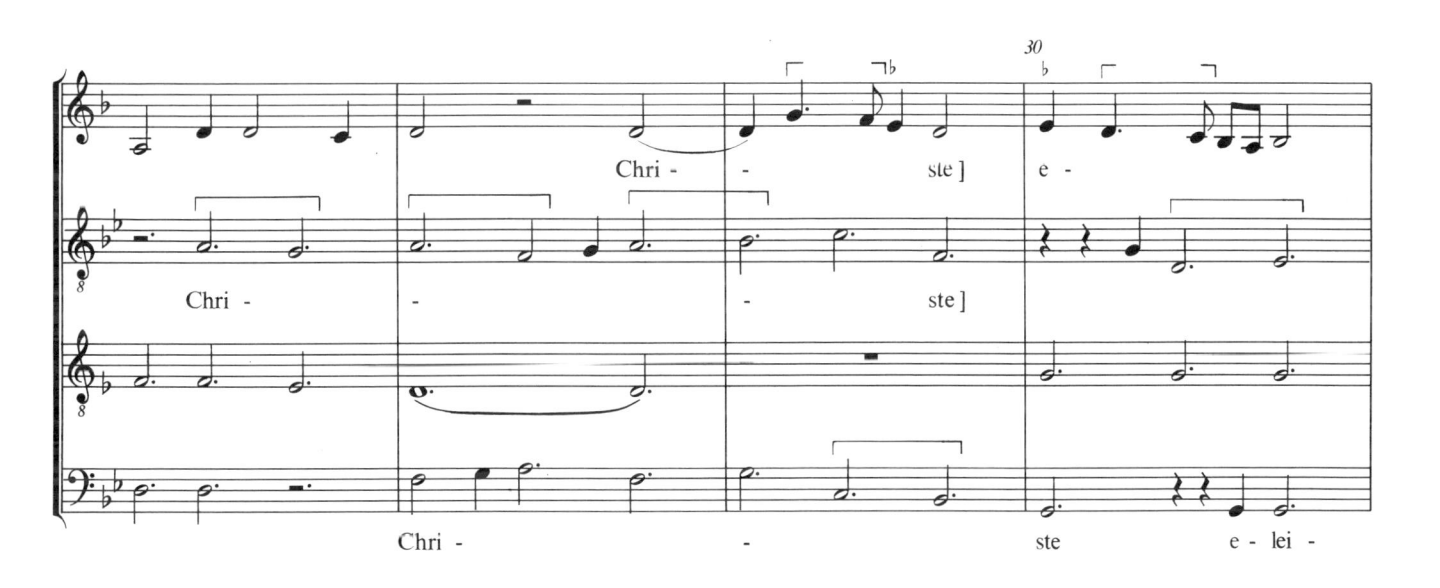

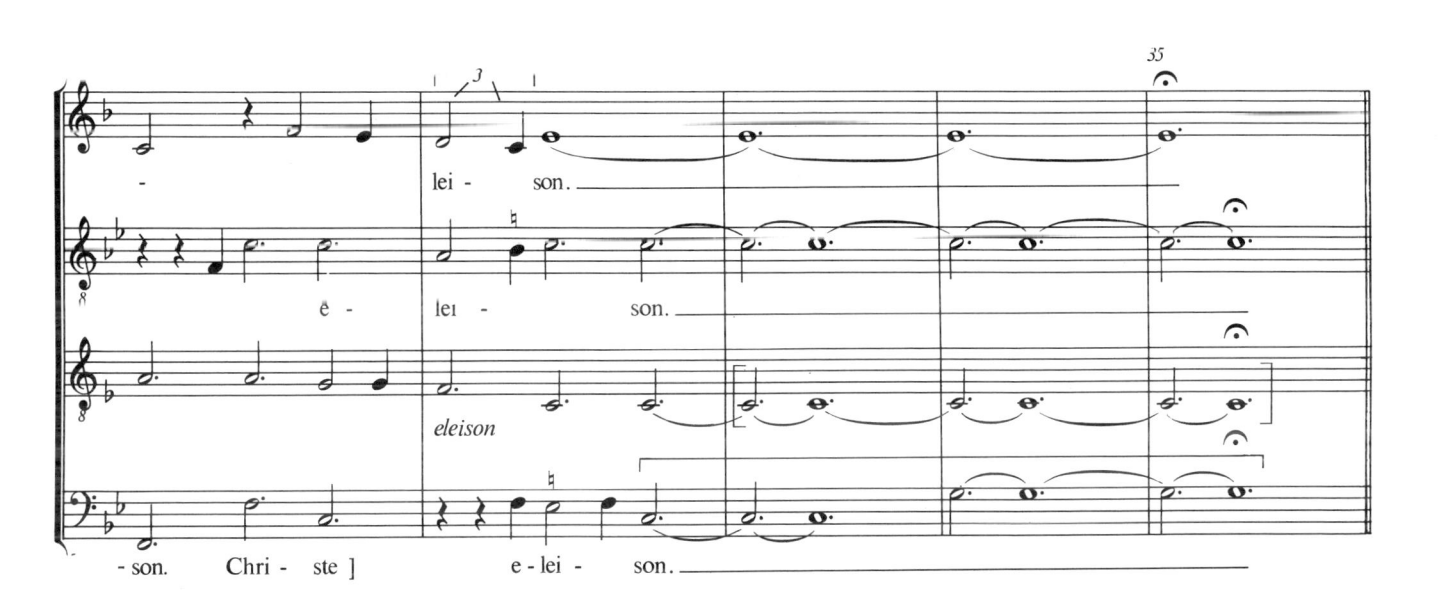

78

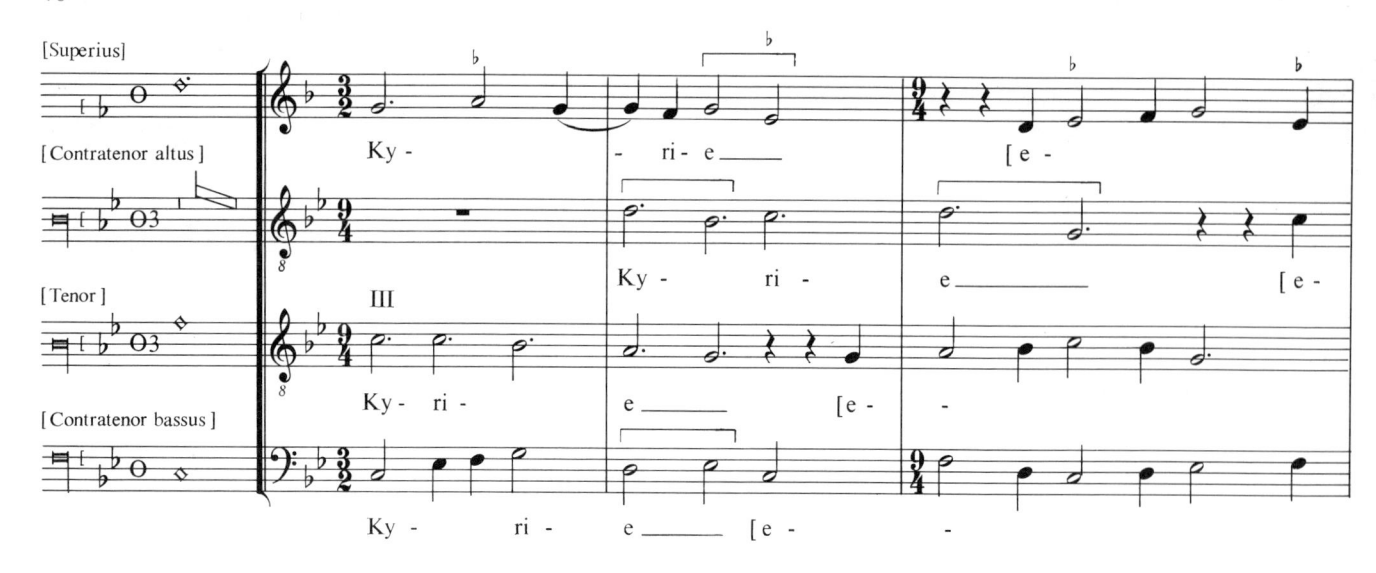

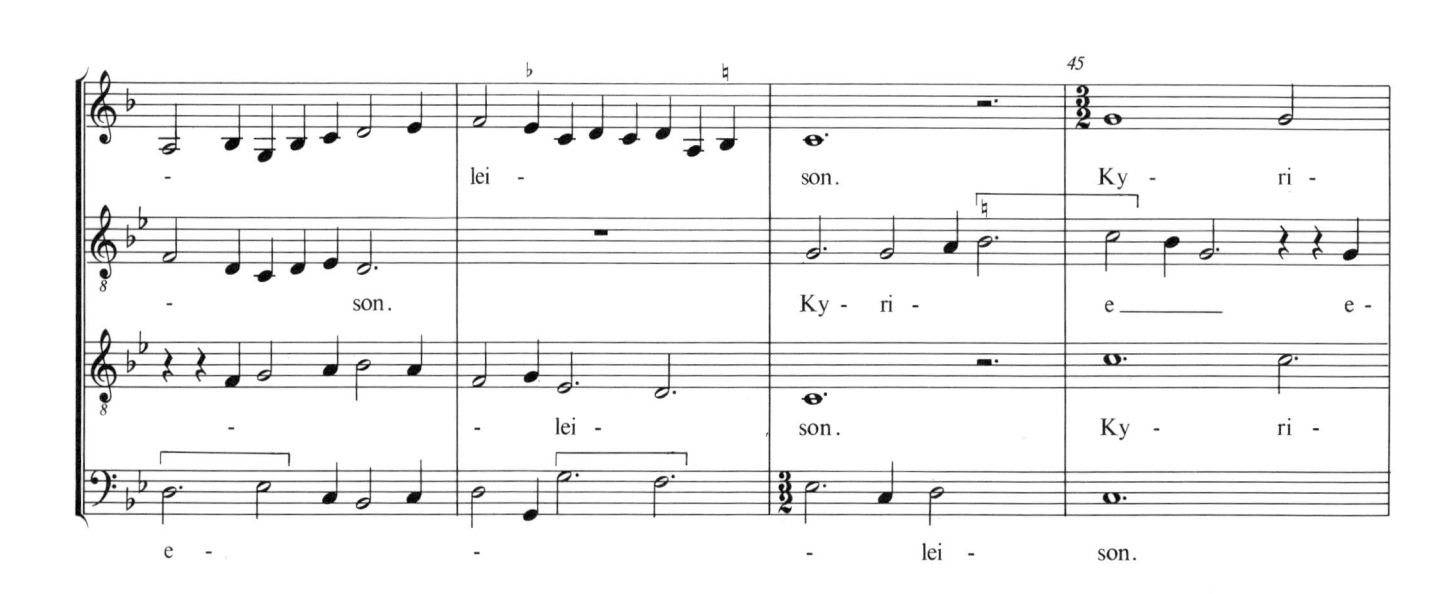

79

Gloria in excelsis Deo

15
A - do - - ra - mus te. Glo - ri - fi - ca -
-mus te. Glo - ri - fi - ca -
A - do - ra - mus te. Glo - ri - fi - ca -
- mus te.
- mus te.
- mus te.]
.S.
20
Gra - ti - as
Gra -
I
a - gi - mus ti - - bi pro - pter ma - gnam glo -
- ti-as [a - gimus ti - bi pro - pter ma - -

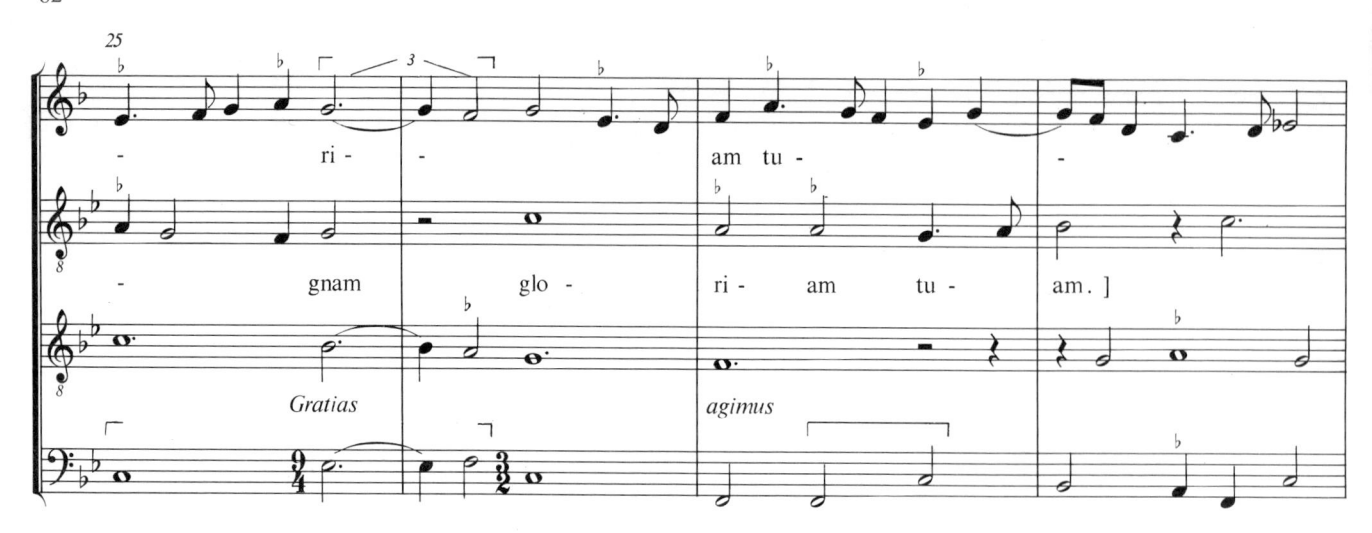

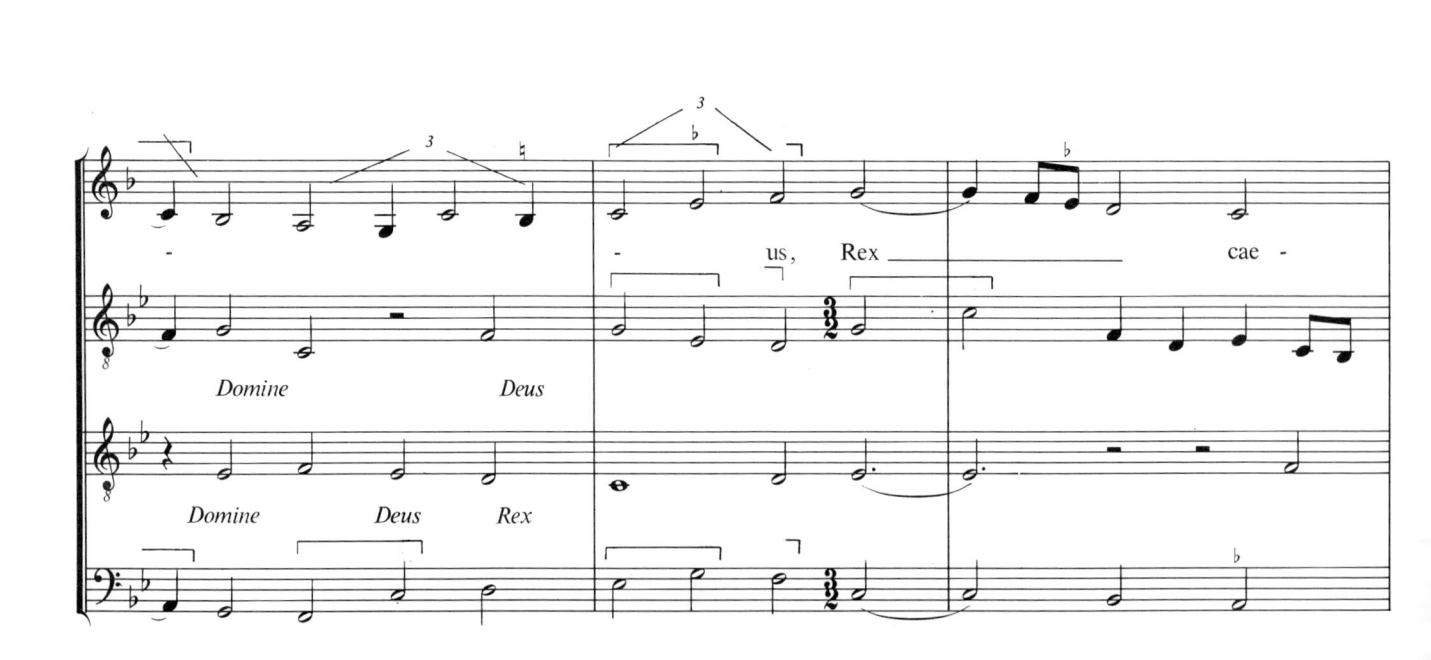

-ri - -i - am tu- -am.

gnam glo - ri - am tu- am.]

Gratias agimus

Do - mi - ne De-

-us, Rex cae -

Domine Deus

Domine Deus Rex

83

-le - - stis, De - us Pa - ter o - mni - po - - tens. Do - - mi - ne Fi - - li u - ni - ge - - ni - te Je - su

Do - - mi - ne [Fi - - li u - ni - ge - ni - te Je -

Do - mi - ne ———— Fi - - li u - ni - ge - - ni - te [Je -

50
Chri - ste. Do- mi- ne De- us, A -
- su Chri - ste. Do- mi- ne De - us, A- gnus
- su Chri - - - ste. A -
55
- gnus De - i, Fi - li-
De- - - i, Fi- li- us
- gnus De - - i Fi-
60
- us Pa- - - tris.
Pa- tris. Fi- - li- us Pa-
- li- us Pa- - -

Qui tol- lis pec- ca- - ta
- tris. Qui tol- lis pec- ca- - ta
- tris.
65
mun- di, mi- se- re- re no- -
mun- di, mi- - se- re- re
70
- bis. Qui tol- lis pec- ca-
no- bis. Qui tol- lis pec- ca- ta mun- -
Qui tol-

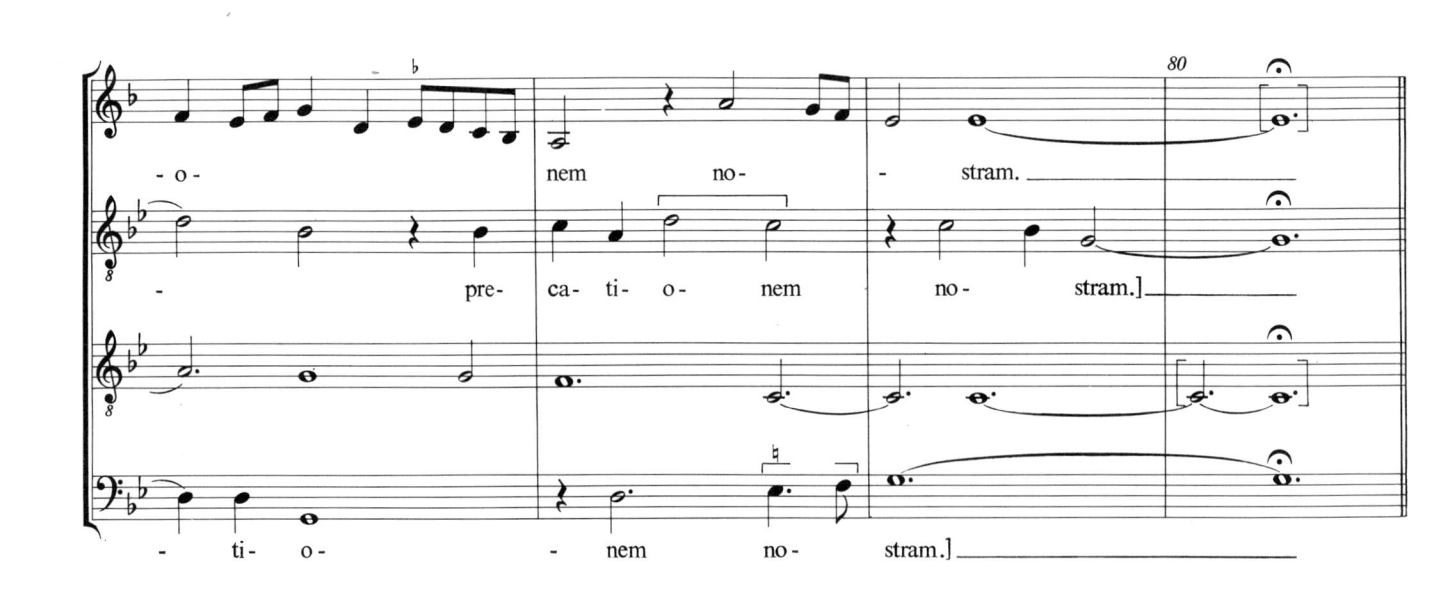

-ta mun-di, su-sci-pe de-pre-ca-ti-
-di, su-sci-pe de-
-lis pec-ca-ta mun-di su-sci-pe de-pre-ca-

-o-nem no-stram.
-pre-ca-ti-o-nem no-stram.]
-ti-o-nem no-stram.]

[Superius]

Qui se-des ad dex-

Contra[tenor altus]

Qui se-des ad dex-te-

Tenor

[Contratenor] bassus

90
-te- - - - - ram Pa- tris, mi- se-
- - - ram Pa- - tris,
95
100
-re- re no- - bis. Quo- - - ni- am tu
mi- se- re- - re no- - bis. Quo- - -
105
so- - lus san- ctus. Tu so- - lus Do-
-ni- am tu so- - lus san- - ctus.
110
- mi- nus. Tu so- lus Al- tis- - si- mus, Je- -
Tu so- - lus Do- mi- nus. Tu so- lus Al- tis- si- mus
115
120
.S.
- su Chri- ste. Cum San- - - -
.S.
Je- su Chri- ste.
III
Cum sancto
Tu solus Altissimus [Cum San- - -

125
cto Spi-
spiritu
cto
130
135
-ri- tu, in glo-
.S.
Spi- ri- tu in glo-
140
ri- a
ri- a De-

89

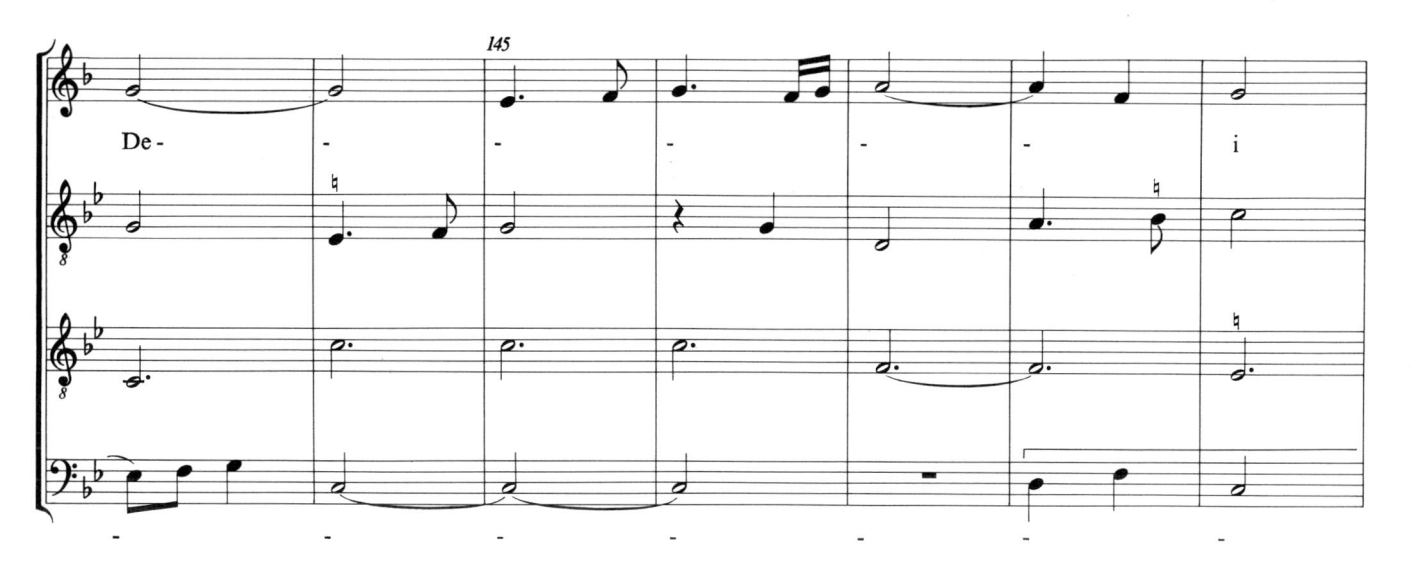

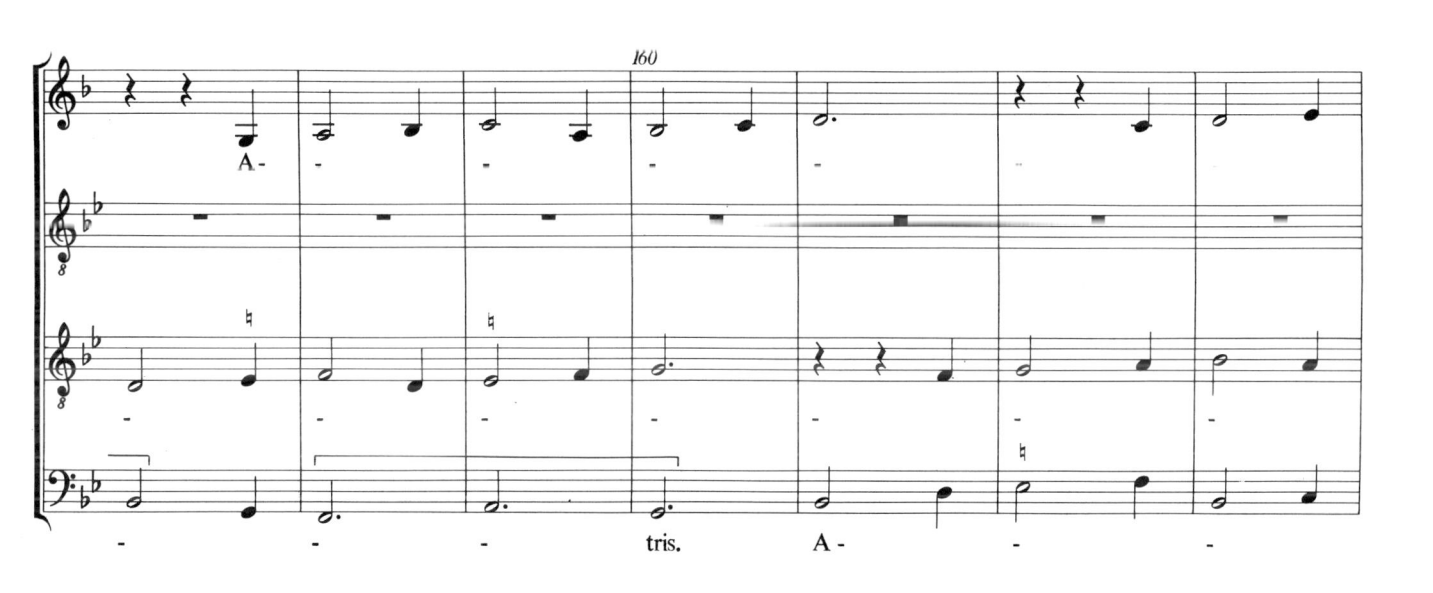

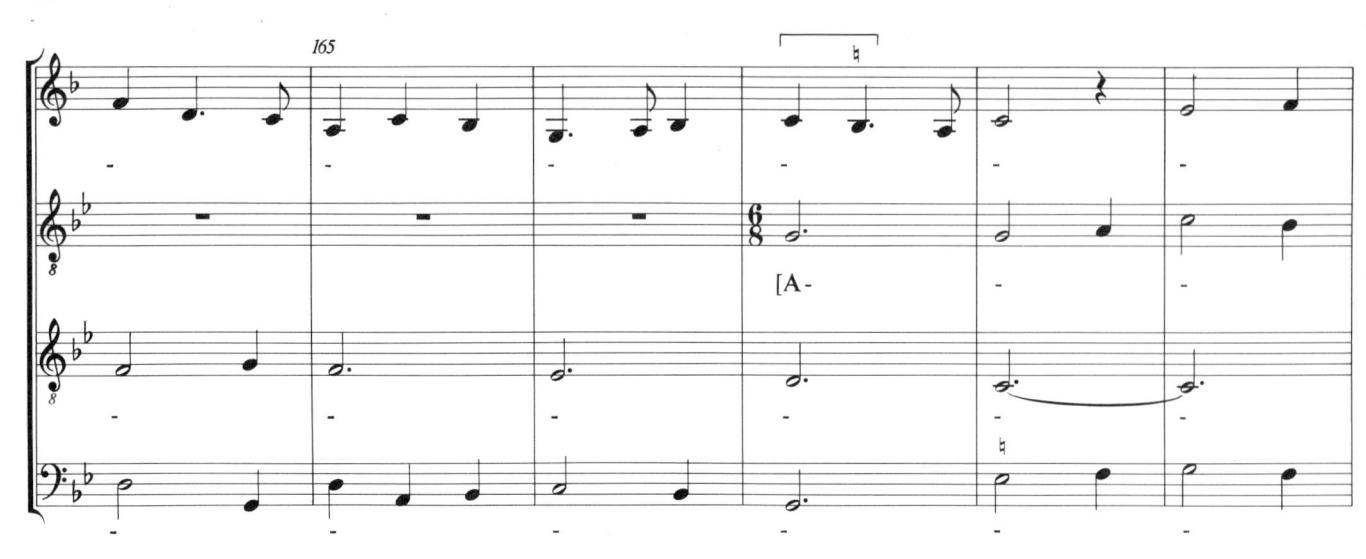

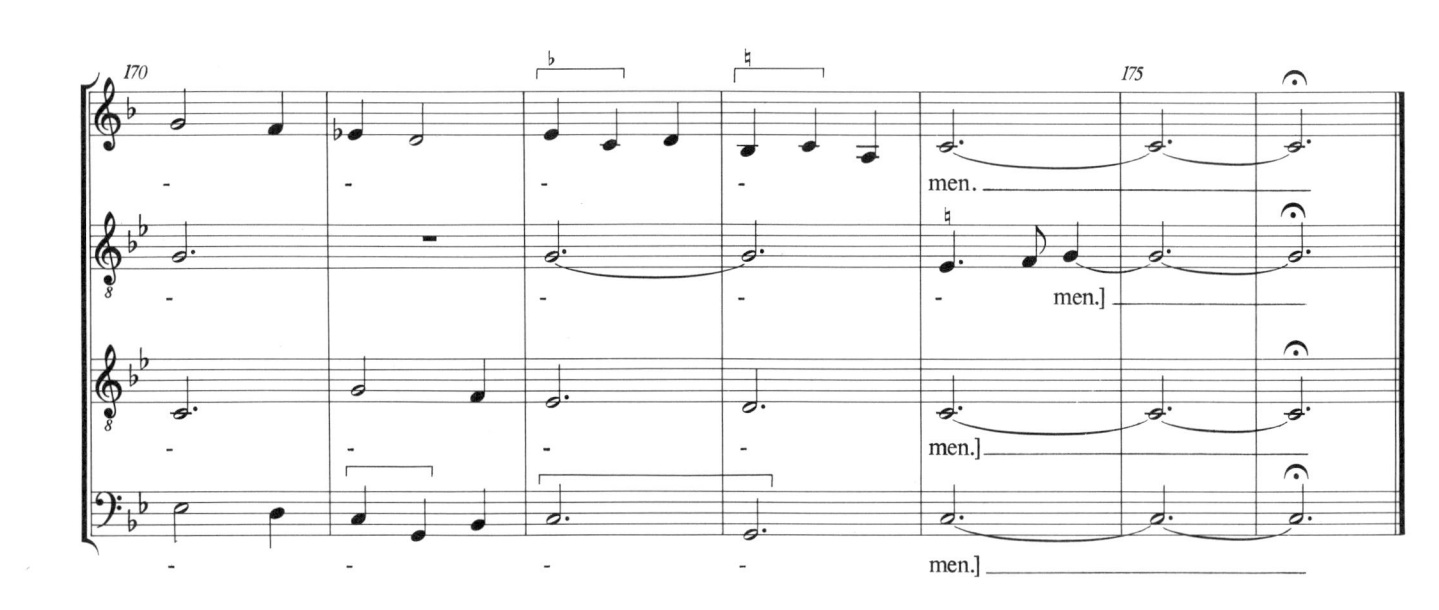

Credo in unum Deum

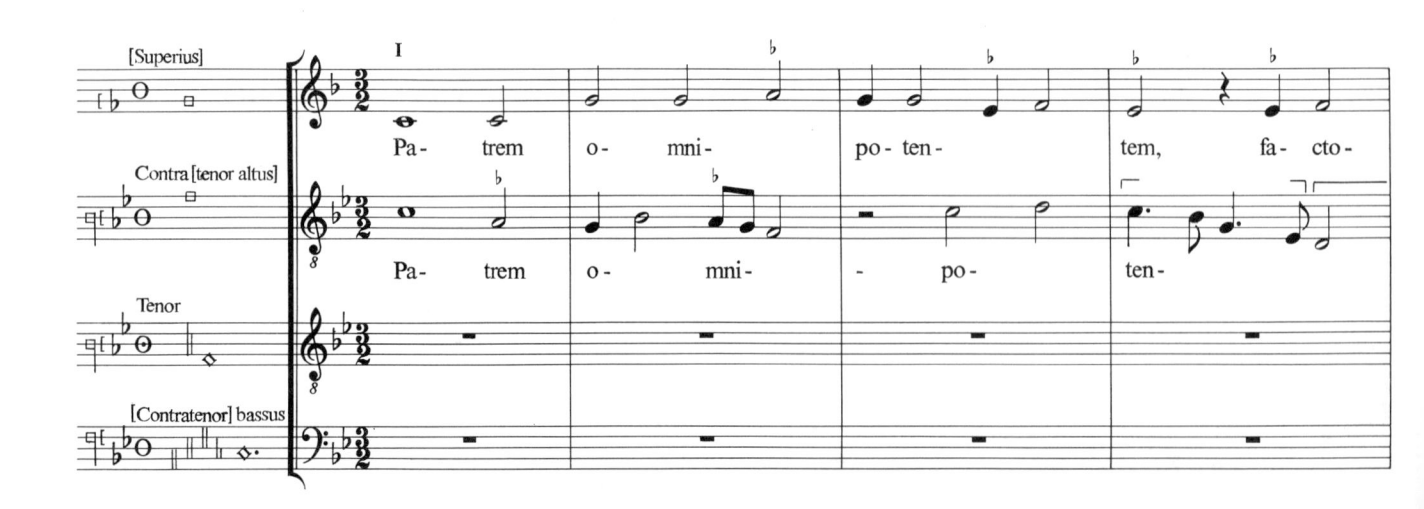

-rem cae- - - - li et
-tem, fa- cto- rem cae- li et ter-
ter- rae, vi- si- bi- li- um o- mni- um et
-rae, vi- si- bi- - - li- um o- mni- um
in- vi- si- bi- - li- um.
et in- vi- si- bi- - li- um. Et in u-
I
Et in
Et in u- num Do- mi- num Je- sum Chri- stum, Fi- li- um De- i u-
-num Do- mi- num [Je- sum Chri- stum,] Fi- li- um De- i u- ni- ge- ni-
Et
unum

25
- ni- ge- - ni- tum. Et ex Pa- tre na- tum an-
- tum. [Et ex Pa- tre na- tum an- te o- mni- a
in unum Dominum ENTRE-
- te o- - mni- a sae- - cu-
sae- cu- la.] De- um de De- o,
PRIS SUIS
30
- la. De- um de De- o, lu- -
lu- - - men

35
-men de lu- - - - mi-
[de lu- mi- - - ne,
40
- ne, De- um ve- rum de De- o ve- ro.
De- um ve- rum] de De- o ve- ro.
Ge- ni- tum, non fa- -
[Ge- ni- tum, non

45
- ctum, con- sub- stan- ti- a- lem
fa- - ctum,] con- - sub- stan- ti-
consubstantialem
50
Pa- tri: per quem o- - mni- a
- a- lem Pa- - tri: per quem o- mni- a
55
Qui pro- pter nos ho- mi- nes, et pro-
fa- cta sunt. [Qui pro- pter] nos ho- mi- nes, [et pro-
II
con

-pter no- stram sa- lu- - tem
-pter no- stram sa- lu- - - tem
substantialem
60
de- scen- dit de cae- lis. Et in- car- na- - tus est
de- scen- - dit de cae- lis.] Et in- car- na- tus
65
de Spi- ri- tu San- - cto ex Ma- ri-
est [de Spi- ri- tu San- - cto ex Ma-

70
-a Vir- gi- ne: et ho- mo fa- ctus est.
-ri- a Vir- gi- ne:] et ho- mo fa- ctus est.
75
Cru- ci- fi- xus e- ti- am pro no- bis:
Cru- ci- fi- xus [e- ti- am pro no- bis:
80
sub Pon- ti- o Pi- la- to
sub Pon- ti- o Pi- la- to]

85
pas- sus,] et se- pul- - tus est.
pas- sus, et se- pul- tus est.
[Superius]
Contra [tenor altus]
Tenor
[Contratenor] bassus
I
Et in Spi- ri- tum San- ctum, Do- -
Et in Spiritum Sanctum
Et in Spiritum
Et
90
- mi- num, et vi- vi- fi- can- tem: qui ex Pa- tre Fi- li- o- que pro- ce-
ENTREPRIS SUIS
in Spiritum Sanctum

-dit. Qui cum Pa- tre et _____ Fi- li- o si- mul a- do-ra- tur, et con- glo- ri- fi- ca- tur: qui lo- cu- tus est per Pro-

105
-phe- tas. Et u- nam, San- - ctam ca - tho-
110
-li- cam et a- po- sto- li-
Et
-cam Ec- cle- si- am. Con- fi- te- or u- num bap- tis-
unam Sanctam
Confiteor
unum
Confiteor
Confiteor

115
-ma in re- mis- si- o- nem pec- ca- to- rum.
III
Et ex- spe- cto re- sur- -
120
- re- cti- o- nem mor- tu- - o- rum. Et
125

vi- tam ven- tu- ri sae- cu- li. A-

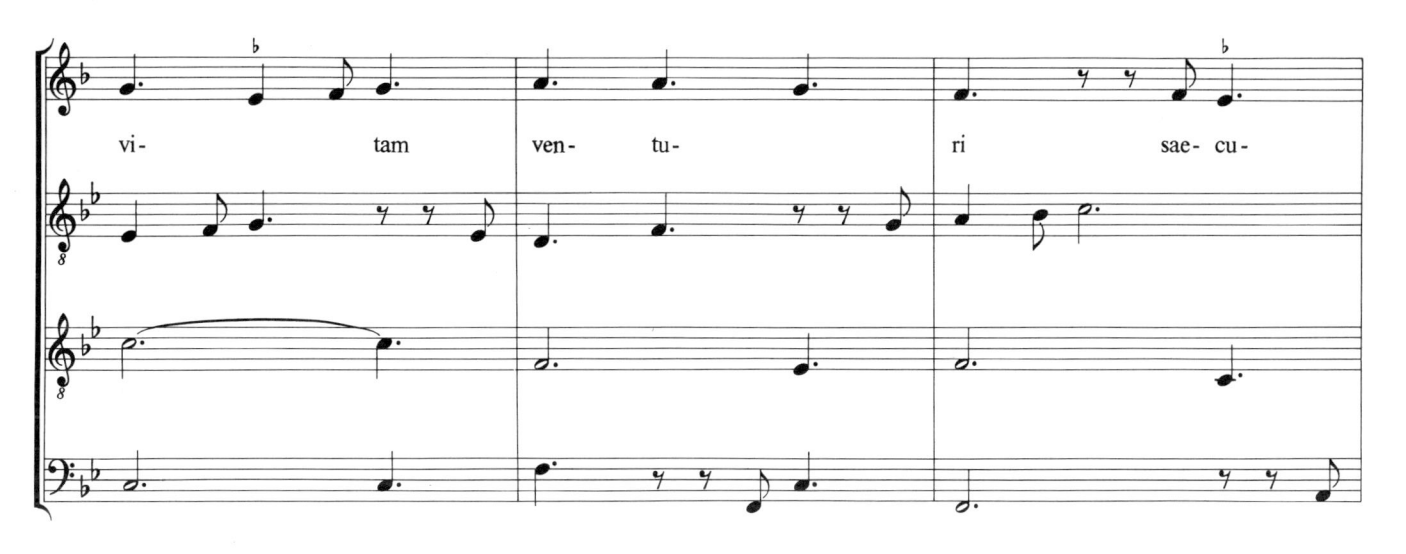

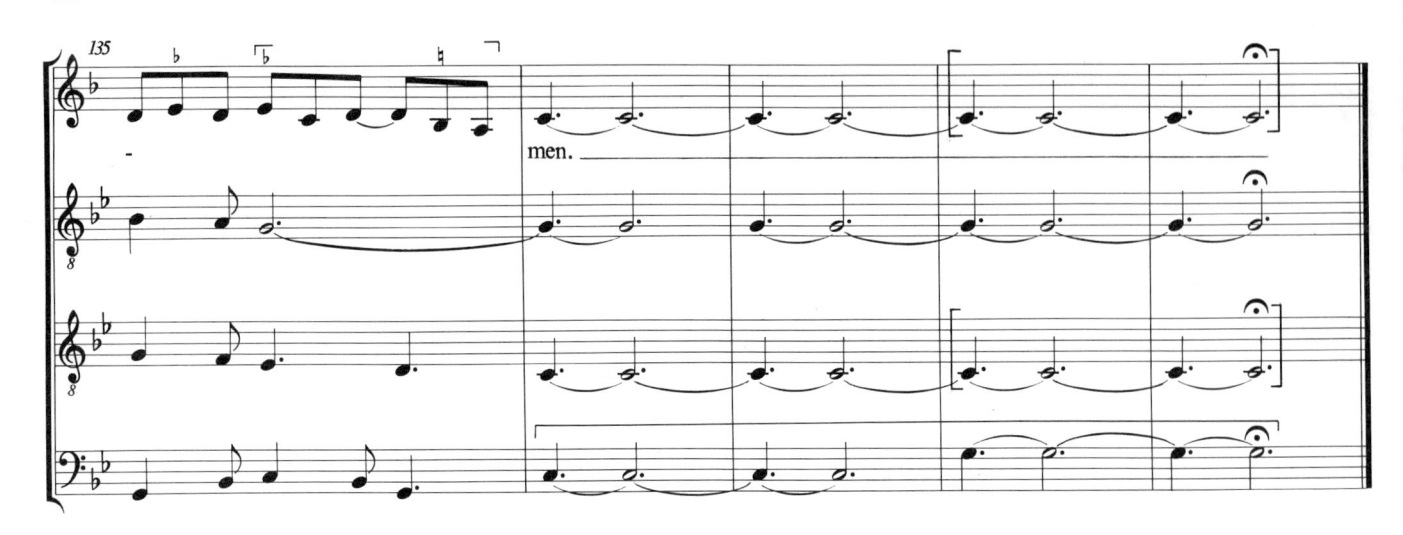

Sanctus

103

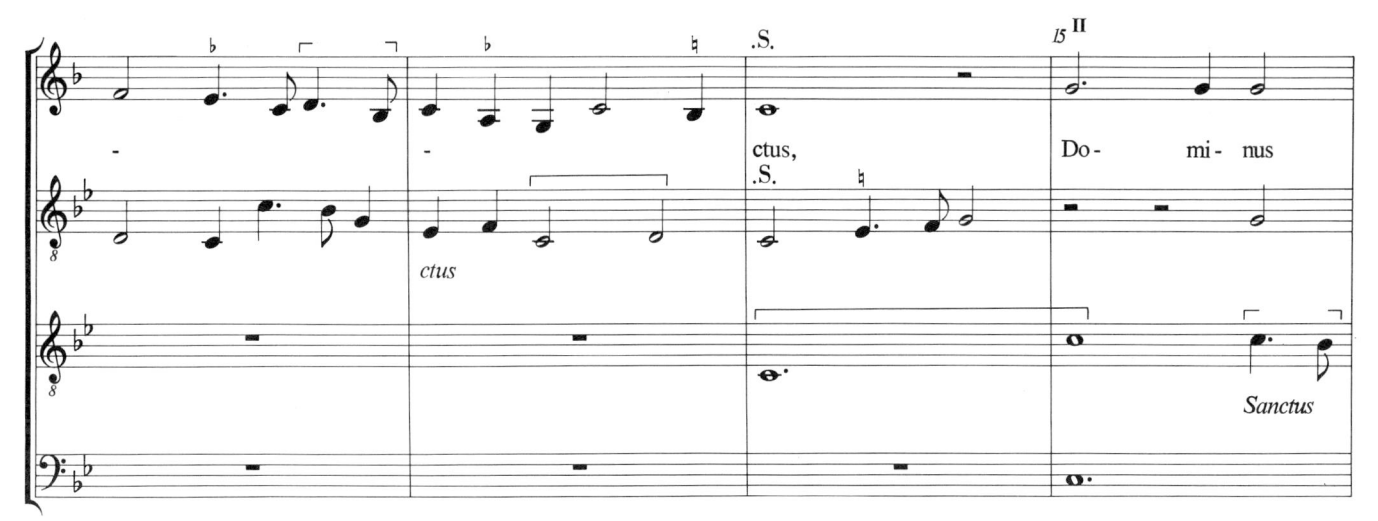

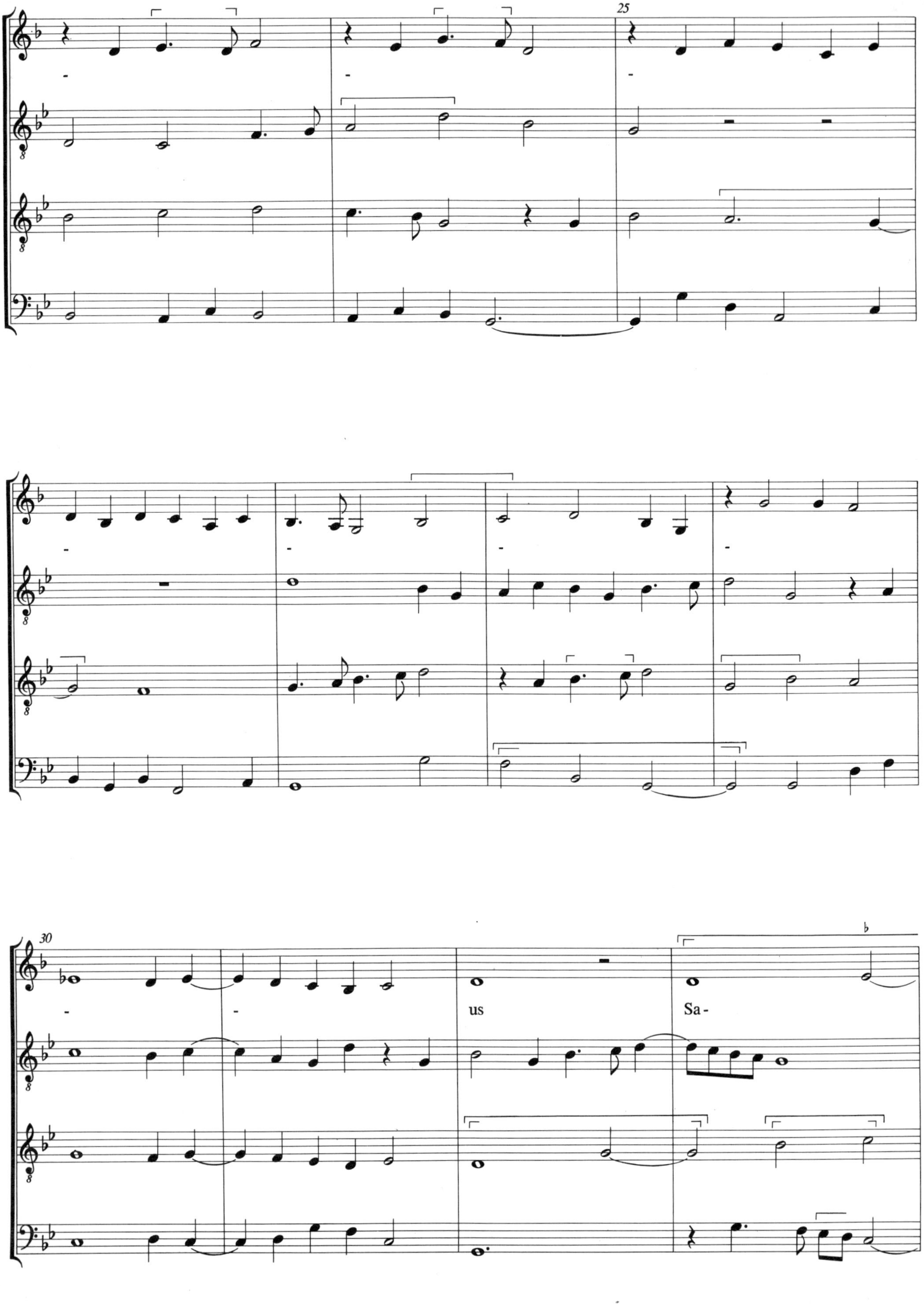
25
30
us
Sa-

105

55
glo - - - -
glo - - - -
60
- ri- - a tu- -
- ri- - a tu- -
65
- - - - a.
- - - - a.
[Superius]
Contra[tenor altus]
Tenor
[Contratenor] bassus
70
Ho- - - - - san- -
Ho- - san- - - -
Ho- - san- - - -
Ho- - - san-

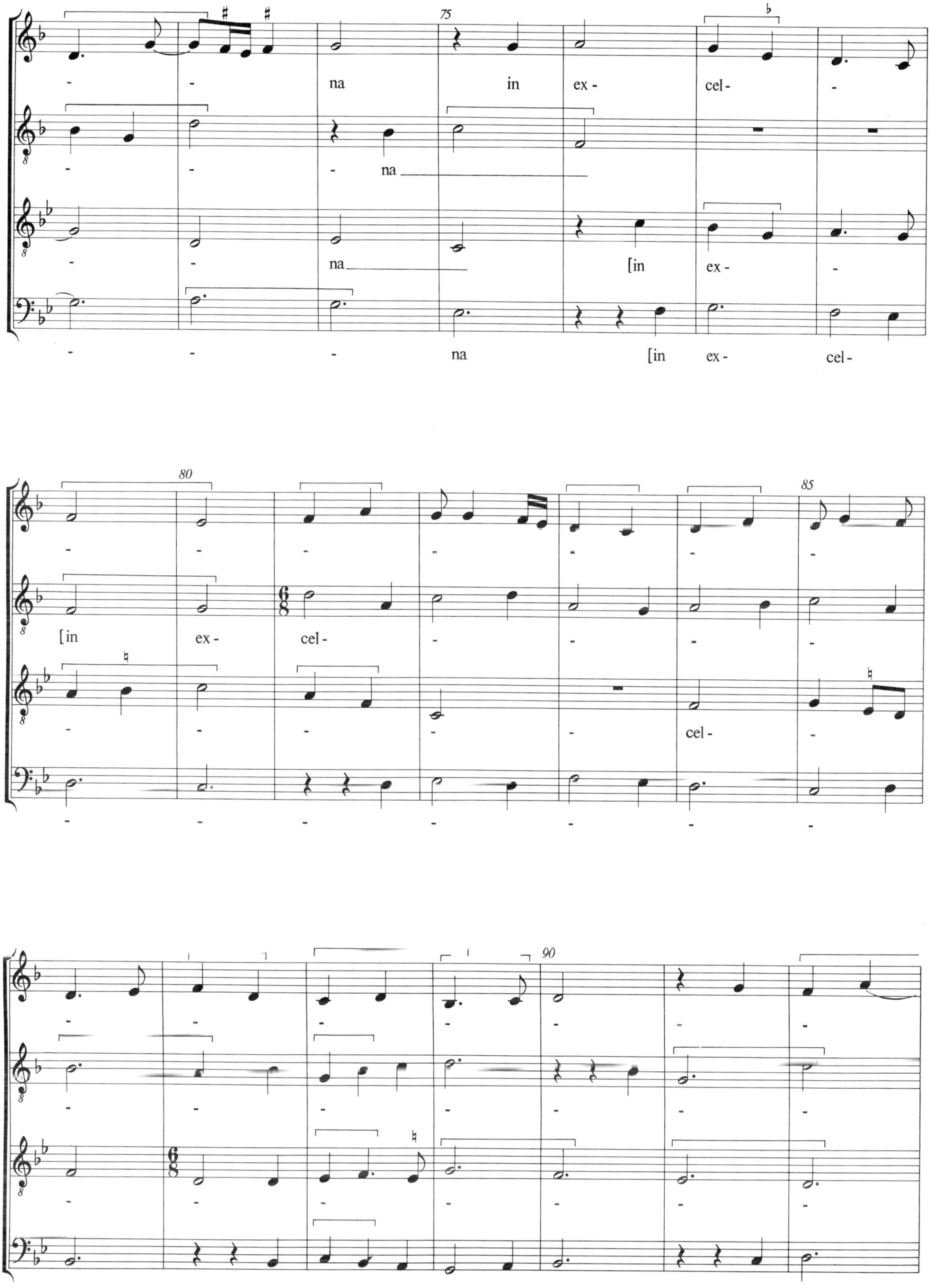
75
na
in
ex -
cel -
na
na
[in
ex -
na
[in
ex -
cel -
80
85
[in
ex -
cel -
cel -
90

sis.
sis.]
Benedictus tacet
sis.]
Benedictus tacet
sis.]
[Superius] duo
[Contratenor altus] duo
Be- ne-
di-
Be- ne-

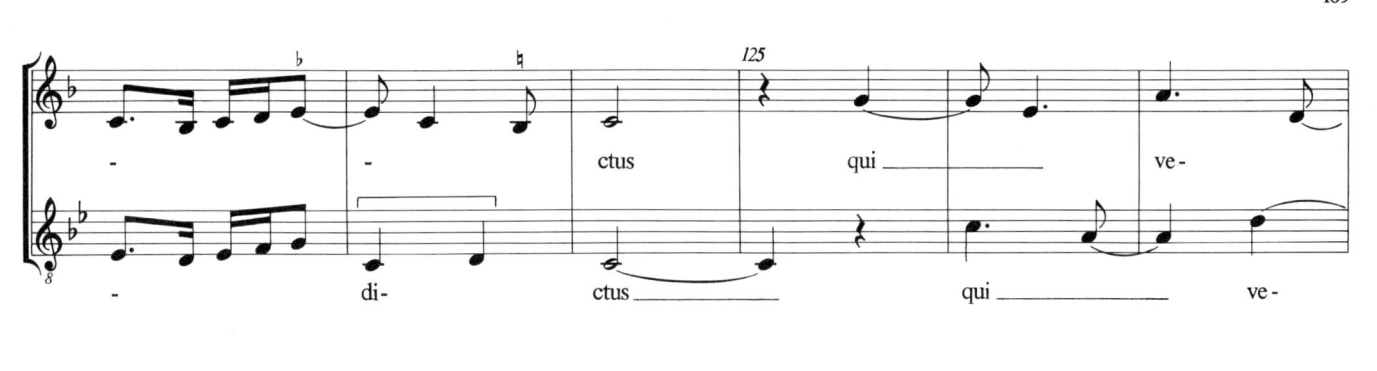

[Hosanna ut supra]
mm. 66-100

Agnus Dei

*The second line is sung in the Da Capo repeat.

112

113

[4] Mass: O gloriosa regina mundi

Kyrie

20
- - - lei- son.
Christe tacet
- son. Ky- ri- e] e- lei- son.
- lei- son.
- lei- - - son.
[Superius]
Tenor
Contra[tenor bassus]
25
30
Chri- - ste [e- - -
Chri- - ste [e-
Chri- ste [e- - -
- - - - lei-
- lei- - - -
- - - -
35
40
- son. Chri- ste e- - - -
son. Chri- ste e- - -
- lei- - son. Chri- -

45
- lei- - son. Chri- - ste] e-
- lei- son. Chri- - ste] e-
- ste e- - - - lei-
50
- - - - - lei- - -
- - - - - lei- -
- son. Chri- - ste] e- -
55
60
- - son.
- - - son.
- lei- - son.
[Superius]
[Contratenor altus]
Tenor
[Contratenor bassus]
65
Ky- ri- e
Ky- ri- e

70
Ky- ri- e
[e- -
Ky- ri- e
[e-
[e- lei- -
75
[e- - lei- - son. Ky-
- - - lei- - -
- lei- - - son. Ky- ri- e
- - - son. Ky- ri-
80
-ri- e e- - - -
- son. Ky- ri- e e-
e- - - - -
-e e- - - -

118

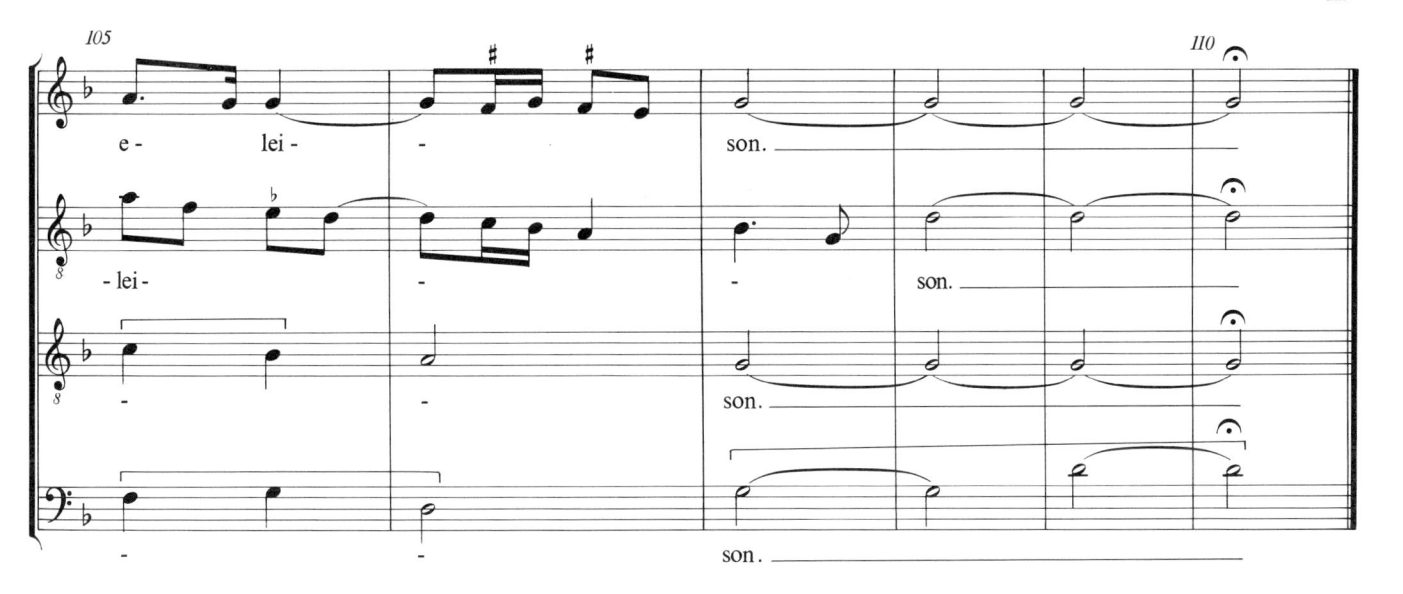

Gloria in excelsis Deo

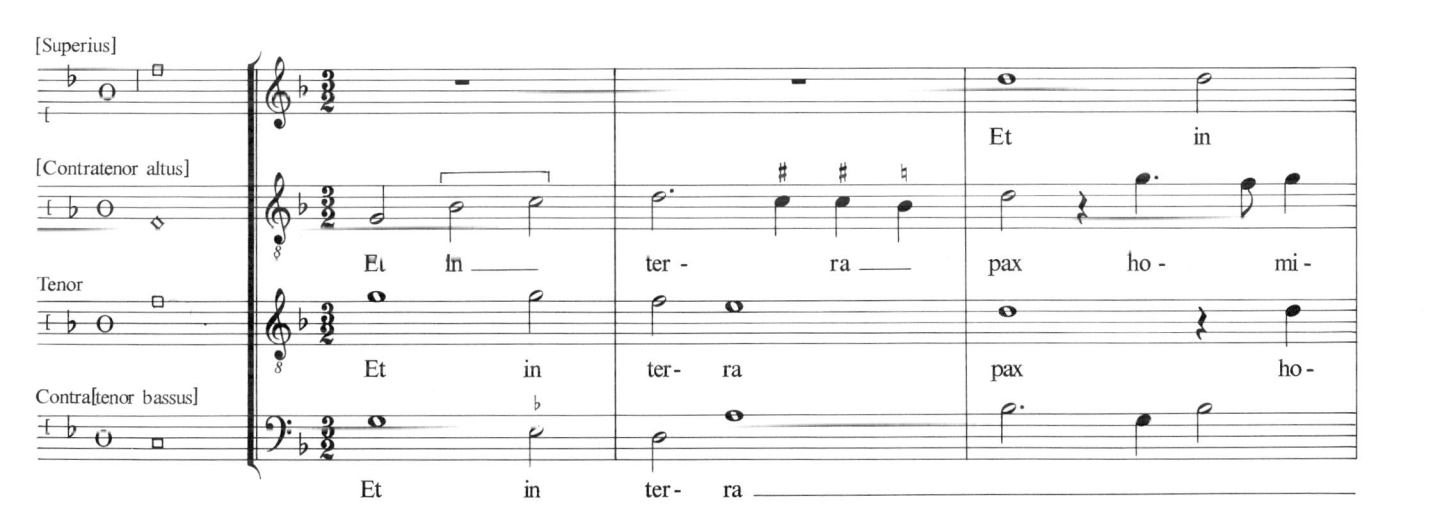

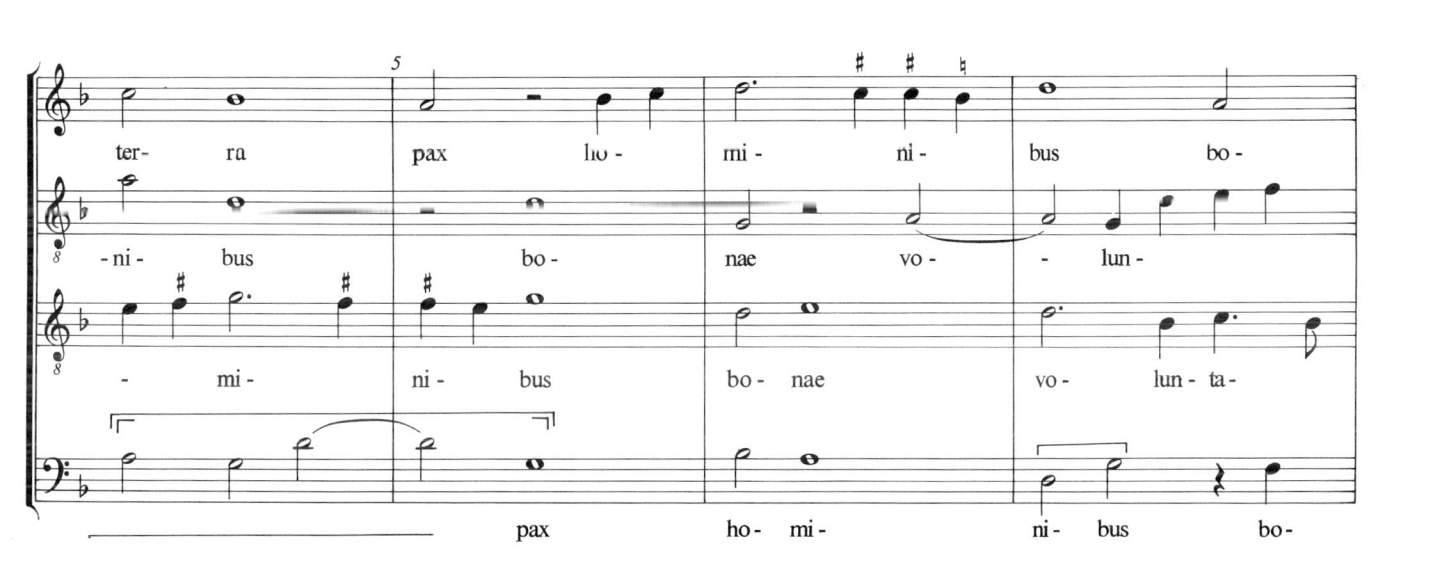

10
-nae vo- - lun- ta- tis. Lau-da- - mus te.
-ta- tis. Lau- da- mus te.
- - tis. Lau- da- mus
-nae [vo- lun- ta- tis.] Lau- da-mus te. [Lau-da-
Be- ne- di- - ci-mus te.
A- do-ra-
te. A- do- ra- mus te.
te. Be- ne- di- - ci- mus te. A- do-
- mus te.] Be- ne- - di- ci- mus te. A-
15
- - mus te.
Glo- ri- fi- ca- mus
- ra- - mus te.
- do- - ra- mus te. Glo- ri- fi- ca- mus

20
Glo- ri- fi- ca- - mus te. Gra-
te. [Glo- ri- fi- ca- mus te.] Gra-
Glo- ri- fi- ca- mus te. Gra-
te. Gra- ti- as
- ti- - as a- gi- mus ti-
- ti- as a- - gi- mus ti- bi
- ti- as a- gi- mus ti-
a- gi- mus ti- bi
25
- bi pro- - pter ma- gnam
[pro- pter ma- - gnam] glo- -
- bi pro- - pter
pro- pter ma- gnam

glo - - ri - am tu -
- - ri- am tu- - am. ___
ma - gnam glo - - ri- am ___ tu -
glo - ri- am ___ tu- am.
30
- am.
Do- mi- ne ___ De- us, ___ Rex ___
- am. Do- mi- ne ___ De-
Do- mi- ne ___ De- us, Rex cae- le-
35
o- mni-
___ cae- le- - stis, De- - us
- us, Rex cae - - le- - stis, De-
- stis, De- us

- - po- tens. Do-
Pa- ter o- mni- po-
- us Pa- ter o- mni- po- tens.
Pa- ter o- mni- po- tens.
40
-mi- ne Fi- li u- ni- ge- ni- te
- tens. Do- mi- ne Fi- li u- ni- ge- ni- te
[o- - mni- po-
Je- - su Chri- -
Je- - su Chri- - ste.
Je- su Chri- - ste.
- tens.]

45
-ste. Do - mi - ne De - -
— Do - - mi- ne De- -
Do - mi- ne De - -
[Do - mi - ne De - -
50
- - -
- - - us,
- - -
- - -
- us, A - gnus De - i,
- us, A - gnus De - i, Fi - li -
- us, A - gnus De - i, Fi - li -

55
Fi- li- - us Pa - -
A - gnus De - i, Fi- li- us Pa -
- us Pa - - -
-us Pa - - -
60
- - tris.
- - tris.
- - tris.
- - tris.]
[Superius]
[Contratenor altus]
Tenor
Contra[tenor bassus]
65
Qui tol - lis pec - ca - ta mun - - di,
Qui tol - lis pec - ca - - ta mun -

126

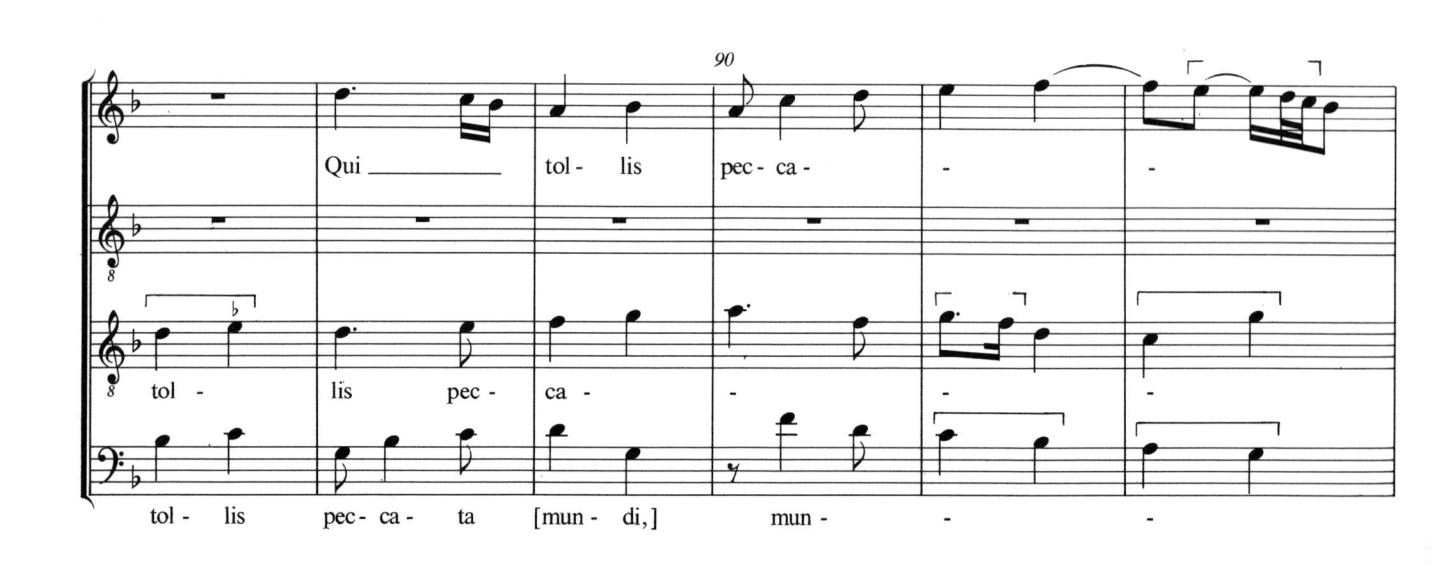

127

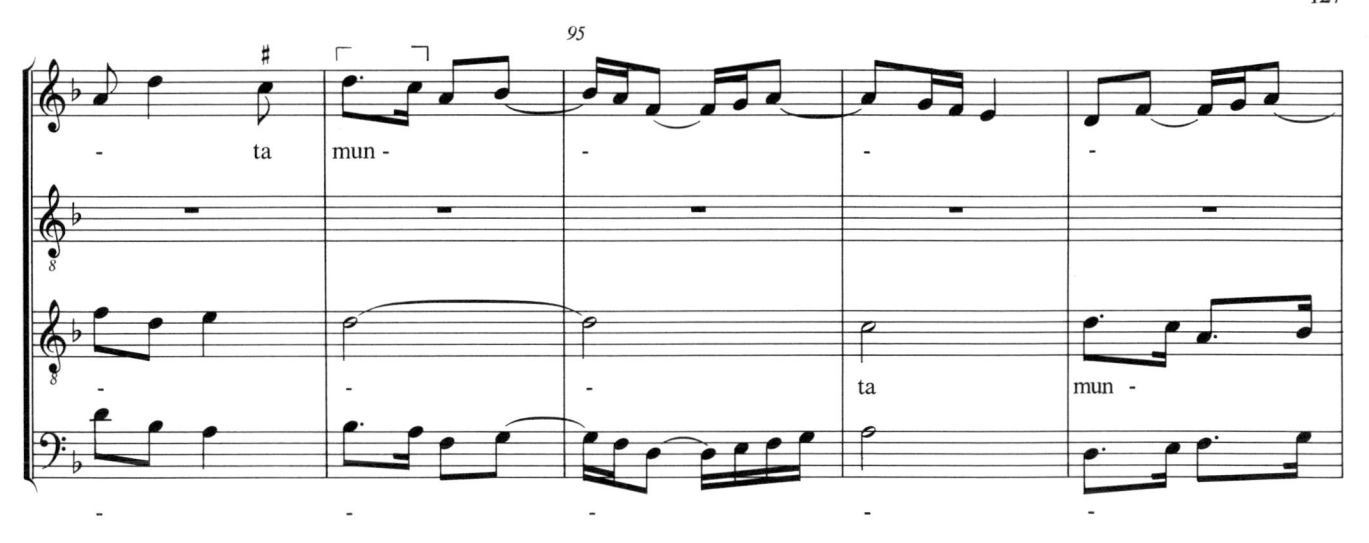

110
115
-o- - nem no- stram.
-nem no- - stram.
-o- nem no- - stram.
-nem no- - stram.
[Superius]
[Contratenor altus]
[Tenor]
[Contratenor bassus]
120
Qui se- des ad dex- te- ram Pa- tris,
Qui se- des ad dex-
Qui se- des ad dex- te- ram
Qui se- des ad dex- te-
125
mi- se- re- - re no- bis.
- te- - ram Pa- tris, mi- se- re- re
Pa- tris, mi- se- re- re no- bis.
ram [Pa- tris, mi- se- re- re no-

130
135
Quo - ni - am tu so - - lus san - - ctus. Tu
no - bis. Quo - ni - am tu so - lus san -
Quo - ni - am tu so - - - lus san - ctus.
- bis. Quo - ni - am tu so - lus
140
so - - - - lus Do - -
- ctus.
Tu so - - lus Do - - -
san - - - ctus.
145
- - mi - nus. Tu so - - -
[Do - - - - mi -
- mi - nus. Tu so - -
Do - - mi-nus. Tu so -

150
-lus Al - tis - -
- nus. Tu so - lus Al - tis -
- - lus Al - tis -
-lus Al - tis - -
155
- - si - mus Je - - su Chri -
- si - mus, Je - - - su
- si - mus, Je - - su
- - si - mus, Je - - su
160
- - - ste. Cum San -
Chri - - ste. Je - su Chri - - -
Chri - - - ste. Cum San -
Chri - - ste. Cum

165
170
- cto Spi - - - ri -
ste. Cum San - cto Spi - - ri -
- cto Spi - ri - - tu
San - - cto Spi - - ri -
175
- tu, in glo - ri - a De - - i Pa -
- tu, in glo - ri - a De - i Pa
in glo - ri - a De - - i
- - - tu, in glo - ri - a De - i
180
- tris. A - - - - -
- - - tris. A -
Pa - - tris. A - - - -
Pa - - tris. A - - -

Credo in unum Deum

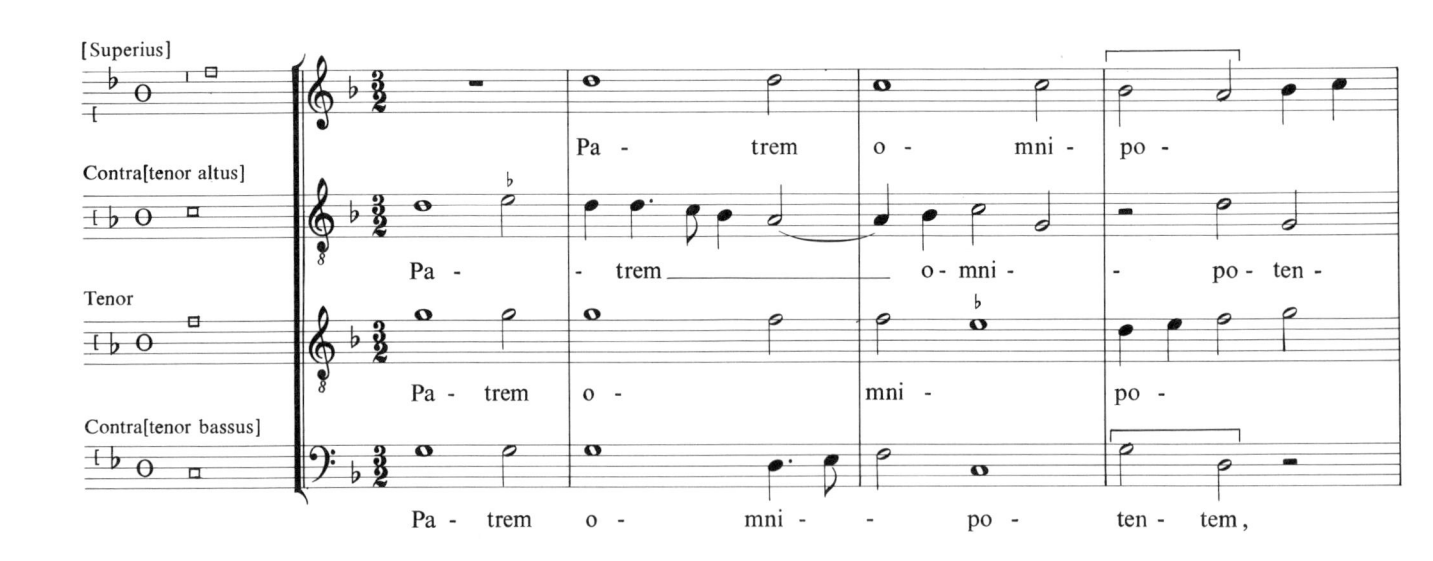

10
-li et ter-rae, vi-si-bi-li-um o-mni-
-li et ter-rae, [vi-si-bi-li-um o-mni-um et in-vi-si-bi-li-
-rae, vi-si-bi-li-um [o-mni-um]
ter-rae, vi-si-bi-li-um o-mni-um et
15
-um ct in-vi si bi li-um. Et in u-num
-um.
et in-vi-si-bi-li-um. Et in u-
in-[vi-si-bi-li-um.
20
Do-mi-num Je-sum Chri-stum, Fi-li-um De-i u-
-num Do-mi-num Je-sum Chri-stum, Fi-li-um De-i
Et in u-num Do-mi-num Je-sum Chri-stum, Fi-li-um

-ni - ge - - - ni - tum.
Et ex
u - ni - ge - - - ni - tum. Et
De - i u - ni - ge - - - ni - tum.
25
Pa - tre na - tum an - te o - - mni - a
ex Pa - tre na - tum an - te o - - mni -
De - um de De - o, lu - men de lu - mi -
30
De - um ve - - rum de De - o ve -
sae - cu - -
- a sae - -
- ne,

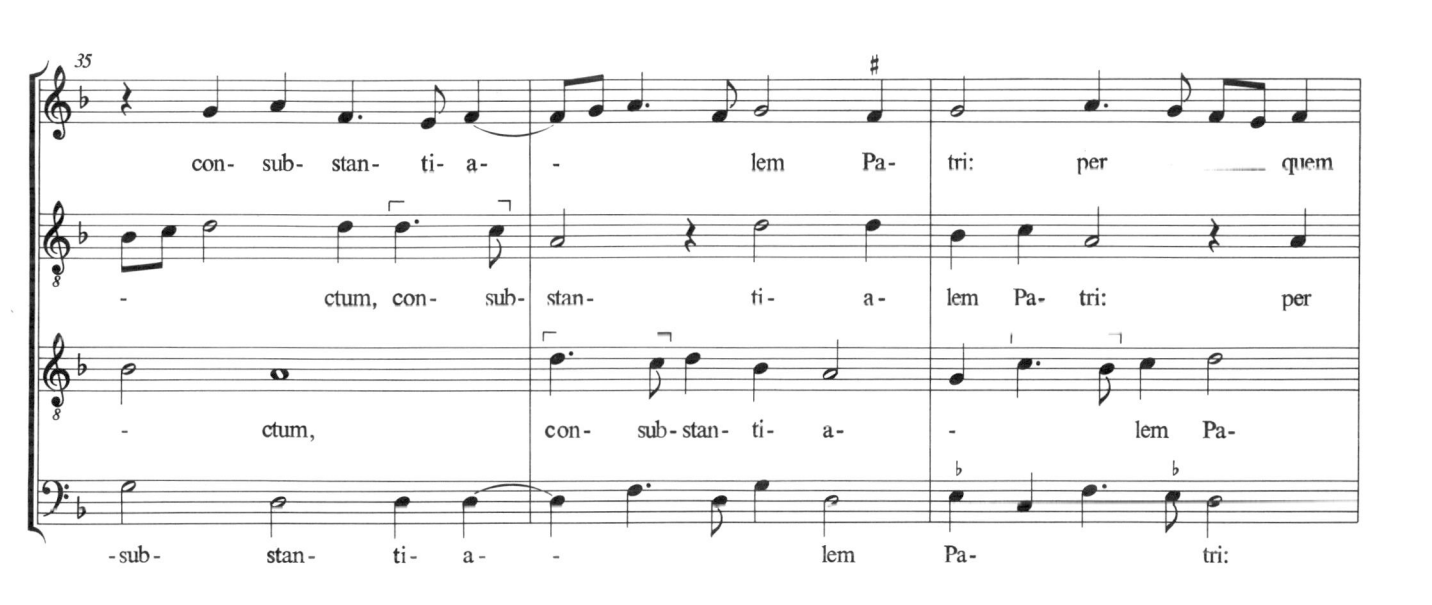

-ro. Ge- ni- tum, non fa- ctum,
-la. Ge- ni- tum, non fa-
-cu- la. [Ge- ni- tum, non fa-
Ge- ni- tum, non fa- ctum, con-

con- sub- stan- ti- a- lem Pa- tri: per quem
-ctum, con- sub- stan- ti- a- lem Pa- tri: per
-ctum, con- sub- stan- ti- a- lem Pa-
-sub- stan- ti- a- lem Pa- tri:

o- mni- a fa- cta
quem o- mni- a fa- cta
-tri:]
per quem o- mni- a fa- cta

sunt. Qui pro- - pter nos ho- mi-
sunt. Qui pro- pter nos ho- mi- nes et
Qui pro- - pter nos ho- mi- nes et pro- pter no-
sunt. Qui pro-pter nos ho- mi- nes,
45
-nes, et pro- pter no- stram sa- lu- tem de- scen- dit de cae-
pro- pter no- stram sa- lu- tem de- scen- dit
-stram [et pro- pter no- stram] sa- lu- tem de- scen- -
et pro- pter no- stram sa- lu- tem de- scen- dit de cae-
50
- - lis. Et in- car-
de- scen- dit de cae- lis. Et
- dit de cae- lis. Et in- car- na- tus est
- lis. Et in- car- na- tus est, Et in- car- na-

137

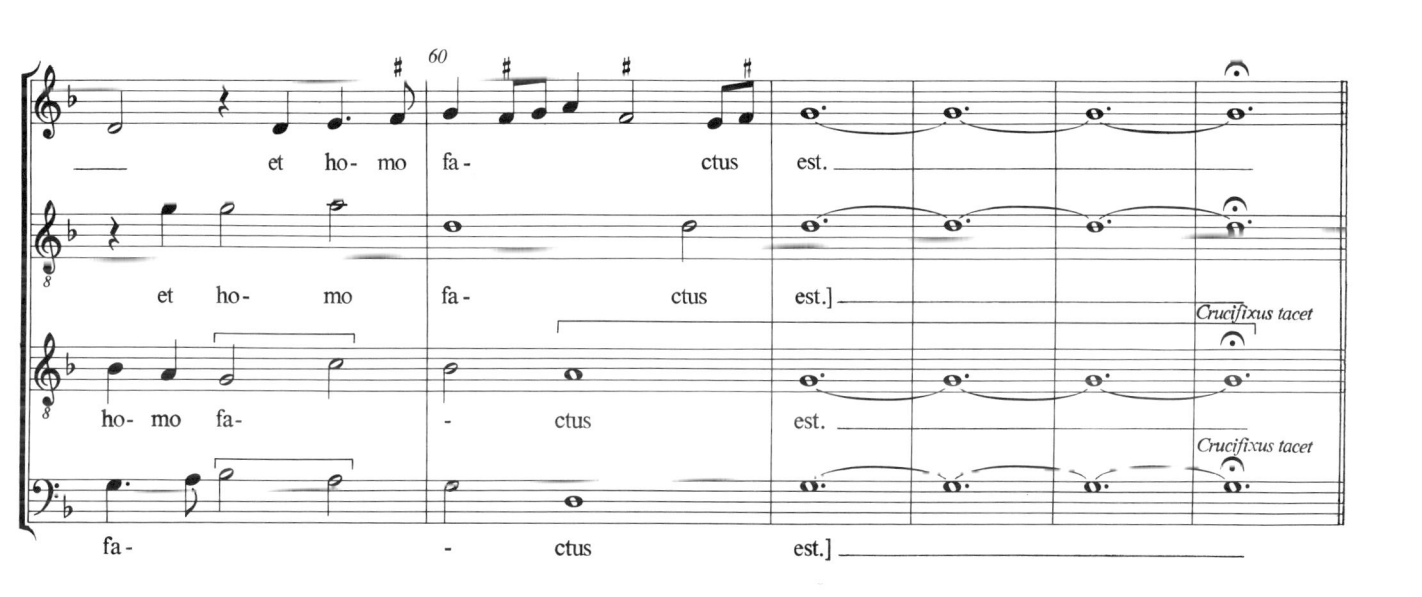

138

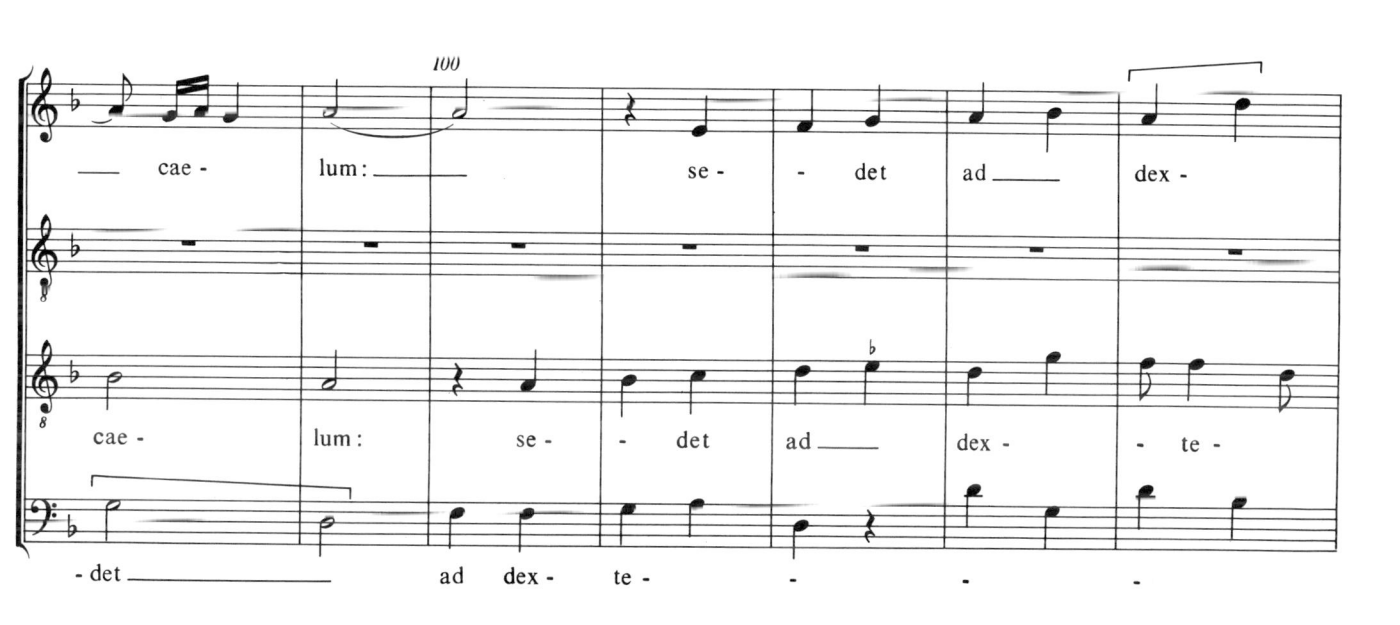

tertia die, secundum Scripturas.
tertia die, secundum Scripturas.
a die, secundum Scripturas. Et a-

-pturas. Et ascendit in
-pturas. Et ascendit in
-scendit in caelum: [se-

caelum: sedet ad dex-
caelum: sedet ad dexte-
-det ad dexte-

105
- te - - - ram Pa - - tris.
- - - - - ram Pa -
- ram Pa - tris. Et i - te - - rum
110
115
Et i - te - - rum ven - tu - - rus est cum glo - - ri - a,
- tris. Et i - te - rum ven - tu - rus est cum glo - ri -
ven - tu - rus . est cum glo - - ri - a, ju - di - ca -
120
ju - di - ca - - re vi - vos et mor - - tu -
- a, ju - - di - ca - - re vi - vos et mor - tu - -
- re vi - vos et mor - tu - os:

125
-os:
cu - jus re - - gni non e - rit fi -
-os:
cu - jus re - gni non e -
cu - jus re - gni non e - rit fi -
130
Et in Spi - ri - tum San - - ctum, Do - mi - num, et
-nis.
Et in Spi - ri - tum
-rit fi - nis.
-nis. Et in Spi - ri - tum San - - ctum,
135
140
vi - vi - fi - can - - - - tem:
San - ctum, Do - mi - num, et vi - - vi - fi - can - tem:
Do - mi - num, vi - vi - fi - can - - tem:] qui ex

145
qui ex Pa - tre Fi - li - o - que pro - ce -
qui ex Pa - tre Fi - li - o -
.S.
Pa - tre Fi - li - o - - que pro - ce -
150
- dit. Qui cum Pa - tre et Fi - li - o si - mul a - do - ra -
- que pro - ce - dit. Qui cum Pa - tre et Fi - li -
- [dit. Qui cum Pa - - tre et Fi - li -
155 .S.
160
- tur, et con - glo - - ri - - fi - - ca - tur:
- o si - mul a - do - ra - tur, et con - - glo - ri - - fi - ca -
et con - glo - - ri - - fi - ca - tur: qui
- o qui lo -

165
qui lo-cu- - - tus est per Pro-
- tur:
lo- cu- - - tus est per Pro-
- cu- tus est per Pro- phe- - -
170
- phe - tas.
[Et u- nam, san- ctam, ca- tho- - li-
- phe- - tas.
- tas. Et u- nam, san- ctam,ca-tho-li- cam et a-
175
180
Con- fi-
- cam et a- po- sto- - li- cam Ec- cle- si- am.
Con- fi- te- or
- po- sto- li- cam Ec-cle- si- am. Con- - fi-

- te - or u - num bap - tis - ma in re - - mis -
in re - - mis -
u - num bap - - - tis - ma in re -
- te - or u - num bap - tis - ma
- si - - o - nem pec - - ca - to - -
- si - o - - - nem pec - ca - to - - - -
- mis - - si - - o - nem pec - - ca - - to - -
- rum. Et ex - spe - cto re - sur - re - cti -
- rum. Et ex - spe - - cto re - sur - re - cti -
- rum. Et ex - spe - cto re - sur - re - cti - o -
Et ex - spe - cto re - sur -

205
210
- o - - nem mor - tu - o - - rum. Et
- o - - nem mor - tu - o - - rum. Et
- nem mor - tu - o - - rum. Et vi - tam
- re - cti - o - - - nem. Et vi -
215
vi - tam ven - tu - - - ri sae - - cu - li. A -
vi - tam ven - tu - - ri sae - - cu - li.
ven - - - tu - ri sae - - cu - li. A -
- tam ven - - tu - ri sae - - cu - li. A -
220
225
A -

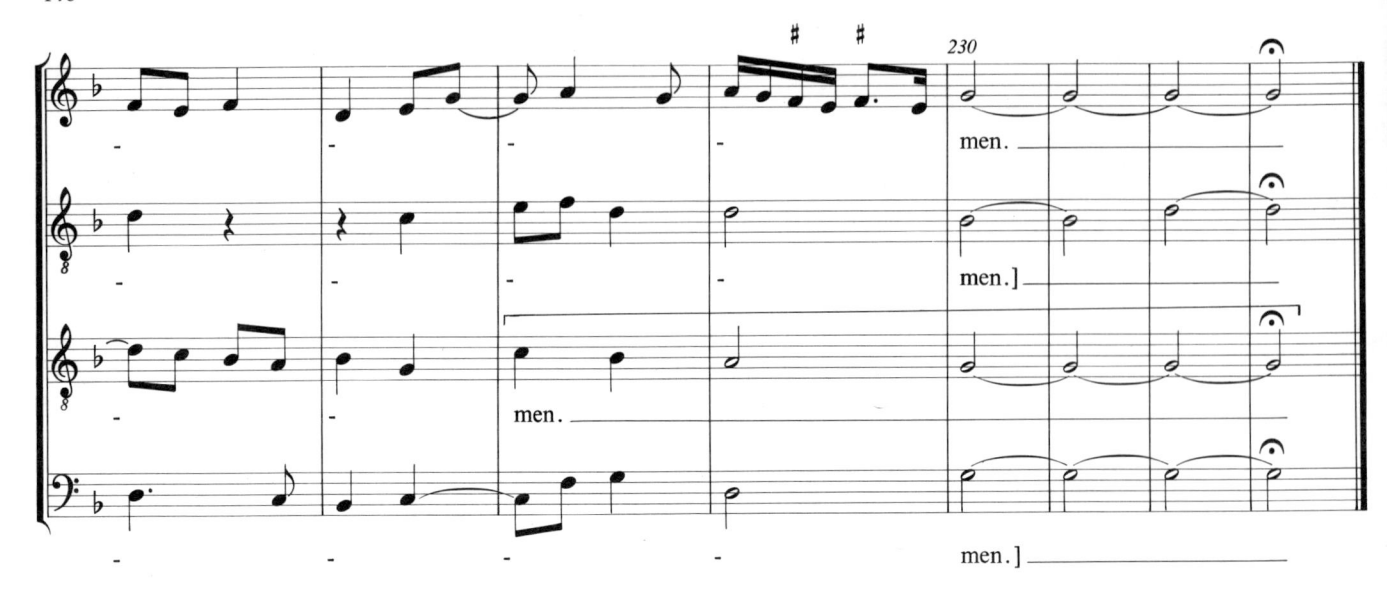

Sanctus

147

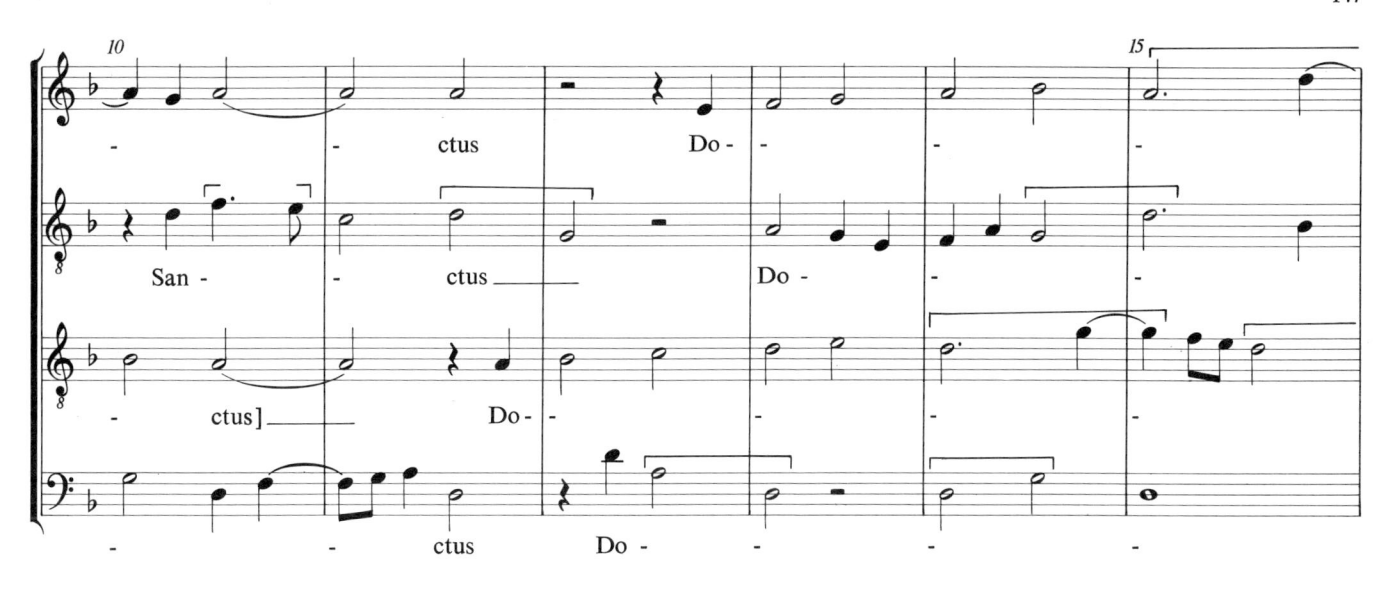

148

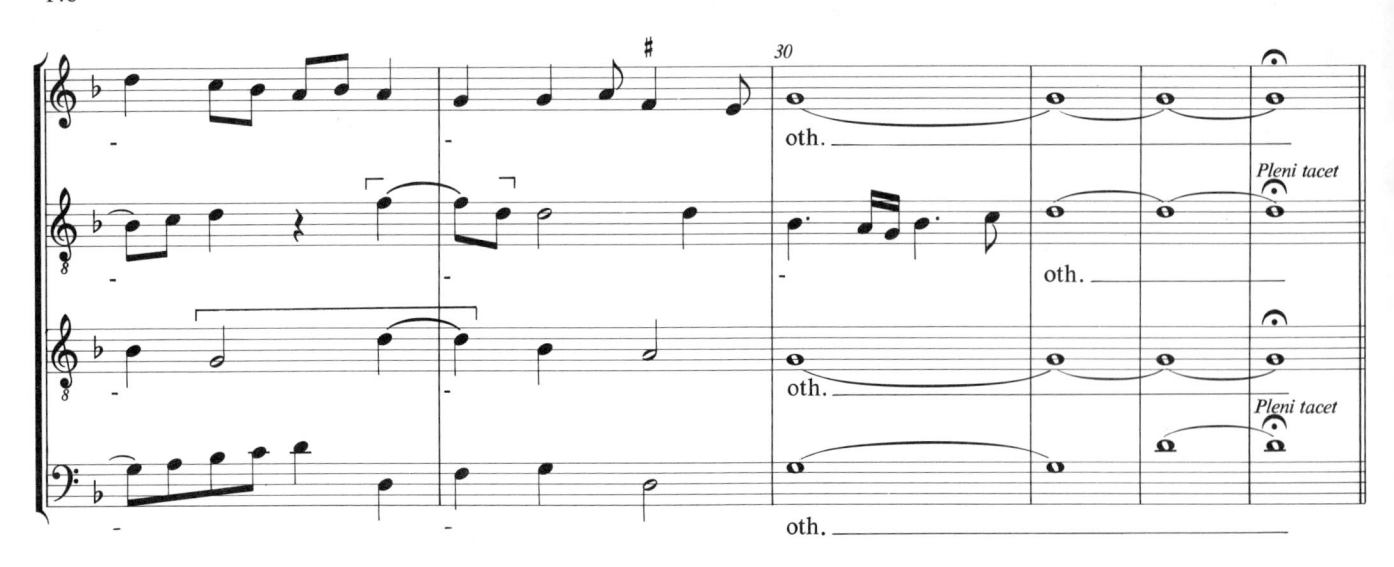

149

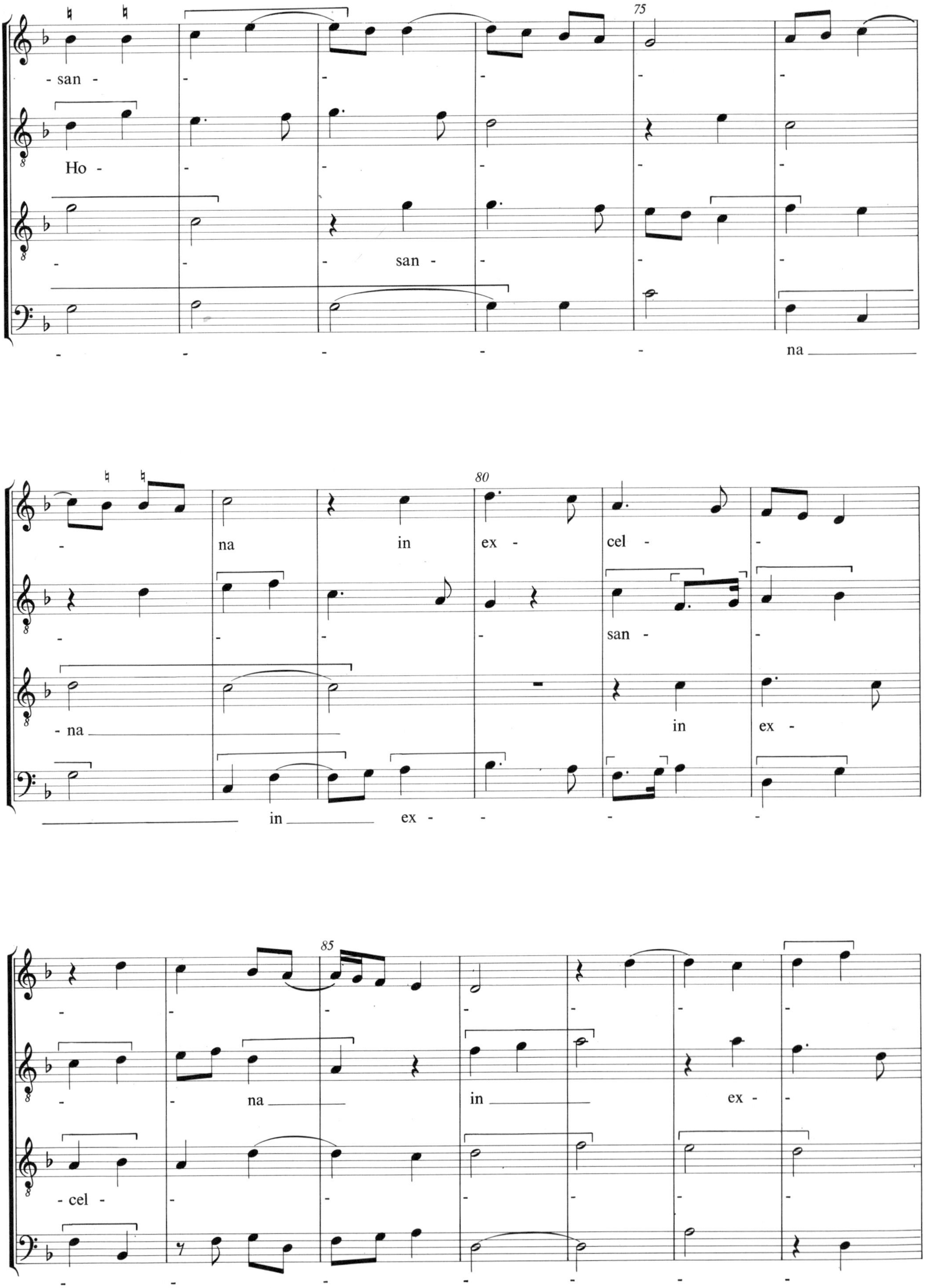
75
san
Ho
san
na
80
na in ex cel
san
na
in ex
in ex
85
na
in
ex
cel

90
cel -
- cel -
95
100
sis.
Benedictus tacet
[Superius]
duo
[Contratenor altus]
duo
105
Be - ne - di - ctus qui ve -
Be - ne - di - ctus qui
110
ve -

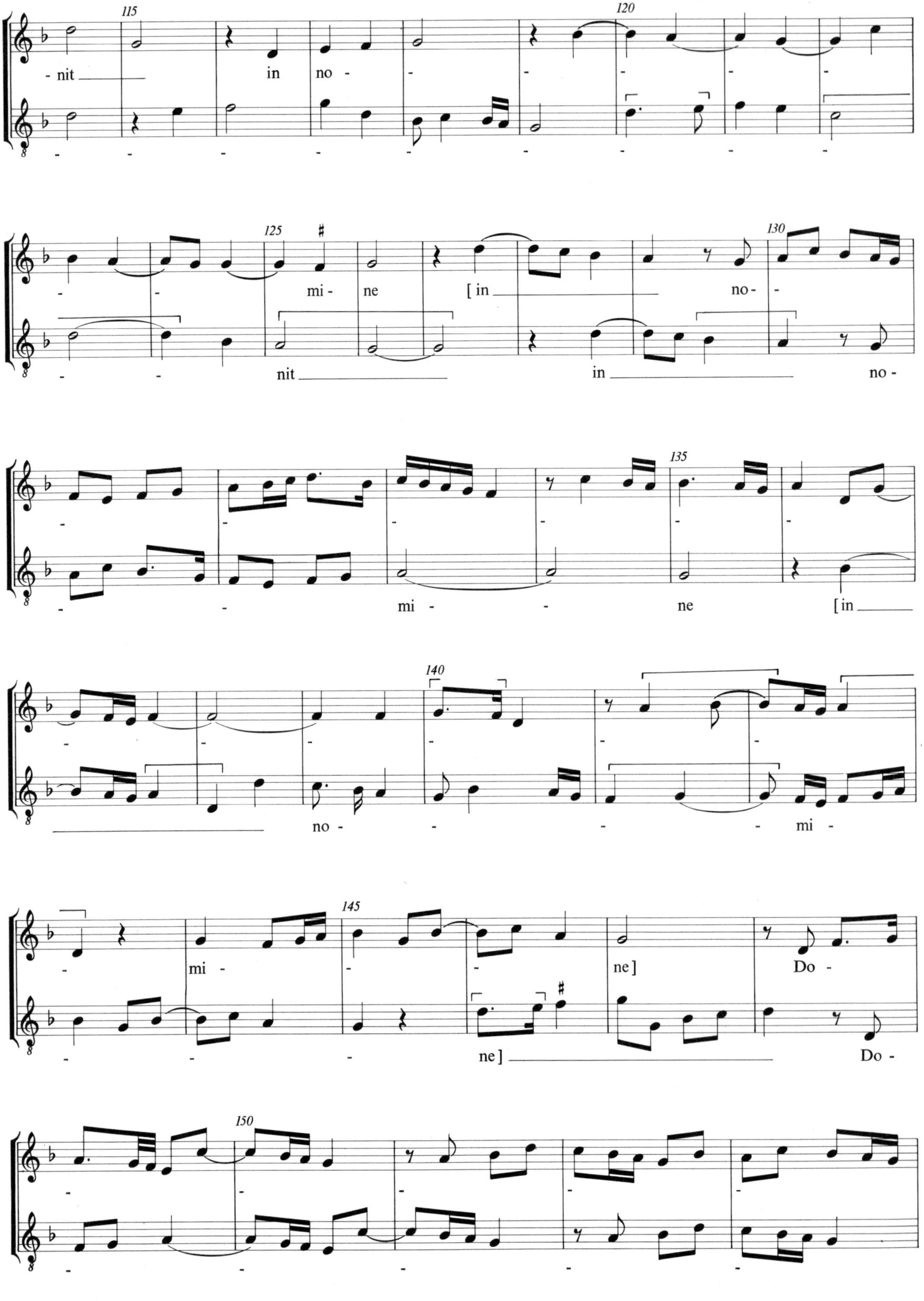
- nit in no - - - - -
- - - - - - - - -
- - mi - ne [in no - -
- - nit in no -
- - - - - -
- - mi - - ne [in
- - - - - - -
no - - - mi -
- mi - - - ne] Do -
- - - ne] Do -
- - - - -
- - - - -

Hosanna ut supra
[mm. 66 - 101]

Agnus Dei

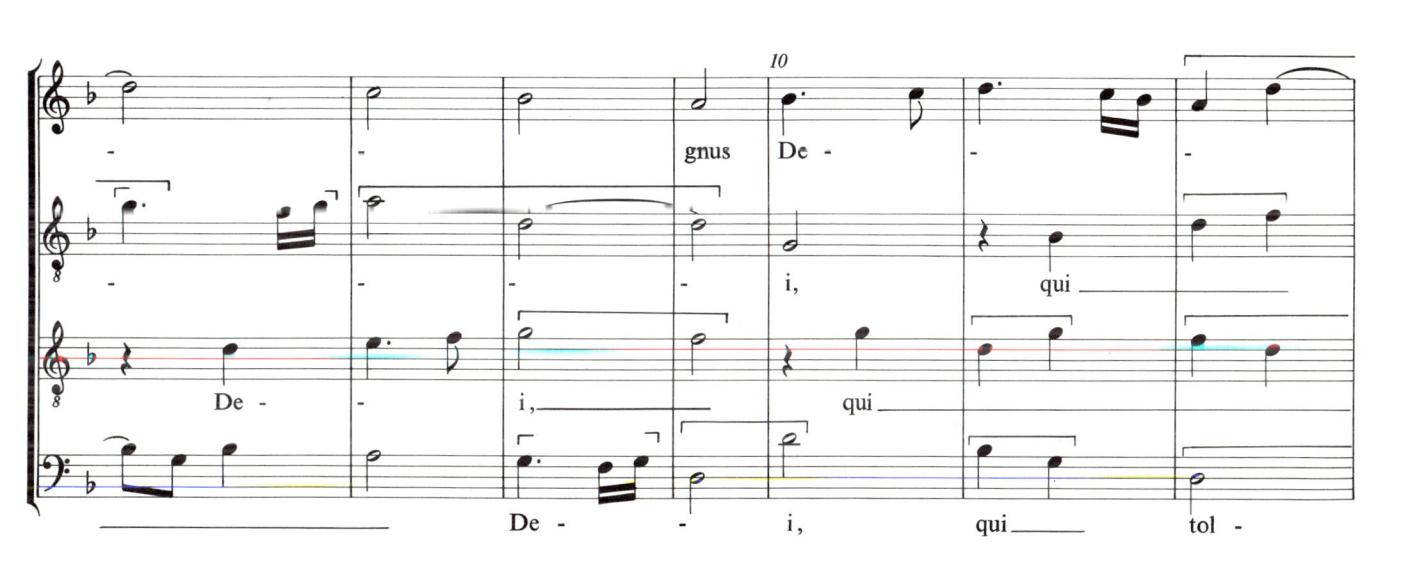

15
- i, qui tol- - -
tol- - lis pec- ca- - - -
tol- - -
- - - - - - -
20
25
- - lis pec- ca- - -
- - - ta mun- - -
-lis pec- ca- - - ta
- lis pec- ca- - -
30
- ta mun- - - - - di:
-di: mi- -
mun- - - - - - -
-ta mun- - - di:

155

[Superius]
duo
[Contratenor altus]
duo
A - - - - gnus De - - - - - - - - - i, qui tol - - - - - - - lis pec - ca - ta mun - - di: mi - se - - re - - - - - -
A - - gnus De - - - - - - - - - i, qui tol - - - - - lis pe - ca - ta mun - - di: mi - se - re - - - - - -

157

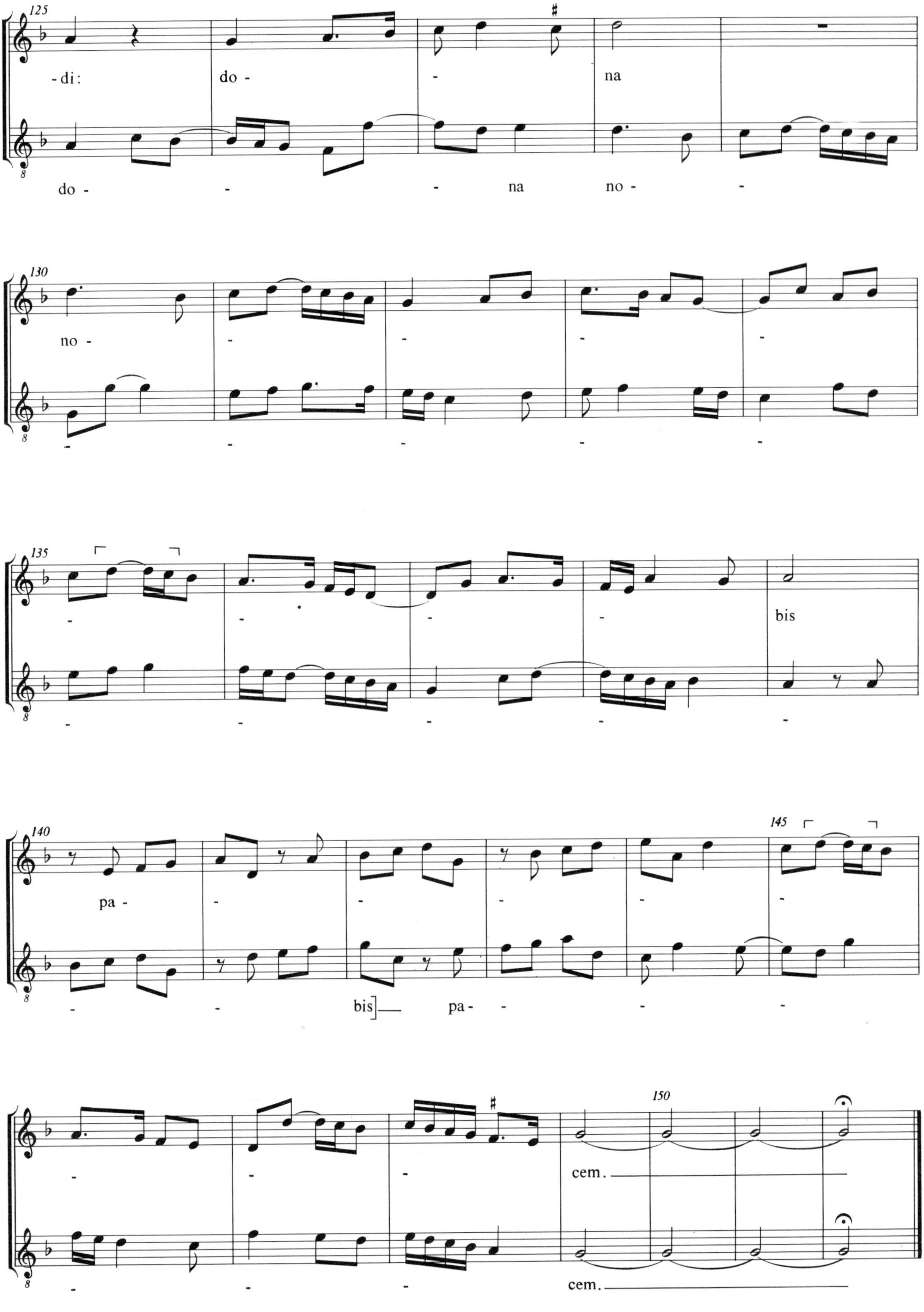
125
-di: do- - na
do- - - na no- -
130
no- - - - -
- - - - -
135
- - - - bis
- - - - -
140
pa- - - - -
145
- - bis] pa- - -
150
- - - cem.
- - - cem.

[5] Villancico: La pena sin ser sabida

sa - be que por su a - mor Soy tri-
-ste to - da mi vi - da.

[Superius]

2. Et finge
3. Por que mas

Contratenor altus

Et finge
Por que mas

Tenor

Et finge de non saber
Por que mas a su plazer

Contratenor [bassus]

Et finge
Por que mas

161

[6] Rondeau: Triste qui spero morendo

15
20
may non mo - re Va
de fo - co in fo - co ar - den -
25
do.
.S.
2. Tri - ste qui te - ne spe -
30

35
-ran- ça A lo su- o tem- - po ser- vu-
40
-to. Tri- - ste chi mai nul- la a-van-ça Si- non
45
pe-na per a-iu- - to.

[7] Rondeau: Ou doy je secours querir

20
25
- le dam - - - - - me et
- gois - - - - - seu - se
- tres vos - - - - tre no -
seul - le dam - - - - -
an - - gois - seu - - - - -
mous - - tres vos - - - - -
30
mais - tres - se,
des - tres - se.
- bles - - se,
.S.
- me et mais - tres - se,
- se des - - tres - se.
- tre no - bles - - se,
♮.S.
2.8. Aul -
6. Puis -
.S.
35
40
2.8. Aul - - - tre - ment ne puis ly - - es -
6. Puis - - - que vous es - tes prin - - ces -
- - tre - ment ne puis ly - es -
- - que vous es - tes prin - ces -
45
- se, Ne res - - con - - fort
- se, Pour fai - - re ung
- - - se, Ne res - - - con -
- - - se, Pour fai - - -

[8] Rondeau: Fortune, par ta cruaulté

- aul - - té, Pour dueil ou pour ad -
huer - - té, Moins suis doub - teux, plus
- heuir - - té, J'ay ris de ta di -
cru - - aul - té, Pour dueil ou
huer - - té, Moins suis doub -
mal - - heuir - té, J'ay ris de
- ver - - - - si - té, Ne pour
ay seur - té, Car j'ay
- ver - - - - si - té, J'ay plai -
pour ad - ver - - - - si - té, Ne
- teux, plus ay seur - té, Car
ta di - ver - - - - si - té, J'ay
do - - - leur que tu m'a - van -
le bas - - - ton d'es - pe - ran -
- sir de ton ac - ta - van -
pour do - - - leur que tu m'a -
j'ay le bas - - ton d'es - pe -
plai - sir de ton ac - ta -

ce,
ce.
ce,
-van- ce,
-ran- ce.
-van- ce,
2.8. Je ne per- dray ma pa- ci- en-
6. J'ay fier- te contre ta puis-san-
2.8. Je ne per- dray ma pa-
6. J'ay fier- te con- tre ta
ce,
ce,
ci- en- ce,
puis- san- ce,
Et ne pen-
Car tout me
-se- ray la- sce- té.
vient de loy- aul- té.
ne pen- se- ray la- sce- té.
tout me vient de loy- aul- té.

SONG-MODEL SOURCES

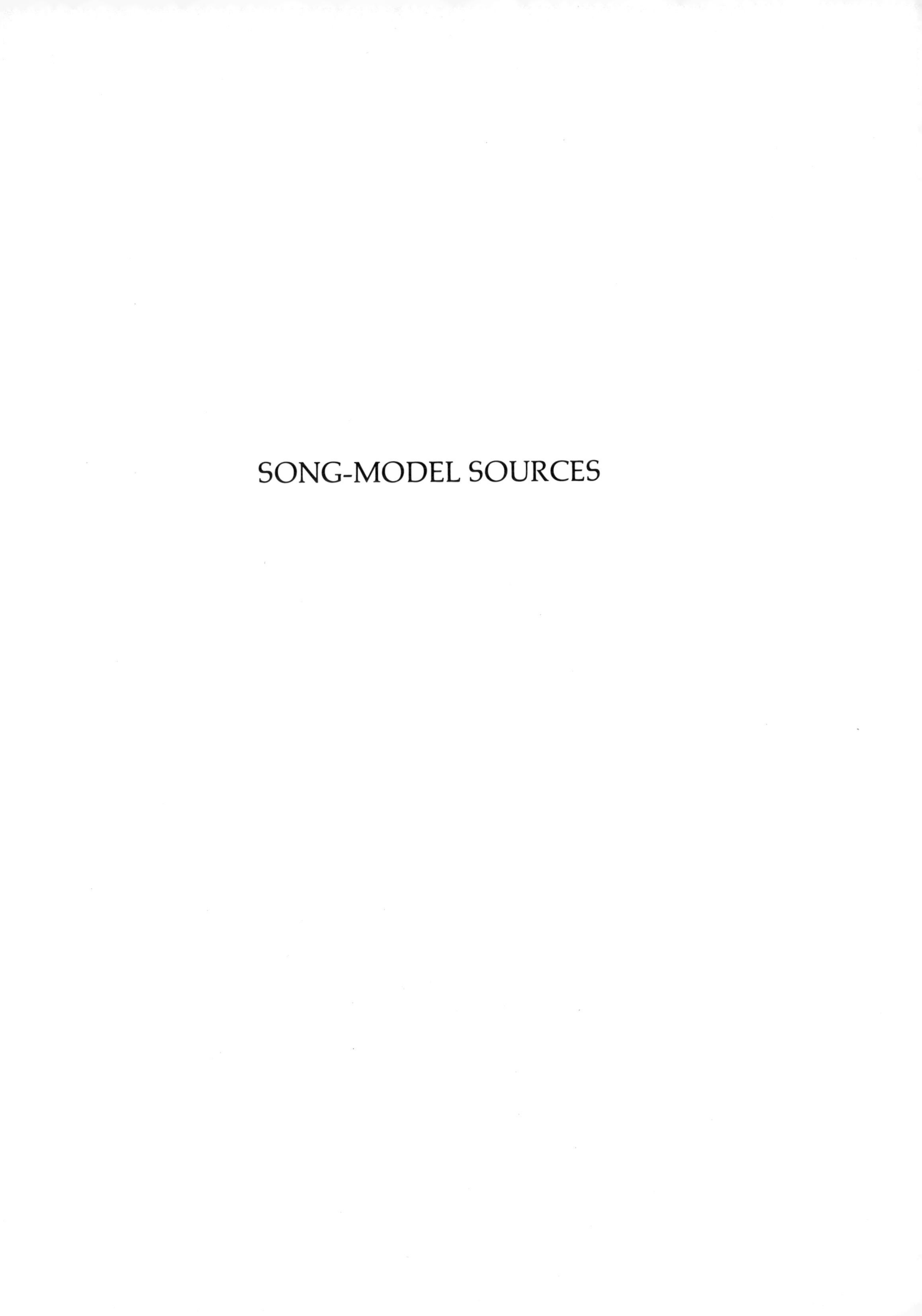

Rondeau: Entrepris suis par grant lyesse

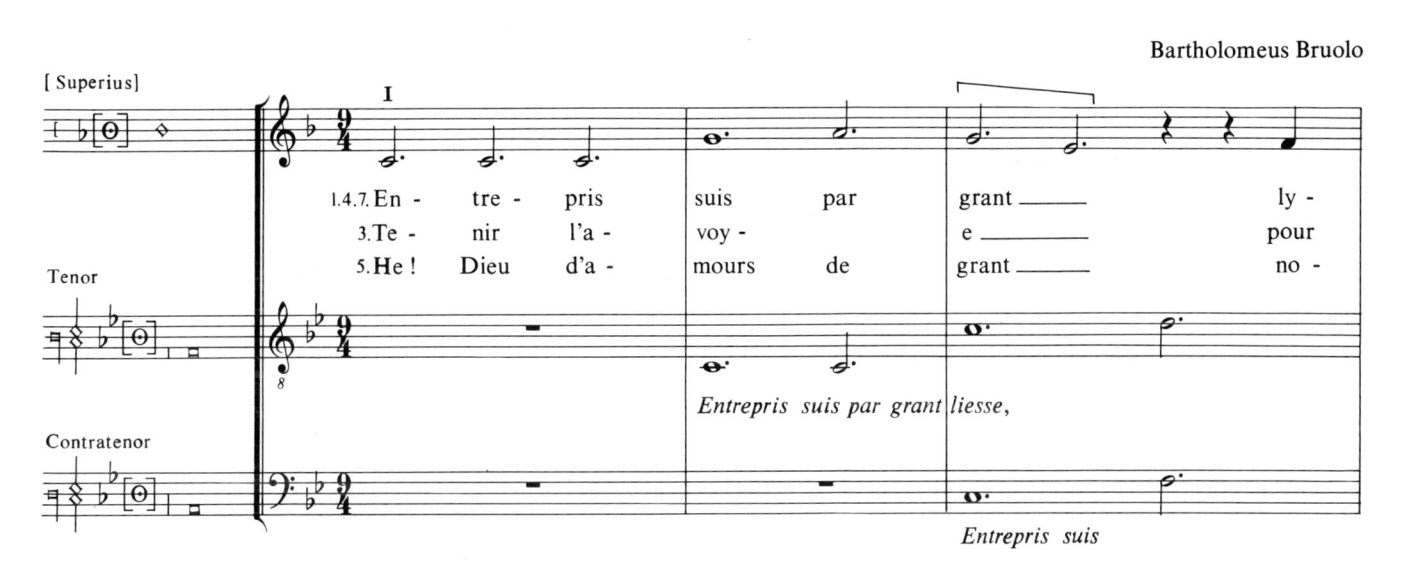

Bartholomeus Bruolo

174

30
.S.
III
-ens de son cler vis,
le siens ar - mis.
ne soit guer - pis,
2.8. En re - pen - sant
6. De sa dou - cheur,
de son cler vis,
35
il m'est a - vis,
par ta mer - cis,
40
Qu'el soit la flour de
Car y le maul que
Qu'el soit
45
gen - ti - les - se.
tant me bles - se.

Song-motet: O gloriosa regina mundi

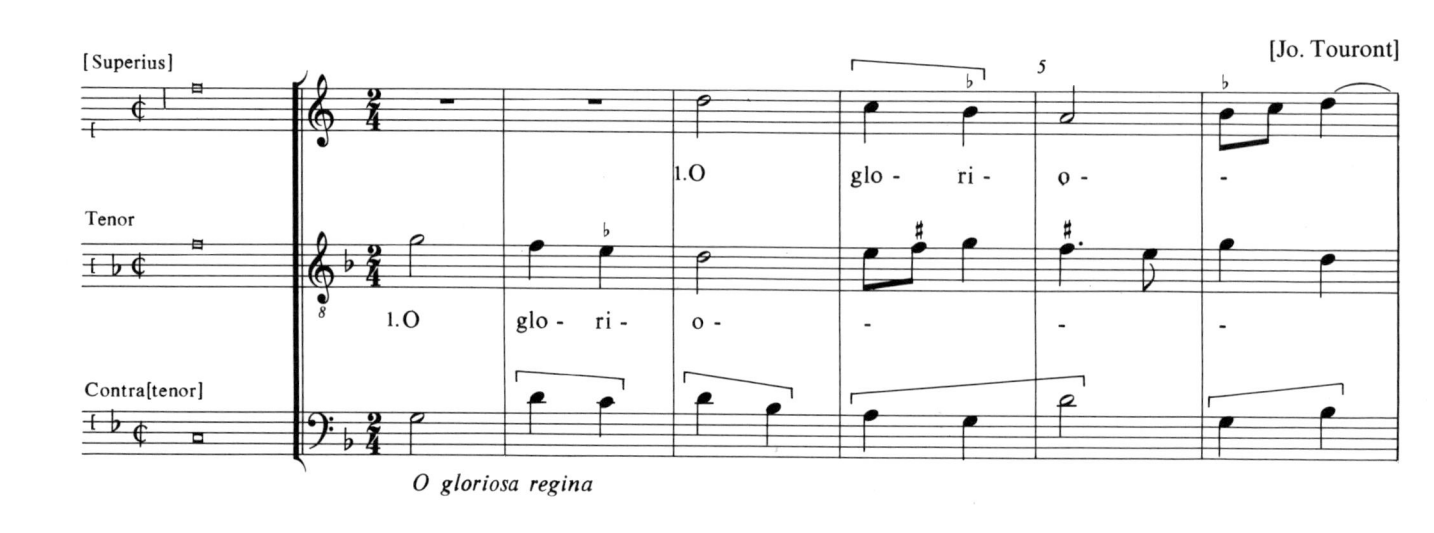

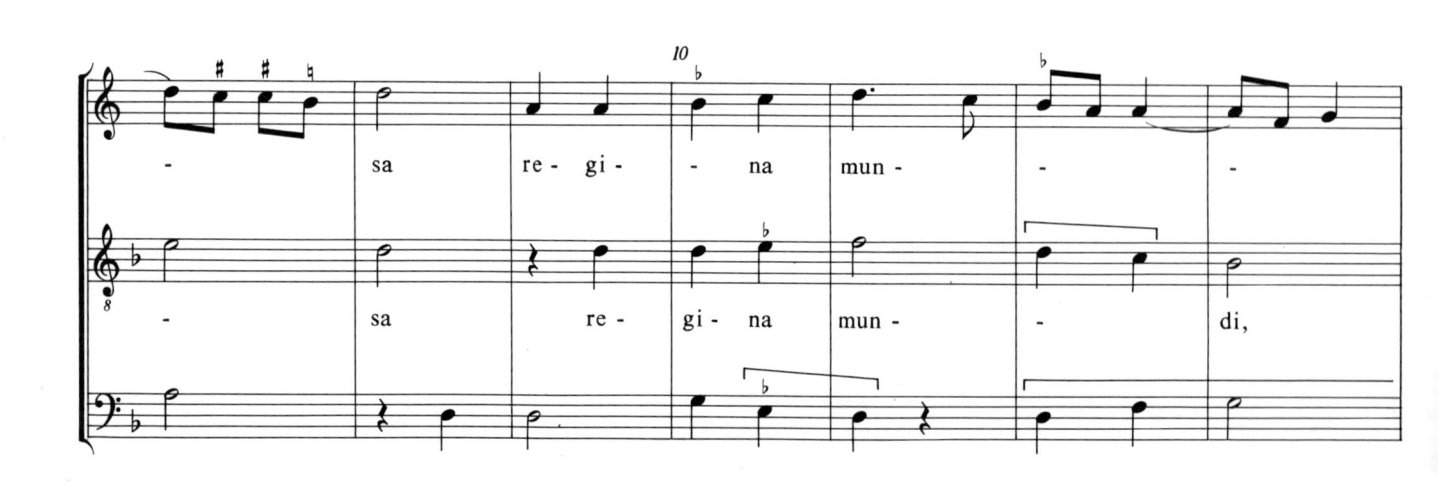

[Jo. Touront]

177

- rem in gen - - - ti- bus.
-rem in gen - - ti - bus.
2.A - ve vir - - go pul - - cher - -
2.A - ve vir - go pul - - cher - ri - -
- ri - ma, In gra - - - -
- - ma, In gra - - - ti -
- - ti - is u - ber- ri - ma, A - - ve
- is u - ber - ri - ma, A - - ve vir - go

vir - go re - gi - a, Sa- lu- - -
re - gi - a, Sa- - lu - - - tem,
-tem, sa - lu - - - tem pro -
sa - lu - - - tem pro - -
- - tu - li - - -
- - tu - li - - -
- - - - sti.
- - - - sti.

M2
.R2383
v.9-10